Development and Governance

Series Editor
Yilin Hou
Center for Policy Research Maxwell School Syracuse University, USA

This series will be devoted to the treatment of "development" and "governance" as two universally urgent issues that underlie many related problems in all countries. Though many other books, even series, already exist to tackle directly or otherwise these issues, this series stands out as a unique set with unique features.

More information about this series at http://www.springer.com/series/13392

Yilin Hou • Qiang Ren • Ping Zhang

The Property Tax in China

History, Pilots, and Prospects

Springer

Yilin Hou
Center for Policy Research the Maxwell
School of Citizenship and Public Affairs
Syracuse University
Syracuse
New York
USA

Ping Zhang
School of International Relations and Public
Affairs
Fudan University
Shanghai
China

Qiang Ren
Central University of Finance
and Economics
Beijing
China

ISBN 978-3-319-38357-6 ISBN 978-3-319-10049-4 (eBook)
DOI 10.1007/978-3-319-10049-4
Springer Cham Heidelberg New York Dordrecht London

Softcover reprint of the hardcover 1st edition 2015

Printed on acid-free paper

Springer is part of Springer Science+Business Media (www.springer.com)

Preface

This monograph is a special policy report on the creation, pilot implementation, and possible wide adoption of the real property tax at the local level in China. As is known, China has gone through a series of reforms in various areas in the past three decades. The reform to establish and adopt a local property tax is a very new endeavor but a very important one that carries wide and deep implications and will change the landscape of public finance, intergovernmental relations, and local governance in the country. In this sense, it is not exaggeration to say that such a reform goes way beyond mere economic or financial reform. It is a fundamental change to the financing of public service provision, the relationship between local governments and tax payers, and the status of localities in the government structure, among others. Thus, this monograph will be of great interest to policymakers in China—it provides a timely study of the policy process of establishing the tax and of the preliminary result of pilot experimenting the tax in two metropolitans. (As an update, a Chinese version of this report is simultaneously being published in China.) This monograph is also of huge benefit to other countries that are considering adopting or reforming their versions of the local property tax, to see what lessons the Chinese experiment has to offer. Meanwhile, this monograph is intended for researchers in public finance and public policy as a first study of the Chinese experiment in levying the local property tax: it contributes to the literature and policy practice in several important ways as we elaborate in the text. As a policy report, this monograph is not yet deep in details of methodology, due to limitations in data and in access to the inner workings of policy making. Our subsequent research will offer progress in those aspects.

Syracuse, NY, USA
November 2013

Yilin Hou

Acknowledgements

This monograph is a special policy report of **The China Local Property Tax Project**. This project was initially funded by a grant from the *Lincoln Institute of Land Policy*, Boston, Massachusetts (2011–12) and the Stanley W. Shelton Professor Fund at the School of Public and International Affairs, University of Georgia. The manuscript preparation and revision in 2013 was sponsored by the Center for Fiscal Development (CFD) at the Central University of Finance and Economics, Beijing, China. In the process, Qiang Ren was funded by the China Overseas Studies Scholarship Fund to stay for a year at the University of Georgia and Ping Zhang was funded through arrangements by the Graduate School of the University of Georgia. We express our sincere gratitude to all these organizations for their generosity and support.

The authors also express sincere thanks to scholars in Chinese academic institutions who provided suggestions for the project, to officials at the Ministry of Finance and the State Tax Administration of the Chinese Central Government for sharing their policy insights, and to finance and tax officials in the relevant departments of Beijing, Shanghai, and Chongqing Municipality Governments for accepting our interviews in 2011 and 2012.

Dr. Jerry Miner, professor of economics emeritus at the Maxwell School of Syracuse University read through the manuscript in Spring 2014 and offered many valuable insights that help make this manuscript more readable to the audience in the English world.

Book Note

Preamble: A Note on China's Housing Sector

China's urban housing sector experienced significant changes after the founding of the People's Republic in 1949 (Ye et al. 2006). One way to summarize these changes is to break the 70-plus years from 1949 to 2012 into three periods. The first period (1949–1978) was the command economy, when housing was provided by the government or state owned enterprises as a fringe benefit ("welfare" in Chinese official lexicon), with a nominal rent, to all who worked for the public sector, mostly in urban centers. In the second period (1979–1997), changes were incrementally introduced with deepening economic reforms. A typical feature of this period was a double-track system that grandfathered the old benefit/welfare housing in combination with new, other methods of housing provision including the market. The third period started in 1998 with market-based housing provision.[1]

Under the benefit/welfare housing policy of the first period, the rents collected were not enough even to recover the cost of basic maintenance; the government was simply not able to provide adequate housing to the increasing population. As a result, the living conditions of urban residents (employees of the public sector) continuously deteriorated—the (urban) per capita housing space declined from 4.5 m^2 in the early 1950s to 3.6 m^2 in the late 1970s (Li 1998).[2] The miserable conditions made a reform necessary and urgent.

China's reform of its housing sector was initiated in the second period, largely motivated by the pursuit of mechanisms to provide adequate housing for its citizens while reducing the excessive financial burden of managing a massive public housing stock (Deng et al. 2009). Several changes were incrementally introduced in the provision and allocation of housing in the 1980s and the early 1990s. A new mechanism was to split, at varying ratios, the construction cost between employees

[1] Some scholars in China divide China's most recent real estate market (since the late-1980s) into four phases: initiation and exploration (1987–1991), abrupt expansion (1992–1993), contraction and recession (1994–1997), and recovery and continuing expansion (since 1998). For details, see Liu and Huang (2004).

[2] One square meter is about 10.7 ft^2.

and the state; meantime, rents were increased in order to be adequate for covering the maintenance costs. The achievement of introducing these changes was obvious: By the end of the 1990s, per capita housing of urban residents more than doubled, increasing to almost 10 m^2 (Wang 2003).[3]

Dramatic, systematic reforms occurred in 1998—a central government document put a formal stop to the old practice of public employers (government or institutions) constructing or buying new housing for their employees, [4] placed in its place was a new mechanism—employers provide employees with cash subsidies for home purchase on the market. Adoption of this mechanism marked the turning point of China's housing reform (Deng et al. 2009). Thereafter, China's housing market developed very fast against the background of accelerated urbanization of the country's huge rural population (Liu and Huang 2004). Around the 2010s, the government had come up with separate strategies that target different income groups in an increasingly divergent economy. The government stays out of the market of up-scale (large, high quality) housing that is for high income households and the markets of a wide range of price options for middle income households. On the other hand, subsidies are provided in financing "economical housing" that is exclusively for low income households. From the supply side, low- to middle-income households are supported by the *Economical and Comfortable Housing* (ECH) program and the *Housing Provident Fund* (HPF) program. In addition, the *Cheap Rental Housing* (CRH) program was especially designed to help low-income households.[5]

The ECH and the HPF programs have been the main drivers in promoting the country's home ownership. Several sources claim very high ownership rates: Deng et al. (2009) put it at 80 % in 2004; the 2010 China population census shows 90 %. [6] We suspect that these high numbers are skewed, because close to 50 % of the surveyed households lived in rural areas, meaning their housing was self-built rather than provided by employers or purchased from the market. As a matter of fact, home ownerships in mega cities like Beijing and Shanghai and developed provinces such as Guangdong and Zhejiang are all below 60 %, which is roughly comparable

[3] Wang (2003): "There are three different housing space measures used in Chinese statistics: living (*juzhu*) space, usable (*shiyong*) space, and construction (*jianzhu*) space. Living space refers to the space one sleeps in, the bedrooms. Usable space includes not only bedrooms but other usable space within a housing unit as well, such as living room, corridor, bathroom, and kitchen. Construction space includes common areas outside a housing unit (such as an apartment) but shared by residents in a complex (e.g., stairs, common corridors). Over time, the most common measure for housing has shifted from relying on living space to construction space. There are no published standards for conversion among the three, but the rule of thumb used by many is that living space is 75 % of the usable space, and usable space is 75 % of construction space. In other words, construction space is twice the living space." All housing space parameters used in this book refer to "construction space" if not otherwise specified.

[4] The document was the "State Council Decision on Further Deepening the Reform of the Urban Housing System and Accelerating Housing Construction."

[5] See Deng et al. (2009) for a comprehensive review of the three programs.

[6] For details, see http://www.joneslanglasalleblog.com/APResearch/residential-research/chart-of-the-day-home-ownership-rate-in-china, retrieved on July 14, 2014.

to most OECD counties.[7] That is, even home ownership rates in these most wealthy cities and provinces do not necessarily correlate with the country's highest levels of household income. Nevertheless, the above measures of housing reform did effectively boost China's per capita construction space of urban residents. It increased to 29.2 m^2 by 2010, with the per capita living space around 15 m^2.

Land Ownership Issues

In China, the property right of (urban) land belongs to the state, [8] which sounds similar to the case in the UK. For real estate developers, the first step of their business is to acquire the right to the use of urban land for housing construction. In almost all cases, a local government that is in charge of the jurisdiction where vacant or to-be-redeveloped lots sit, sells via a set of formal public bidding process the land use right to developers on behalf of the central government. The length of the use right varies: it is up to 70 years for residential use, 40 years for commercial use, 50 years for industrial and institutional use, and 50 years for mixed use. After obtaining the use right with full payment to the local government, a developer builds housing on the acquired lot, and finally sells constructed housing units on the market.

Hence, the retail price of housing includes the cost of construction, paid to the developer plus his profit, and the transfer fee of land use right, paid to the local government via the developer's purchase of land use right. From 1998 to the writing of this manuscript, the latter had become an increasingly higher portion of the total price of housing. There have been multifarious reasons for the frenzy by local governments to sell land use right at higher and higher prices. The most striking reason is the seemingly insatiable local need for cash in order to finance the ever increasing demand for better infrastructure and more public services; then top local officials can claim the new infrastructure and services as their achievements, the so-called GDP championship, that pave the way for their promotion to higher positions.[9]

With a home purchase, the owner of a housing unit bought and own the property right of the unit, the physical structure, and the "slice" of land use right corresponding to his/her unit. This slice of land use right is constrained to the remaining years under the 70-year limit from the date of his/her purchase. The limited land use right has been the cause of huge confusion and numerous problems for developers, housing owners, and the government. The Damocles' sword is: What happens if/when the 70-year limit falls tomorrow? Policymakers have been shy of an answer; legal scholars have been discussing and some cry for a constitutional amendment.

[7] The US home ownership in 2012 was around 65%. See U.S. census, http://www.census.gov/housing/hvs/files/qtr413/q413press.pdf, retrieved on July 11, 2014.

[8] In theory, this is also true of agricultural land though in practice farmland is owned "collectively." Rural homestead is a fuzzy issue unique to rural residents.

[9] Zhou (2008) is an excellent explanation of this incentive mechanism behind selling land use right for work achievements by local governments.

However, so far the 70-year land use limit has not caused major social unrest in the housing market. Probably, all parties including the general public hold the expectation that a solution will somehow be available by that date; the sky will not fall.

Soaring Housing Prices

With the above said, it is not difficult to understand why housing prices in China have soared since the late 1990s. The media and the general public repeatedly, even bitterly complain that housing is not affordable for households with average incomes. According to the *Global Financial Stability Report* by the International Monetary Fund, the year-2011 ratios of mean housing price to average annual income in Beijing and Shanghai hit 22.3 and 15.9, respectively, much higher than Hong Kong and Tokyo, whereas this ratio for other major cities in the world including New York, London, Singapore, and Toronto, was from 4 to 7 (IMF 2012). As of this writing, signs have emerged that the growth rate of housing prices is becoming less steep for the coming years. The housing market is experiencing some fundamental changes after a decade of frenzy.

On the other hand, more and more people are holding multiple housing units. This is a divergent group who fall roughly into three sub-groups. First are the new rich with piles of assets from business, technological innovation, or corruption who mostly possess up-scale housing at the best locations in mega cities, for their own occupancy, for their children, and for investment (these people have been shying away from the lukewarm stock market for years). Then, there are long-time public employees and city residents who acquired several units in their city of residence and employment, often through the several waves of housing reform. For example, they may have purchased the earliest benefit/welfare unit, then purchased a new unit at subsidized price via the cost-split construction initiative, and recently bought a better and larger unit as their main residence or as the new nest for their child to get married in. These households are asset rich, at least on paper, though they are not necessarily rich income wise. Finally are the relocated households who used to live in the next-to-city line villages or crowded downtown slums. When rapid expansion of urban centers and downtown redevelopment came to their "turf," they usually could obtain, out of hard and harsh negotiations, several units in return for agreement on relocation. The size and number of housing units under their name are lot more than their household needs, including for their children's wedding, though their units may not be of high quality or at the good locations. These households may be cash poor but they are definitely asset rich within their income group. Almost all such households have become landlords, renting out excess housing for income. Many new and up-scale units stay vacant—owners are concerned that renters may be careless and not take good care of these valued assets, giving rise to ghost complexes, even communities. There are no reliable data available on what proportion of the total properties stock are rented out or vacant.

Facing the most difficulty in acquiring housing are new immigrants into cities. These are either rural-turned-urban newcomers or career seekers from smaller cities. The former have no family financial support—their parents are still in poor rural homes, and their meager, hard-earned income is a drop in the sea for acquiring urban housing. The latter come to central cities for a dream career or any career, but they cannot afford buying and their parents housing asset in the smaller, home city is a mere dwarf in front of the prices of central city housing. These new immigrants are the customer base of rental property.

The above is a little background for western readers of this manuscript. This little book is merely an early stage report of our project. The field calls for vast amounts of detailed work and deserves a thorough investigation before we can systematically estimate the effects of property taxation reform in China which is reserved for subsequent stages of research.

Syracuse, NY, USA Yilin Hou
August, 2014

References

Deng, L., Q. Shen, and L. Wang. 2009. Housing policy and finance in China: A literature review. University of Michigan working paper prepared for US Department of Housing and Urban Development. http://www.chinaplanning.org/Publications/Lan%20Deng%20-%20Housing%20Policy%20and%20Finance%20In%20China.pdf.

International Monetary Fund (IMF). 2012. Global financial stability report: The quest for lasting stability. Washington, DC: IMF.

Li, R. 1998. Residential houses going to the market. *Beijing Review* 41 (20): 14–17.

Liu, H., and Y. Huang. 2004. Prospects of real estate markets in China-challenges and opportunities. Tsinghua University working paper. https://www.housingauthority.gov.hk/hdw/ihc/pdf/phmc1112.pdf.

Wang, F. 2003. Housing improvement and distribution in urban China: Initial evidence from China's 2000 Census. *The China Review* 3:121–143.

Wang, Shing-Yi. 2011. State misallocation and housing prices: Theory and evidence from China. *American Economic Review* 101 (5): 2081–2107.

Zhou, L. 2008. Local governments in transition: Incentives for officials and governance. Shanghai: Gezhi Publishing House.

Introduction

China started its housing reform in the late 1990s to encourage "home ownership"; the term entails full property rights and transferability of housing on the real estate market. With progress of this reform, home ownership among the Chinese people has been increasing rapidly. In the early years of this century, the Chinese government placed on its agenda a new reform to institute a "real property tax." At that time, the tax on "real property," a concept that in the Chinese context covers the structure but not the land on which the structure stands, was called the *wuye* tax (物业). The term referred only to the structures or the housing units on the land, to distinguish it from a real property tax that covers both the land and the structures. In October 2003, the Chinese ruling party made a decision "to reform current taxes and charges on real estate, and levy a *wuye* tax (real property tax) when it is necessary while eliminating related charges."[10] At that time, the goal of the *wuye* tax reform was to rearrange the existing taxes on the transaction and possession of real properties. Also, the central government hoped to make the *wuye* tax an important revenue source for local governments and rationalize intergovernmental fiscal relations between the central, provincial, and other local governments. Beginning in 2003, as China's economy gradually recovered from the Asian financial crisis that started in 1998, the real property market entered a period of rapid expansion. And speculation in real property was rampant. In the last ten years, the price of real property in most cities more than tripled. This problem has been more severe in metropolitan areas, such as Beijing, Shanghai, and Guangzhou than the rest of the country, especially small cities. Meanwhile, local governments have obtained large amounts of revenue from selling the use rights of state-owned lands. In response to this abnormal market, the central government has frequently adopted monetary, fiscal, and administrative measures in an effort to "regulate" or more exactly control, the market.

Against this background Shanghai and Chongqing, two metropolitan areas, began to levy a real property tax on residential housing on January 28, 2011. As expressed in official documents, the short-term goal of this new tax is to curb sky-rocketing

[10] It was passed on October 14, 2003 by the third plenary session of the Chinese Communist Party's 16th Central Committee. The resolution was titled "CPC Central Committee's Decision on Some Issues of Improving Socialist Market Economy..

housing prices. Beyond this apparent objective, we assume that the Chinese central government may be "muddling through" in an effort to determine whether the property tax can be one stone that "targets multiple birds." Among these "birds" are stable own-source revenue for localities, the readjustment of intergovernmental relations, and the improvement of local governance in the long term. If we are correct in making this assumption, then the pilot local property tax prepares China for some fundamental reforms in tax administration, local governance, and government structure in the next few decades.

In this monograph, we argue that the local property tax is one candidate for the "magic" bullet; the installation of local property tax can help solve multiple problems that are deeply rooted in society and the result of many previous reform measures. Our analyses unfold as follows. Chapter 1 offers a three-stage framework of China's financial reforms. Its focal point is that China is now in the third stage wherein it needs to reform the underlying operating mechanisms in order to improve local governance. Chapter 2 highlights a comparison between two frameworks that have appeared in China. Under the first, local governments depend on land transfer fees (on use right purchase) to finance infrastructure, and under the second, localities shift to real property tax. Chapter 3 defines the modern real property tax and explains why China urgently needs to introduce this tax as an institution. Chapter 4 considers the requirements and background of implementing a modern real property tax. Chapter 5 traces the history of real property taxes in China and compares them with the modern real property tax in developed countries. Chapter 6 analyzes the pilot real property taxes in Shanghai and Chongqing and compares them with their counterparts throughout the history of China and with the modern real property tax in western countries. Chapter 7 describes the implementation of the pilot real property taxes in the two metro cities and the effects of each pilot tax on local own-source revenue and housing price. Chapter 8 offers the outcome and analysis of the surveys of residents and government officials on their perception of the pilot taxes. Chapter 9 conducts a simulation of real property tax that can be collected with a broad tax base at a relatively low tax rate. Chapter 10 concludes with policy recommendations for the Chinese government in its effort to conduct the third stage of financial reform and improve local governance.

Contents

Chapter 1
Three Stages of China's Financial Reforms

Beginning in late 1978 or early 1979, China's reform in China has endured almost three and a half decades. An important component of the country's comprehensive reform program has been the overhaul of its financial systems. Finance, as the bloodline of government operations, necessarily underlies fundamental changes in any country's political and state systems as well as its economic and social structures. To a large extent, government finance is "technical" in the sense that it is neutral regardless of the political and state systems and the economic and social structures of a country. This important feature of finance makes it an ideal forerunner of any reform efforts and a testing ground for new measures.

The above statement is quite true of China's reform in the past three and a half decades. Before any reform in the political and state system was even attempted, changes had to occur so as to provide the resources for action and incentives for innovation. Prior to adopting radical reforms of the economic structure or introducing new social norms, observable and unobservable adjustments emerged quietly in the means of government revenue and the ways of program outlay. After all, institutional adaptations happen gradually; but the ways and means of government operations have to move ahead to pave the path for other aspects to evolve. This description is an accurate summary of the relationship between financial reforms and other reforms of China's fast-paced transition and growth so far.

China's fiscal systems from 1978 to 2012 are a gold mine to explore. In examining how these reforms unfolded over the 35-year period and laid the foundation for other dimensions in China's systemic overhaul, a previous study (Hou 2009) formulated a two-stage division, according to which financial reforms in the first 15 years (1978/1979–1993) were efforts mainly aimed at readjusting the country's financial system; those in the second 15 years (1994–2008) were aimed at introducing innovations into its financial system. In this monograph, we build on this previous work to propose that a third stage has started. The main task of this third stage is to go deeper in overhauling the system, integrating past innovations into a network while resolving some hard problems that were unsolvable in the past, and addressing new problems that have emerged with the innovations under the restraints of some persistent, old institutions. In the following, we offer details on this three-stage analytical framework of China's financial reforms, with our focus on the third stage.

Y. Hou et al., *The Property Tax in China*, Development and Governance,
DOI 10.1007/978-3-319-10049-4_1

1.1 Stage One: Readjustment for Growth and Development

The core functions of modern government are to safeguard social stability, promote economic development, and through the first two functions, to provide public services and raise the living standards of citizens. The basic roles of central, regional, and local governments are all set up around these three functions (Hou 2008). However, under the old, prior-1979 regime, the three functions were not conducted properly; at least the latter two concerning economic and living standards were not. At the initial phase of reforms, most of the components of the regime were very hard to break, but it was easiest to loosen the centralized management, or control, of the financial system.

Measures were taken on three dimensions: within the government, with state-owned enterprises (SOE), and with individual citizens. Regarding the first, the reform was to decentralize revenues and outlays from the center to the provinces (and provinces then followed suit to grant more control to localities). Concerning the second, the measure was to place SOEs on profit contracts to make them fully accountable for their liability to the government, which conversely provided incentives for them to make profits for themselves. With reference to the third, the reform measure was to relieve individuals from the grips of the state so that every laborer could make his/her own living, and even a fortune, by working hard with his/her skills and means of production. In urban areas, the reforms gave rise to family businesses; in rural areas, farmers got rid of the old "communes" to grow crops on their contracted land and sell produce in the market. In summary terms, measures in these three dimensions were the Chinese route for growth and development.

Thus, financial reforms first broke the ice; however, the old regime remained largely unchanged, which gave rise to new problems. One of the problems was shrinking revenue for governments, particularly central and provincial governments because lower levels of government pocketed the largest share of incremental profits from decentralization, and enterprises harvested the initial benefits of the contract system. Among individuals, farmers received the largest fruits of increased output, yet, the rural income increase rate soon lagged far behind that of urban residents. In urban areas, the self-employed became rich ahead of all others. Both effects caused income disparities among the population, and the gap widened over time. A third prominent problem was the gap in growth and income between regions at both the aggregate and the individual levels. The coastal region developed earlier and faster than the interior and western regions because of their locational advantage in attracting foreign investment and cheap labor from the other regions.

These three, among many other problems, were not treatable under the old regime or with temporary adjustments to the old regime. In a practical sense, those problems were part of the price for the fast growth route the country had chosen for itself. The problems only worsened as the country's growth accelerated and maintained momentum. Solving them would be possible only when wealth accumulated to allow for drastic changes, and public impatience reached a critical point.

1.2 Stage Two: Innovations for a New Financial System

In the second stage, policy innovations were introduced to build a new financial system in accord with the generic principles of public finance, thereby solving the problems that occurred in the first stage. In a nutshell, those problems could only be tackled by the means of fiscal federalism. The goal of the new financial structure was to finance the opportunity for equal access to basic public services for every citizen regardless of the location of residence or type of household registration (urban versus rural). The economic and political rationale was to strive for equity between regions and income groups, thereby, to achieve and maintain social stability.

Two major policy innovations were introduced, each taking approximately five years. The first (1994–1998) adopted a separate central versus local tax system, under which the center collected a larger share of the major taxes (value added tax, and later, the personal income tax);[1] provincial governments, and their localities, split the remainder part of these taxes. The new tax structure provided the financial capacity for the central government to play its key roles in macroeconomic stabilization and financing nationwide public services. The second (1999–2003) established the central–local structure of fiscal transfers for basic public services and gradually increased central input into these services. As the center collects the largest share of revenues, it naturally shall finance a large part of those services. Beginning in 2004, the new public finance structure has demonstrated substantial impacts, with annually increasing amounts of transfers for education, public health, social security, and public housing.

The new financial structure has also caused unintended consequences that manifest as four problems. First, tax revenue is top heavy at the central level, light in the middle in the provinces, and minimal at the bottom with local governments, whereas the responsibilities for basic services provision are laden at the bottom with localities. These two problems exist at the same time. The center keeps the most resources, but has the least direct responsibility; the local level has the least own-source revenue, but must bear most of the direct services provision. The middle level, provinces, collects some, but inadequate, own-source revenues to help out the localities; yet, they often wait for actions from the top. A third problem arises from the first two: as revenue sources and responsibilities do not match, no one level can be held accountable for results. The top criticizes the bottom for the malpractice in using transfer funds; the bottom complains about the lack of resources for task overload.

Meanwhile, local officials are incentivized to fulfill all tasks set by their superior levels because they are appointed by their bosses—thus career considerations have driven most top local officials to resort to informal, even illegal means of financing for infrastructure and development, including selling the use right (up to 70 years) of state land for cash and borrowing huge sums via local financing vehicles. The

[1] These two major shared taxes are collected by the State Tax Administration through its local branches. The central government keeps 75% of the value–added tax and 60% of the personal income tax.

former means has been a cash cow, accounting for nearly half of total own-source revenue in many localities for over a decade. Indeed, land sales have constituted a large amount of the input into infrastructure that has provided tangible benefits; on the other hand, land price has added considerably to the cost of new housing, which has pushed up housing prices, distorting the market and causing bitter public complaints. The latter means, hidden borrowing, has piled up long-term liabilities that in many cases are multiple times over annual local revenue. Finally, waste occurs everywhere, as no one is held accountable for any specific task.

1.3 Stage Three: Toward Efficiency and Accountability

We propose that China is now situated in the third stage of its financial reforms with the following goals: fully addressing the four major problems arising out of the second stage, establishing accountability, and raising efficiency in public expenditure. These reforms will by no means be easier than those in the first two stages, though resource wise, the country is much wealthier than before.

First and foremost, the goal is to refine the intergovernmental fiscal system by more closely matching responsibilities with revenue sources. Specifically, this goal is intended to readjust the distribution of taxes, not necessarily to increase the overall tax to gross domestic product ratio between the layers of government thereby granting localities a reliable and stable source of revenue. Enriching the bottom level is that single piece of "stone" that can strike several birds: correcting the previous top-heavy revenue structure, helping to rectify distortionary local financing practices, and granting localities more autonomy.

The second goal is to re-establish the revenue-to-service link for accountability. A new source of revenue is not a free lunch for local governments; rather, the money imposes a set of restrictions on the behavior of local officials. Newly added revenue is earmarked exclusively for public services, linking the new tax to specific services that are undersupplied: education, public health, public safety, and local infrastructure. This revenue-to-service link will explicitly place accountability of officials into the hands of local tax payers, forcing the government to move closer to the people (Shah and Shah 2006).

With the revenue-to-service link established, local residents/tax payers will possess a much louder voice than before. In a real sense, they have paid a tax to purchase the right of demanding the type, amount, and quality of services by revealing their preferences. This model of "public choice" for service bears support from theoretical and empirical studies in improving the efficiency of public expenditure, raising the satisfaction of tax payers, and curbing corruption. As a result, local governments will not be forced, but will strive to get closer to the people they serve.

Last, but perhaps most important, such a reform of the financial system will help advance reforms in other aspects of the overall regime. For example, more public choice in local services plants the seed for the direct election of top local officials who are held in a reporting relationship to their voters rather than to their bosses in a higher level government who appoint them. Public choice will also boost demand for free migration among the population that, in turn, will further increase competition among local governments for revenue sources and ultimately high efficiency.

The core of this third stage reform that this monograph examines in the Chinese context is the real property tax as a financial means and a socio-political institution. As a financial means, the real property tax is merely a source for government revenue; but as a socio-political institution, the real property tax plays multiple roles, as previously described. We envision this tax will serve the country well in this unfolding, deeper than ever, stage of financial reforms. No doubt, introducing and adopting an institution is never an overnight task; it may take years even decades to arrive at fruition. This is why, we believe in its value, and want to spend time and energy dissecting the evolution, working mechanisms, and prospects of this potentially "magic" device.

a higher level government who appoint them. Public choice will also be less dominant for free migration among the population. This in turn will further decrease competition among local governments for revenue sources and ultimately harm efficiency.

The core of this third stage reform is that this more grand-scale [illegible] in the Chinese context is the real property tax as a financial instrument or a sociopolitical institution. As a financial device, the real property tax is merely a means for government revenue; seen as a sociopolitical institution, the real property tax plays multiple roles, as previously discussed. We envision this tax will serve the country well in the [illegible] [illegible] stage of financial reforms, however, [illegible] adopting an institution is never an overnight task. [illegible] were [illegible] decades [illegible] [illegible] In this book, we [illegible] this [illegible] and theory, discussing the evolution, ongoing predicaments, and prospects of this tax in the mainland Chinese.

Chapter 2
Transition of Local Revenue Systems

It is clear that China is tentatively transitioning or attempting to transition from an old local revenue system that relied exclusively on land transfer fees (LTF) from selling land use right to a new system that changes the one-time fee into a regular tax alongside a different use for the revenue. In this chapter, we provide a more detailed analysis of the transition process.

2.1 The Old System: Land Transfer Fees

By Chinese laws, all land is the property of the sovereign state, i.e., the central government. This has never been changed, even after the Property Right Law was promulgated in 2007. The exercise of the property right over state-owned land, however, has almost always been by local governments instead of the central government. From 1949 to 1980, transference of the right of land use had been between governmental entities or organizations affiliated with government. Deviation from that old practice started in the early 1980s as a means to attract foreign investment; it was part of the country's overall opening and reform program. A 1981 Guangdong Provincial People's Congress interim rule over land use granted the use of state-owned land for investors to build factories and run businesses for which the investor would pay a "land use fee".[1] In December 1987, the first public auction for the use of land (8588 m^2 for a lease term of 50 years) was conducted in Shengzhen city, the first case of land use right as an asset listed on the market for exchange. In the next April, the National People's Congress amended the Constitution with a clause on "legal transfer of the land use right within the provisions of the law."

Revenue from the transfer of the land use rights was split initially between the central and local government and was all earmarked for exclusive use on infrastructure. In 1993, part of the central-local compromise for adoption of the tax–sharing system was to grant localities exclusive control over land transfer revenue (to compensate for their loss of revenue from the new tax system). That compromise

[1] 1981年广东省人民代表大会常务委员会公告第六号公告:《深圳经济特区土地管理暂行规定》。.

Y. Hou et al., *The Property Tax in China,* Development and Governance,
DOI 10.1007/978-3-319-10049-4_2

Table 2.1 Local revenue from sale of land use right (land transfer fees) and its ratio against total local outlays 2008–2011 (in millions of RMB Yuan). (Source: Chinese Ministry of Finance, "Report on central and subnational governments' budget implementation of past fiscal year and budget of current fiscal year," http://www.mof.gov.cn/.)

	2008	2009	2010	2011
Subnational general budget expenditure	49,993	63,202	74,959	94,334
Subnational fund budget expenditure	12,928	14,292	30,299	37,486
Subnational land transfer fees	10,375	13,965	29,110	33,166
Ratio(%)	16	18	28	25

Chinese governments use a multiple budget system that includes General Budget, Fund Budget, and State-owned Enterprise Budget

The ratio equals subnational LTF over the sum of subnational general budget expenditure and subnational fund budget expenditure

triggered an increasing transfer of land use right by local governments and over time "cultivated" local dependence on LTF. In fact, the central government at the time of the compromise did not realize that a temporary measure would develop into such rampant use or that the total transfer revenue could reach such amounts.

By objective observation, the overdependence by local governments on LTF is rooted in a loophole in the country's financial system that embeds a mismatch between revenue sources and service provision responsibilities among central, provincial, and local governments. In simple terms, the new separate tax regime assigned major taxes and designated the largest share of the shared taxes to the central government, leaving localities with minor taxes and the smallest share of the major taxes. However, localities were assigned most of the responsibilities of basic services provision; thus, their own-source revenue is always short of the tasks on their shoulders.

Meanwhile, top local officials all target high growth rates of the local economy for their own legacies with local residents and for their career prospects at higher positions, with the latter possible mainly from grand achievements on the former. Thus, it only became rational for local officials to maximize the discretionary assets within their control, LTF, which is a very brief version of the complicated "(government) land coffer" story. Table 2.1 offers data from public sources, for the years 2008–2011, on the size of the land coffer and its contribution ratio to total local outlay. The ratio was 16% in 2008 and peaked at 28% in 2010.

Needless to say, the huge amounts of LTF played a very positive role in raising the urgently needed financing for urban infrastructure, which paved the way for fast economic growth, as has been observed everywhere in the country in the past two decades. But problems also arose. One example is that most of the raised funds were used on urban construction so that the gap in facilities and services has been enlarging between urban and rural areas. Another example is that some local governments did not adequately compensate relocated residents or resort to simplistic measures in relocation, which has caused numerous tragic incidents even social unrests. The biggest problem is that the stock of land is limited; thus, this route for fund raising is unsustainable for long-term growth.

There has been some research in this regard. Anderson (2011) examines the effect of LTF in China (the fees paid at the time of development) on development timing and structural density. He argues that charging the LTF may delay development and the impact of LTF on structural density depends on the situation of a municipality (growing or declining). As an extra cost on land, LTF increases the structural density in a growing municipality and decreases the structural density in a declining municipality. Thus, removal of the LTF may speed up development.

2.2 The New System: Local Property Tax

It is high time that China switched into a new system—the local property tax (LPT), as the means to overcome the problems caused by the rampant sale of land use rights and over-reliance on LTF. As we have argued in a few other places in this monograph, the change from land rent to property tax is to place finance on a regular and contractual basis that facilitates financial planning and supervision. Anderson (2011) also argues that switching to the property tax (if it is designed as a unified ad valorem tax on both land and improvements) will be more favorable to development timing. Another recent study (Hong and Brubaker 2011) examines issues in integrating the property tax into the current local public finance system in China. With empirical results, they are optimistic about switching from land-leasing to the property tax—as long as local governments devote revenue from the property tax to public services in their jurisdiction, the land value will not see a drastic decline.

Starting from the 1994 "separate taxes system", Chinese local governments have been relying on central transfers for about half their annual outlays. Under the *Initial Equilibrium*, the **revenue equation** for local governments is:

$$R_{t,j,i} = F_{land} + G_{(dis+spe)} + T_{(b+vat+fees)} \tag{2.1}$$

The term "local government" refers to that in an urban district or a rural county, respectively. R is total revenue of local government i of province j in year t. Total revenue includes own-source revenues and fiscal transfers. F is "land transfer fee" that a local government attains by selling land use rights. G is fiscal transfer from the central government and provincial government. Transfers can be classified as discretionary transfers (*dis*) and special transfers (*spe*). The former can be used for any purpose without strings attached; the latter can be used only for designated purposes. $T_{(b+vat+fees)}$ are other own-source revenues from the business tax (T_b), value-added tax (T_{vat}), and other fees (T_{fees}).

On the expenditure side, the initial **expenditure equation** is:

$$E_{t,j,i} = C_{ecn} + S_{(edu+hth)} + A_{(psn+ope)} \tag{2.2}$$

E is total local expenditure from own sources and fiscal transfers. C_{ecn} is outlay on infrastructure for economic development. $S_{(edu+hth)}$ is outlay on key public services education and public health. $A_{(psn+ope)}$ is outlay on government administration, which consists of personnel expenses (psn) and operational expenses (ope). It is important to separate personnel expenses from operational expenses because in the Chinese context, the government payroll is large and usually rigid; operational expenses are more flexible in comparison and can be subject to cuts more easily than personnel expenses.

There exist corresponding relations between terms in the revenue equation and the expenditure equation. Land transfer fees (F_{land}) are typically used for infrastructure (C_{ecn}) to facilitate economic development and attract business investment. Special purpose fiscal transfers (G_{spe}) are typically designated for education and health services ($S_{edu+hth}$); discretionary fiscal transfers (G_{dis}) are mostly for personnel and operations.

The "land transfer fee" is the price paid by developers to a local government for the right to use a land parcel for up to 70 years. Given this long window of the use right at a one-shot fee, we take it as infinite in terms of government budgeting. This price for land use per unit is a function of the local economy (developed, under- or undeveloped; urban, suburban, or rural) and the specific location (downtown, mid-, or up-town). The final price is determined through open bidding. The **land transfer fee equation** is:

$$F_{j,i} = \gamma\mu\rho L \tag{2.3}$$

The equation does not carry the year marker (t) because revenue from LTF is irregular and unstable. It is not a guaranteed recurring income, and the amount fluctuates from year to year. γ is the ratio of the total fee that is allowed to be kept at the local level as own-source revenue; the rest is to be remitted to the central and provincial governments. μ is a binary of 1 and 0, 1 being urban and 0 rural. ρ is the location index, $0 < \rho < 1$. 1 indicates prime location like downtown; 0 is farmland that is prohibited from development. L is the stock of land in a jurisdiction.

The **fiscal transfer equation** is:

$$G_{t,j,i} = Zr\mu_{(dis+spe)} + P\mu(1-w)_{(dis+spe)} \tag{2.4}$$

Z stands for central government transfer programs; P for provincial transfers. r is the region designation of 1, 2, and 3. It is linked to economic development of the province: 1 for the eastern or developed provinces; 2 for interior or underdeveloped provinces; and 3 for western or undeveloped provinces. Using this designation as a multiplier, central transfer programs distinguish the provinces by their extent of development, for equity between provinces. μ is the urban marker since property tax is levied only in urban areas (including the county seat or metro townships in rural counties). w is the indicator of within-province, local economy or tax base, $0<w<1$; it is used by the provincial government in distributing provincial transfers, for equity between local jurisdictions.

After three decades of high-speed industrialization, in particular residential housing development in the past 15 years, urban land for construction is facing severe restrictions; additionally, land supply is limited and land transfer fees are very unstable. China started in early 2011 to introduce the LPT. We can assume that if the introduction is smooth, then overtime LPT will be an effective tool for sustainable local revenue (Dye and England 2010), particularly for Chinese local governments that now rely heavily on LTF.

Introducing the property tax brings in a *New Equilibrium*, under which the **revenue equation** changes to:

$$\mathrm{R}_{t,j,i} = F_{land} + P_{t,j,i} + G_{(dis+spe)} + T_{(b+vat+fees)} \tag{2.5}$$

The land fee is maintained because it will stay for a long time as a local revenue source and exert downward pressure on expansionary land use, though revenue from this source remains unstable and irregular. The new addition is the property tax as extra revenue, P, that is regular, recurring each year; more importantly, this new revenue is stable because market values of existing property parcels tend to be stable. The **property tax equation** is:

$$P_{t,j,i} = \tau v n \tag{2.6}$$

τ is the rate set for the LPT. Different from other existing taxes whose rates are set by the central and/or provincial governments, this LPT rate is (will be) set by local governments. v is the benchmark value of residential property as an eligibility test for the LPT. n is the ratio of total property stock subject to the tax. In the pilot property taxes in Chongqing and Shanghai, the benchmark value, v, has been set at a very high level (only targeting luxury housing, for now) in order to mitigate the shock of the tax to the middle class or other house owners. In the long run, this benchmark will decrease to broaden the tax base; ultimately, all (urban) residential property will be subject to the tax.

Once property tax revenue streams in, the **expenditure equation** adjusts also:

$$E_{t,j,i} = C_{ecn} + S_{(ph+edu+hth)} + A_{(psn+ope)} \tag{2.7}$$

Specifically, property tax revenue is now designated for a new service, public housing (*ph*), as has been planned for in Shanghai and Chongqing. In the future, it is expected to provide extra resources for education and public health also.

2.3 Local Discretion and Decentralized Service Choice

It has long been established in the public finance literature that public service provision by local governments maximizes economic efficiency from their proximity to service recipients and thereby better, real-time information about citizen demands and preferences for public services (Tiebout 1956). More recent studies provide further evidence that despite its over-strict assumptions, the Tiebout model remains valid when local preferences are similar in localities where most "residents can benefit from those goods" (Gruber 2007, p. 281). China-specific studies reveal that regional decentralization and fiscal incentives have played a significant role in the process of China's economic development from 1970 to 1999 (Jin et al. 2005).

As evidenced in the literature, local governments "dependent on grants have little autonomy" (Fisher 1996, p. 211). Fiscal independence to some extent determines the level of political autonomy; China's economic development process has also showcased this tendency. The institutionalization of the LPT is a major step in this direction. We can represent the degree of fiscal independence with B, the ratio of own-source revenue against total revenue, $(Ros/Rtot)^{-r}$; the superscript is to take into account the gap in economic development between the three regions (eastern, interior, and western).

With increasing revenue from the LPT, local governments will be able to afford more own-source outlay on services thereafter, in particular outlay on education and public health, which will capitalize into the local tax base, v, so that the relationship between local public service outlays and local own-source revenue is increasingly clear and tight. This closer link of own-source revenue to service provision will help bring about democratic governance by holding local government accountable for service provision and the quality of services, which in turn will capitalize into the property value in a jurisdiction. This loop will form a favorable cycle.

We can represent this loop with D, the ratio of LPT revenue against total own-source revenue, $(P/Ros)^{-w}$; the superscript takes into account the within-province differences in economic development (w). Earmarking property tax revenue for specific uses establishes the tax-service link. Making transparent the LPT levy and collection and basing the use of the LPT revenue on formulae will help institutionalize the link, which enforces democratic governance via public oversight of tax administration and the local government budget (use of LPT revenue). The above equations will be substituted or combined to formulate workable and testable propositions.

Based on the aforementioned theoretical framework, we formulate the following hypotheses:

- H1: Levying the LPT will provide a stable revenue source for local governments.
- H2: Increased own-source revenue to be designated for local public services will closely link the local revenue to service provision, more truthfully reflecting resident preferences and demands.
- H3: Increased own-source revenue will reshape intergovernmental fiscal relations, granting local governments more autonomy.

With that said, the immediate next argument is to make the property tax a local tax as a means to increase local autonomy in making taxing and spending decisions. Thus, decisions for the type, quantity, and quality of services to provide will be local issues through mechanisms of collective decision-making, like public budgeting and voting. These are among the best ways to bind local governments to local residents and tax payers, increase transparency, hold officials accountable for results, and ultimately improve the trust between the citizenry and government. These are topics we refer to again and again in this monograph.

Chapter 3
Real Property Tax for Chinese Local Governments

In this chapter we expand Sect. 1.3 with deliberation on the rationales for the real property tax (RPT) as the administrative tool and fiscal institution that has the potential to solve multiple problems China now faces. We first define the RPT then explain how the tax is a fiscal and budgetary institution and how it can reshape the relationship between the higher and local governments. Finally, we discuss how this tax can raise the efficiency of public service provision. With all these deliberated we complete the circle of why China now needs a local property tax.

3.1 Defining the Real Property Tax

The modern RPT displays some distinctive features with its base, rate structure, revenue elasticity, efficiency, and equity. The base of RPT is land and structures on land. The tax is levied on all land and structures that are residential, commercial, and industrial except specific exemptions, for example, land and buildings owned and used by government, religious, and nonprofit organizations in the United States. Thus defined, the tax *base is very broad*, which is a key element in the efficiency of a tax because the broad base minimizes possibilities of behavioral distortion by individuals, households, and businesses.

The RPT uses an *ad valorem* rate structure; The tax levy is a percentage of the market value of the property (both the land and the structure). In this sense, it is a proportional tax, not progressive or regressive. However, housing is a normal good with a positive income elasticity of demand. As the income or wealth level of an individual or household increases, they tend to purchase and own, or invest in, larger and better houses in better, more desirable locations. As a consequence, they end up paying higher amounts of this tax relative to others with lower income or wealth. This "new view" of RPT (in the academic literature) shows a potentially progressive aspect of the tax. On the other hand, generally a person or a household, over its lifetime, will acquire higher incomes and accumulate more wealth, and naturally will own better homes than when their incomes are low. In this life cycle perspective, everyone will move up in their living standards and pay greater amounts of

Y. Hou et al., *The Property Tax in China*, Development and Governance,
DOI 10.1007/978-3-319-10049-4_3

taxes later rather than earlier in their lives. Improvements in income and quality of life enlarge the tax base and makes the tax burden proportional, rather than progressive. This feature increases the tax's *equity* and also substantively contributes to the political *feasibility* of the tax because most individuals and households, in most years of their lives, will take this tax as fair.

Another important feature of the RPT is the cyclical stability of revenue for government from this tax, relative to revenues from other taxes. The income elasticity of individuals and households on residential property is positive, but smaller than unity, and the increase in housing consumption typically lags behind income, which leads to a smaller than unity revenue elasticity. That is, it is an inelastic tax: in boom years of the economic cycle, government revenue from this tax will be shy of the growth rate of GDP or income, but in bust years, reduction in RPT revenue will be less drastic than that of other taxes that have higher elasticity. This feature makes RPT a more stable revenue source over the economic cycle in comparison to elastic taxes such as the income tax and the consumption (or sales) tax. Cyclical stability of revenue is more valuable to local governments than to national or regional governments because localities have a smaller revenue portfolio than higher level governments. The RPT revenue makes up 50–70 % of total local government revenue, but localities have to provide key public services whose demand tends to be countercyclical. That is, during bust years, residents rely more on local public services than during boom years.

The modern RPT is typically a local tax, which is true not only in the US but also Australia and some European countries. Localities exercise full discretion over the use of revenue from the tax and also the tax rate (in the US though the RPT rate is subject to caps specified in state laws). The localization of RPT is a natural requirement of the tax due to several reasons. First and foremost, regular, accurate, and appropriate appraisal or assessment of property values has long been known as the weakest link of the RPT but is key to the efficiency and equity of the tax. Lack of, or lag in, appraisal will compromise the tax on these two grounds. In the government hierarchy, local governments are much better positioned than the higher levels in obtaining real time, full information (registry) regarding the tax base. Thus, the administration of the tax is best placed within the local level rather than other levels in order to overcome the (lack of) information problem. Advances in information technology in the past two decades have made appraisal much less of a time-consuming and mistake-prone process; the local level still remains the best agent to administer this tax.

Second, a local RPT acts as a benefit tax, when used mostly to finance key local public services such as basic education, health, public safety, streets, and recreational facilities. The explicit direct link between tax payment and services places a demanding requirement for transparent and democratic procedures and processes in its administration. Generally in each budget cycle, the tax rates and exemptions are fully and openly deliberated through public participation, then decided upon via referendum. The adopted budget becomes a public document to facilitate effective supervision of expenditures and program implementation, to hold local officials accountable to taxpayers, and to curb corruption and correct malpractices. This is how, and why, we believe that the property tax works, or should work, as *local property tax* (LPT) for better governance in direct democracy or in transition towards democratic governance.

So far the discussion has been from existing knowledge about the practice and research in western countries, or property taxation of the western style as we know it. Inquisitive readers would challenge why a western practice is taken for granted as proper in the Chinese context. Chapter 5 answers this question by tracing the root of this tax back to Chinese economic and financial history.

3.2 LPT As a Fiscal and Budgetary Institution

Once defined as the LPT, we need to pursue how the tax works and how it changes the operation of local governments. Since property taxation is placed at the discretion of localities, it offers own-source revenue. The working mechanism of own-source revenue differs fundamentally from that of other sources. The amount of revenue from this source is potentially large because its base is a basic life necessity that is housing and a factor of production for businesses. As the economy develops and personal income increases, the tax base trends up despite some short-term cyclical caves along the long-term upward trend. In the United States, the share of LPT in total local revenue was historically high, up to 100 %; however, it has remained in the 50–70 % range during the past half century as intergovernmental transfers have assumed an increasingly larger share. Further, the LPT revenue is more stable than elastic taxes, as discussed in Sect. 3.1, which suits well the unique role of local governments as providers of basic services. The combination of revenue stability and abundant in-stream revenue over time offers a rich endowment to local government financial capacity. It is in this sense that we say the LPT is a fiscal institution.

Further, since the LPT revenue is used to finance basic services, it serves as a direct link between local own-source revenue and local program outlays. This direct link functions fully because of the proximity between local officials and residents and through the public budgeting process. Local officials reside in their jurisdiction, meet other residents on a daily basis, and know the preferences, likes as well as dislikes, of the community. It is this proximity that grants the local level the informational advantage over the other levels. The knowledge of resident preferences is a double-edged sword: taxpayers assume and expect officials to meet their demands. If officials perform well, residents will take the performance for granted. If their performance is below the expectation, blame from residents is imminent. Citizen supervision is constant in an informal way. Moreover, all taxing decisions and spending choices go through the regular budgeting process, whether the local budget cycle is annual or biannual, in an open and transparent environment, which provides multiple formal checkpoints for oversight via venues like public hearings. In this view, the LPT also serves as a budgetary institution that places local officials and taxpayers (residents and voters simultaneously) in a close, inseparable bond. This bond is unique to local governments at the frontline of public services provision.

3.3 LPT and Intergovernmental Relations

With the real property tax installed as a local fiscal and budgetary institution, the LPT inserts subtle changes into the relationship between localities and their higher levels. With dependable streams of own-source revenues as a mainstay of total local revenue, localities become self-sustained; the financial basis for local autonomy now exists. With regular, constant oversight from local residents, accountability of local officials is linked to taxpayers, not to bosses in higher level governments. This mechanism works regardless of the political or state system of a country but is especially apparent where direct election is in place. Local financial autonomy thus builds a natural bridge to local autonomy in other, related aspects. These changes brought in by the local property tax are substantive; they reshape the operational landscape of local governments.

In other words, the above changes are inherent with local discretion over the RPT. As long as the LPT is adopted, those changes occur by default over time. This raises the question of whether the above changes are positive or otherwise. The answer to this challenge is a definite, positive yes. Along with the arguments we made in the first chapter on the functions of modern government, roles of local government in providing services, and the unique advantages of the local level vis-à-vis other levels, local autonomy is necessary and beneficial for the government sector to fully accomplish its responsibilities.

3.4 LPT and Efficiency in Public Service Provision

The LPT as a fiscal and budgetary institution not only reshapes intergovernmental fiscal relations, it also effectively raises the efficiency of the local sector in public service provision. The formal and informal venues of public input and participation in the budgeting process, as discussed in Sect. 3.2, facilitate more direct revelation of the true and often changing preferences of local residents. With the direct link between tax payment and benefits received by local residents, local taxing and outlay decisions fully incorporate the collective demand of taxpayers. In places where majority voting is adopted, the demand of the median voter is the collective choice. Among many different options, this is the one that achieves the highest citizen satisfaction and political acceptability of local policies, maximizing efficiency improvement.

Needless to say, caveats exist. First, this efficiency gain is "economic efficiency" in policy analysis; it is not necessarily equal to or even does not lead to allocative efficiency. The gain in economic efficiency is no guarantee for satisfaction of every resident, neither is the policy or outcome optimal; it is merely the result of majority voting. Second, it is highly likely that efficiency gains may cause compromises on equity: localities with varying real property value are endowed with divergent own-source revenues, which results in disparity in the quantity and quality of local public services. This last issue, inequality in tax base and disparity in local wealth, is usually addressed with intergovernmental transfers, as is done in developed countries. China has been quickly catching up on this front in recent years.

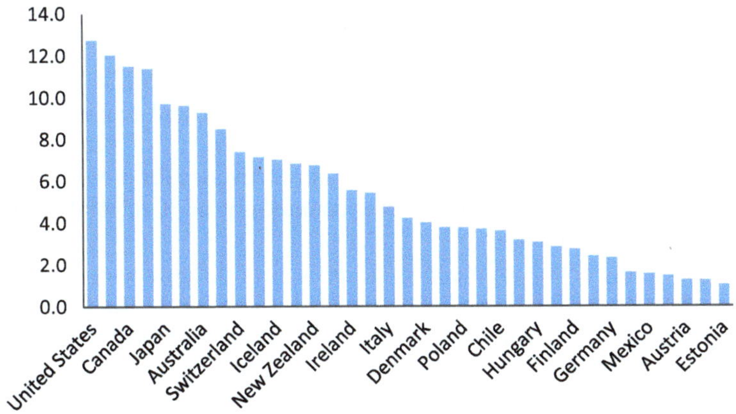

Fig. 3.1 Ratios of property tax revenue in total tax revenue in 2010, OECD countries. (Source: OECD (2012). *Revenue Statistics 2012*. Paris: OECD Publishing)

3.5 Why China Needs a Local Property Tax?

The four aspects discussed above in this chapter present the rationales for an RPT for discretionary local control. They also explain the working mechanisms of LPT as a fiscal and budgetary institution in reshaping intergovernmental relations and raising economic efficiency in service provision. The discussion lays the foundation for our central argument: the LPT is the institution to install in China to help solve the multifarious socioeconomic issues.

Obvious challenges arise: why is the LPT, a western practice taken for granted as proper in the Chinese context? Our answer is embedded in the first section: principles of public finance and mechanisms of financial operation are neutral, or insensitive, to the differences in the political and state systems of context countries. These principles and mechanisms are generic; we expect them to be as applicable in China as have been in other countries.

3.6 Appendix: Property Taxes and the Tax Rate Determining Processes in Typical Countries

3.6.1 A Brief Overview of Property Taxes in Other Countries

In the development process from a natural economy to a commodity economy, taxes from merchandise and income have gradually become an important part of government revenue. However, the property tax is still an important revenue source for governments, especially local governments (Fig. 3.1). In 2010, property tax accounted for over 5 % of the tax revenue in Organisation for Economic Co-operation and Development (OECD) countries; among them, this ratio was more than 10 % in the UK, the US, Canada, and South Korea.[1]

In the US, as of fiscal year 2010, property tax accounted for 35 % of the total combined tax revenue of the state and local governments, and accounted for 75 % of total tax revenues for local governments.[2] In Canada, as of fiscal year 2009, property tax accounted for 16 % of total own-source revenue for province, territory, and local governments; and property tax accounted for 66 % of total own-source revenue for local governments.[3]

With regard to the details of property tax levy, they differ among countries. For instance, in the US, RPT is levied and collected according to the following processes in determining: (1) fair market value; (2) assessment ratio; (3) assessment value; (4) value of exemptions; (5) taxable value; (6) tax rate; and (7) property tax due. There are also differences in property tax/value limitations among the states. In California, due to Proposition 13 that was passed in 1978, property tax may not exceed 1 % of the property's fair market value, and the annual increase rate of assessed value should not exceed 2 %. Under the condition of market transactions, however, the levy of property tax will be based on the fair market price.

In Scotland, England, and Wales, according to the purposes of real estate, commercial or residential (commercial real estate is called "Rates," and residential real estate is called "Council Tax"), the property tax levies are different. For residential properties, they are divided into different grades (Bands). In England and Scotland, the property value is discounted to the value on April 1, 1991 and then divided into eight grades accordingly. In Wales, the property value is discounted to the value on April 1, 2003 and then divided into nine grades accordingly. Each property of a different grade is subject to different tax rates: the tax rate increases as the grade increases.

In South Korea, the property tax includes a LPT and a comprehensive real estate holding tax. The LPT distinguishes taxes on land, residential housing, and commercial housing; meanwhile, the tax rates vary on different types of land and housing. The LPT follows the principle that luxury real estate should be subject to a higher tax rate. The comprehensive real estate tax is collected at a progressive tax rate, and the revenue belongs to the central government.

Even though countries all over the world have imposed different regulations and provisions concerning the property tax, we can still summarize the main characteristics of the property tax in typical countries (USA, Great Britain, Australia, and Canada) as the following:

1. Broad tax base. The vast majority of real estate and land are subject to property taxes, except governments and some nonprofit organizations. For properties eligible for the property tax, the government will often offer certain exemptions.

[1] Source: http://www.oecd.org/ctp/tax-policy/revenuestatisticstaxstructures.htm.

[2] Source: U.S. census, http://www.census.gov/govs/local/.

[3] Source: Revenue and expenditures in Canada: http://www5.statcan.gc.ca/subject-sujet/result-resultat.action?pid=3055&id=3059&lang=eng&type=CST&pageNum=1&more=0.

2. Ad valorem tax. An ad valorem tax means that the property tax is levied based on a certain proportion of a property's fair market value. High value properties are subject to higher property taxes, and vice versa.
3. Inelastic revenue. During boom years, property tax revenues will not grow as quickly as the economy. On the other hand, during a recession, property tax revenues will not fall as intensely as the economy. Compared with other taxes, property tax revenue is inelastic, with stronger resistance to volatility.
4. Important revenue source for local governments. Here, "important" means that property tax revenues account for quite a high ratio of total tax revenue of the local government.
5. Local tax. "Local" means that local governments (under certain constraints) are granted the authority to determine the tax rate and tax base of the property tax; they collect the property tax and determine the use of revenues from the tax.
6. Benefit tax. Property tax revenue is mainly used for basic services, including education, public safety, and local roads, which have very small immediate spill-over effects. Taxpayers are residents living in the jurisdiction; meanwhile, they enjoy the corresponding public services. In this process, the revenues and outlays of property tax payments are interconnected.
7. The revenues and outlays of property taxes are made through a "direct democracy" mechanism. This process happens in a transparent environment and is achieved based on a direct democratic mechanism by local residents. Therefore, it is a process to encourage local government officials to be more responsible and accountable for local services and it is effective at curbing corruption.

3.6.2 The Tax Rate Determining Process

The tax rate determining processes vary among different countries; however, the basic procedure is similar. The property tax rate in a typical nation is often determined through a democratic process in accordance with the so-called procedure "expenditure requirement determining the tax levy." The specific steps are as follows:

1. Determine the amount of public expenditure through the political process. Public spending is determined by the quantity and quality of public services to be provided by local governments. The quality and quantity of public services are chosen by local residents through voting, the public choice mechanism.
2. Determine the proportion of the property tax revenue in total expenditure through the political process. This proportion is often based on the revenue structure of each locality. Local governments first calculate how much revenue they can collect from sources other than property tax and then decide the amount of property tax they need to levy and collect.
3. The local government uses the needed property tax revenue divided by the property tax base to calculate the property tax rate. In many cases, local governments set different tax assessment ratios on different types of real estate. In general, the assessment ratios on industrial and commercial properties are higher than that on residential property; the assessment ratio for residential property is higher than that for agricultural property.

Chapter 4
Creating Local Property Taxes as an Institution: Policy Process in China

In this chapter, we first analyze the policy making process by China's top leadership, then summarize research done by academicians and policy experts in the country, which is then followed by an elaboration on the feasibility of the local property tax (LPT) in China, if it is to be adopted widely in the country. Finally, we list a few remaining challenges that the country will need to address in the process of adopting the LPT.

4.1 A Long and Cautious Policy Formulating Process

The call for a serious feasibility study of the property tax started in official documents of the Chinese Government in the early 2000s. Such official language is seen in documents of the central, provincial, and metropolitan governments. In an October 2003 resolution, the Central Committee of the Chinese Communist Party issued the earliest explicit expression: "Launch a reform of taxes and fees on urban construction; levy a uniform and standardized property tax when prerequisites for it are met, then repeal related fees and charges." That document is the earliest call from the highest organ of the ruling party for the property tax. Two years later, the Party Central Committee called again for the government to "smoothly advance adoption of the property tax" (October 2005 Proposal for Drafting the 11th Five-Year Development Plan).

The advance, however, was not fast. It was another three and a half years before the work report of the Central Government of March 2009 mentioned the motion "to study how to promote a reform of the real property tax." In the same year, the State Reform and Development Commission proposed to "deepen the reform of real property tax and consider levying a property tax," which was soon responded to (in July) by a Shenzhen Municipal Plan to "formulate the technical standards of assessing the property tax base, establish a system of property tax base assessment, and to proactively promote levying the tax in the city of Shenzhen." That was the first round of specific measures by the Chinese government toward adopting an LPT.

Fruition came in the second round when the aforementioned prerequisites were better met. In October 2010, the Party Central Committee called for a third time to

Y. Hou et al., *The Property Tax in China,* Development and Governance,
DOI 10.1007/978-3-319-10049-4_4

"study advancing the reform of the property tax" in its October 2010 Proposal for Drafting the 12th Five-Year Development Plan. Specifically, implementable LPTs started in the metropolitans of Shanghai and Chongqing in January 2011. These two LPTs were levied on some selected categories of housing property on a trial basis as pilots before nationwide adoption in order to accumulate experience and learn lessons. In chapter 6 we offer details on these two pilot LPTs.

After the pilot LPTs had been in place for a year, the March 2012 Work Report of the Central Government included more details: "to accelerate the construction of an urban housing information system, reform the taxation of housing property, and promote the long-term smooth growth of the housing market." The Finance Minister, in response to questions from journalists on March 6, 2013, said that the Ministry of Finance "had intended to further study the promotion plan of real property tax reform on the basis of the two pilots, add more localities on the pilot list, and proactively accelerate the reform in a reliable manner." A summary of the original documents (in Chinese) is provided in Appendix 4.1 to illustrate the policy process on adopting the LPT.

The above excerpts reveal several features of the policy process by the Chinese government. The process was lengthy, lasting about a decade, indicating that it took a while to achieve consensus on the property tax. The process was top-down, starting in all three rounds from the highest policy organ, through the administrative hierarchy to localities. Adoption started from the bottom-up, on a trial-and-error basis to open up a path, which also functioned to accumulate experience and lessons in tax levy and administration. With some first-hand knowledge about this tax, the Ministry of Finance and the Central Government made the final call for wider large-scale trials. The last two points are particularly important: the Chinese ruling party and the Government have always been cautious with new policies; trials and pilots are their means to test public tolerance and political acceptability of a new tax, above and beyond the technical feasibility. This is an important lesson from all Chinese reforms.

4.2 Academic and Policy Research on Adopting the Property Tax

While the government was incrementally exploring this policy, the research community and policy think tanks in the country were diligently doing their part of the work, researching the various aspects of the tax in the Chinese context—after all, the existing literature on real property tax is exclusively foreign and in advanced economies. Despite the lack of an overall consensus, even until now, among academicians about adopting the real property tax, those who advocate the tax have outnumbered and overshadowed those who oppose it. Among the advocates, perspective and viewpoints vary widely.

4.2.1 *Academic Research*

The advocates for a Chinese property tax include An Tifu (2005, 2010), Ma Guoqiang (2011), Gu Cheng (2011), and Liu Rong (2011). In summary terms, support for the tax is built on the following rationales. Property tax is inversely related to housing price; thus, levying this tax will help in suppressing the inflation of housing prices. As a local revenue source, the LPT may become an important contributor to local fiscal capacity. On the purpose of use, LPT revenue can be placed at discretion by localities and dedicated to local public services in order to improve local governance. On the tax base and rate structure, some call for a broad base to include rural residential housing as a way to lower the rate for higher economic efficiency. Others prefer to position the LPT as an adjustment tax of housing consumption to be levied only on luxury housing. Still some others argue for a transition model, a compromise of the above two, which will start from a narrow base, then move to a broader base and lower rate. However, there is also dissent among the advocates. For example, some do not think the tax can help control housing prices or become a major local revenue source.

The voice of the opponents is by no means subdued by that of the advocates. Yang Bin (2007) holds the opinion that the Tiebout model is not at all realistic in the Chinese context where democratic decision making does not exist and "voting with your feet" via free migration is not an option for Chinese citizens. He further believes that the Chinese local government system is distinctly different from that of the US; thus transplanting an American mechanism into China misleads the country. According to Lang Xianping (2010), the free-flowing housing price is controllable only through building an adequate amount of public housing for rent or economical housing for sale. The property tax will not offer any help in this regard. Xia Shangmo (2011) goes to the theoretical basis: It is an outdated theory to regard property tax as an instrument for income redistribution. Real property tax will probably not help to suppress housing prices, but will generate net welfare loss. In Liu Shangxi's (2012) view, the LPT reform in modern China should not set LPT revenue as the policy goal, nor can the LPT become a major revenue source for local governments. At the present level of the national average personal income, LPT is at best an adjustment tax on housing consumption.

4.2.2 *Opinions of Think Tank Researchers*

Among the major government-related think tanks, three have openly expressed their opinions on the LPT. They are the Fiscal Research Institute (FRI) of the Ministry of Finance, the Finance and Economic Strategies Research Institute (FES) of the Chinese Academy of Social Sciences, and the Development Research Center (DRC) of the State Council. Researchers at these think tanks differ from university professors in that these policy researchers are closer to the government, more familiar with administrative practices, and more prone toward application than theory; their opinions often heavily influence policy making. No doubt, think tank researchers are by no means of one voice; but despite some differences among these researchers, their mainstream opinion can be summed up as follows: In the short term, LPT should be narrowly based to readjust housing consumption toward more economical use; in the long run, LPT will incrementally transition into a broad-based real property tax that fits within the Chinese context.

Jia Kang of the FRI (2011) is a typical representative of the practical side of the policy considerations. In his view, adoption of the real property tax is not just a readjustment of the tax system, but also an important step to deepen the reform in matching revenue sources with responsibilities between the different layers of the government hierarchy. Thus, it is a natural move within the medium- to long-term overall planning for the restructuring of the financial regime. In this perspective, adopting the LPT should follow the incremental strategy, starting easy and transitioning into more difficult steps, with the tax base being narrow at first and then gradually being widened, which will ultimately make the tax a mainstay of local own-source revenue. Gao Peiyong et al. (2012) at the FES advocate for a 40 m^2 exemption per household member; floor space above the exemption quota is subject to the LPT. The LPT pilot list is to expand gradually and the experience from Shanghai and Chongqing is to be applied nationwide to promote more economical and rational housing consumption.

Ni Hongri of the DRC (2012) holds the view that the LPT plays a key role in stuffing up major local taxes, maintaining the healthy growth of the housing market, and safeguarding social equity. Thus, it is urgent to introduce the LPT. However, given the current capacity of the country's tax administration agencies, she believes that it is best for the adoption of LPT to stay on a steady and gradual pace. First, trials should start with commercial property to be followed by residential property. She further predicts that a widespread levy of residential property tax is not realistic during the 12th five-year period (2012–2016).

It is clear that even though the policy process has extended for a decade, the academic and policy research communities are far from achieving consensus, which is on the one hand natural. On the other hand, it is emblematic of the magnitude of difficulty involved in a countrywide levy of the property tax on all residential property and in making this tax a major local revenue source. More importantly, when it has been so difficult to convince the educated citizens of the efficacy of the LPT, it will be particularly more difficult to convince all individual tax payers. In the following sections, we turn to those aspects.

4.3 Feasibility of Levying Local Property Tax in Current China

In order to have a perspective on whether the LPT is practicable in the current state of the country, it is necessary to conduct a feasibility study of levying the tax with its political acceptability, technical operability, administrative ease, and revenue adequacy. We examine these one by one.

4.3.1 Political Acceptability

In the western sense, political acceptability refers mainly, if not solely, to the popularity of a policy with the voters; this aspect is also true in China. In the Chinese sense, this term has another aspect—whether the party's top leadership considers the time is right for a new measure. If yes, then they consider whether the top leaders of a province or locality are willing to try it out in their jurisdiction, considering the possible consequences, favorable and unfavorable, intended as well as unintended, for their jurisdiction and their own career. A third, minor aspect is whether the policy is completely western with no Chinese root. In the next section, we will show that property tax has a long history in China; thus this is not a major concern.

Will the Chinese populace support this tax? The answer is not an easy one. Though personal income has been rising fast, in the last two decades with the rapid growth of the country's economy, the total tax burden on average income earners has been heavy, which is especially true if we consider the relatively low quantity and quality of public services. Putting this into technical jargon, the aggregate TAX–GDP ratio is probably not as high in China as in Western European countries, but the tax–income ratio on individual workers is not low in comparable terms; the per capita tax–service (benefit) ratio is low because of low efficiency in service production, rampant corruption, and waste. These factors formulate a vicious cycle that erodes public trust in the government in general, and weakens the political acceptability of any new policy, especially new taxes. This partly explains why the policy process at the top has been long and slow between the first two rounds, as discussed in Sect. 4.1.

On the other hand, the Chinese government has, since 2003, substantially increased input into basic education, public health, social security, and income security, which has won them bargaining room for new policies. This can explain why the policy process accelerated from 2009 onward. In the same period, the real estate sector showed an unprecedented boom. Per capita living space more than doubled from 2000 to 2010, but the housing prices went almost out of control, which caused widespread complaints. Thus, considering all aspects of the issue, the top leaders leaned toward a "go" versus "hold" on the LPT.

The route then taken was to use the old successful strategy of local trials before wide adoption to test the water of public acceptance of the tax; the process was intended to be gradual as a measure to smooth public resentment of tax increases. Specifically, it was to start from the rich and urban areas; thereby came the two metropolitans as pilot cities of the LPT in January 2011.

The choice of the locations of the pilot LPT was based on economic development, potential influence, and willingness of the local top leaders. According to the official documents of Shanghai, the most developed area in the country and among the most troubled with the highest housing prices, the intention of the municipal government (and its leadership) in being a pilot city was to restrain the free-flying price with the new tax. In the official language, it was "to readjust income redistribution and promote social equity, [and also] to guide residents towards rational housing consumption while promoting economical use of urban land."[1] The other pilot city, Chongqing, opted into the new tax trial out of slightly different considerations. Being a very new metropolitan that was created only in 1997, and thus economically underdeveloped, the metro leaders bear no burden in trying new policies, but only seek wider influence. In the words of Mayor Huang Qifan, they weighed more heavily on the potential influence of the tax on the housing market especially on high-end luxury housing.

4.3.2 Technical Operability

In comparison to the political aspect, the technicalities are much easier. As discussed in the next chapter; the LPT and even the housing property tax, dates back by centuries in China. The tax being old, many technical tools have long been in use. In our overall assessment, the technical operability of the LPT presents no major hurdles to its wide adoption in the country; that said, huge tasks lay ahead in preparations by government agencies. Three tasks stand out as the most urgent.

First, create real estate databases, that are to be integrated into a nationwide network. On a fieldwork trip in Shanghai, we witnessed such a local data base in operation. Second, construct a real estate value assessment system and train professional property assessors. This is by far the most difficult and time consuming job. The assessment system should make the fullest use of the proven tools and techniques in advanced countries and be adjusted to the Chinese context. The third is to design the property tax framework. On this, we hold a different view from scholars and policy experts in China. We see as necessary multiple decentralized, locally innovated frameworks rather than a "uniform" or "standard" framework. Given the geographical dispersion of the country, multifarious types of housing features in all parts of the country, and the huge differences in economic development, only locally developed frameworks can apply and prove usable ultimately; any rigid or uniform national standards will be doomed to fail the applicability test.

4.3.3 Administrative Ease

Once the above mentioned database is put in place, information technology can facilitate the administrative side of tax levy and collection, including real time information on market sales and other transactions of all property types. Still, the herculean task lies in property value assessment, as has been true in developed countries that have been levying this tax for decades. It is foreseeable that the biggest challenges and the most frequent and serious complaints from property owners will be in value assessment. A recent study based on interviews of LPT payers in Chongqing provides evidence in this regard.[2]

[1] "上海为啥征房产税:调节收入分配 引导理性选房," see http://www.chinanews.com/estate/2011/01-28/2818903.shtml.

[2] This is a working paper by a doctoral student of the Renmin University, dated December 2012.

4.3.4 Revenue Adequacy

We firmly believe that in the long run, the LPT will become a major revenue source for local governments, once the tax is levied on all real property. In this sense, the Chinese version of the LPT will be as revenue adequate as its foreign counterparts. But in the short run, revenue from this tax will be minimal, as has been shown from the 2011–2012 trial levy and collection in Shanghai and Chongqing. More information will be provided in the following chapters in which we discuss in great detail the pilot LPT in those metropolitans.

4.4 Expansion of Local Property Tax from Pilots to Nationwide

Based on the above analysis, our judgment is that the LPT will spread to all urban areas in the whole country. Recent development among the country's top policy making body has shown strong indications in that direction, though debate in research circles concerning the immediate applicability of the tax remains unsettled.

Before the full expansion becomes reality, policy residuals from the past cry for solutions, at least temporary ones. First, local governments since 1998 have collected land transfer fees through selling the use rights of state-owned land; thus, the market price of housing property already includes an implicit 70-year "land rent". It is legitimate for tax payers to challenge the reasonableness, or "legitimacy," of property taxation on top of that rent. Alternatively, rationale must be provided to fully explain the relationship between the new tax and the price-included land rent. Second, under current Chinese law, all land belongs to the state, which means that housing property owners purchase only ownership of the structure on the land and the use right of the land, but not the property right of the land. A statutory solution will have to be provided as rationale for the land-housing split of property ownership in China. Third, we have envisioned the LPT as a benefit tax that serves as the direct link between tax payment and basic services. How to guarantee that local governments spend the LPT revenue on public services rather than on other items will be an important change in the governance structure. We will elaborate on this in the 9th and 10th chapter. Last but not least, some legal details with regard to the land right demand clarification, for example, the varying length of the land use right between types of housing property (the lease terms are 70 years for residential use, 40 years for commercial use, 50 years for industrial and institutional use, and 50 years for mixed use). Despite all these, the LPT retains its bright applicability in China.[3]

[3] For example, Jia Kang of the FRI also believes there are no unsurmountable challenges to adopting LPT. See "开征房产税仍具可行性," http://finance.eastmoney.com/news/1355,20121207262562832.html.

Chapter 5
Roots of the Real Property Tax in Chinese History

While it is true that the Chinese government has been very open to learning from foreign experiences, especially since the early 1980s, it is also true that Chinese leaders have the inborn inclination to look into the country's long and rich history for wisdom, precedence, and lessons, which is in many ways a smart strategy for acceptability and public resonance. The property tax is no exception. Taking as our second assumption that the Chinese government and the nation as a whole may desire a scrutiny of historical experience, in this chapter, we carefully comb through Chinese historical literature on finance and taxation to trace the use and evolution of the real property tax to thousands of years ago. Our purpose in investigating the history of this tax is to provide a modern, theoretical perspective of property taxation in the tax system of contemporary China. Doing so may contribute to a well-rounded, more comprehensive understanding of an unfolding reform that is currently taking place.

5.1 Property Taxation in Chinese History

In this section, we trace the origin and evolution of property taxation in Chinese history. From this brief historical review, we want to find out whether the property tax was used, and, if so, whether it was a main revenue source in ancient China, in modern China, and in the most recent era until the turn of the 21st century. This review bears much significance as to the evolution of taxation in a country with a long history. More importantly, the historical review generates insight into the possible path of further fiscal reforms in China and provides valuable lessons for other countries as well.

Y. Hou et al., *The Property Tax in China*, Development and Governance,
DOI 10.1007/978-3-319-10049-4_5

5.1.1 *Property Taxation as Mainstay Tax Revenue*

5.1.1.1 Property Taxation Before the Late Tang Dynasty

It has been almost universally true that government revenue in ancient times was tied to land, because agriculture was the base for everything else. Thus, the amount of land owned or cultivated, yield from land, and land-related assets had long been used as the base for the levy and collection of "contribution" from citizens (in Rome and Greece), lords (in Britain and France), and rentiers to the king or emperor. Such a description is true in Chinese history from about the year 2100 B.C. in the slave society to the end of the feudal dynasties (1911 A.D.). During that span of nearly 4000 years, government revenues were collected through/as land rent or land taxes in various forms and under many different names. The core of all those revenue-generating systems was always "property," which in ancient China was almost exclusively land or output from land.

From the years 2070 to 771 B.C. (the Xia, Shang, and Western Zhou Dynasties under the slavery system), the main revenue sources were called *Gong*, *Zhu*, and *Che*. *Gong* (贡), or contribution, was a tax on farmland output in the *Xia* (夏) dynasty, levied at the rate of 1/10th of the unit output from farmland. *Zhu* (助) and *Che* (彻) were taxes on farmland output in the Shang (商) and the Western Zhou (西周) dynasties, respectively, levied at the rate of 1/9th of output.

The years 770 B.C.—220 A.D. (the Spring and Autumn Era [春秋], the Warring States Era [战国], Qin [秦], Western Han [西汉], and Eastern Han [东汉] Dynasties) were periods of transition from a slavery society to a feudal society; the last two dynasties of the above list were also the first powerful and prosperous periods in Chinese feudal society. The main taxes of this millennium were the land tax, head tax, and various forms of *corvee* (力役)[1]. The most important of all these taxes was the land tax, which used a flat rate to calculate the amount of levy. The size of land ownership and the amount of output would be multiplied by the rate; thus, it was a flat or proportional tax.

In the years 220–780 A.D.(the dynasties of the Three Kingdoms Period [三国], Western Jin [西晋], Eastern Jin [东晋], the Southern Dynasties [南朝], the Northern Dynasties [北朝], Sui [隋], and Tang [唐]), the tax system showed more dramatic changes. The so-called *Zu-Diao* (租调) and *Zu-Yong-Diao* (租庸调) systems came into being. These taxes were closely related to the land systems at that time (占/课田制和均田制).

The Three Kingdoms (220–280 A.D.) nationalized uncultivated and unclaimed lands (屯田制) and allocated these lands equally among all citizens, and then levied a fixed amount per unit of farmland (定额地租). On top of the land tax, a household tax (户调), paid in silk or cloth (绢or帛), was levied according to each family's ownership of assets. Households were classified into classes by their possession of assets; the wealthier would have to pay more in household tax. By their nature, both the land and the household taxes were proportional in their rate structure. The Western Jin Dynasty (265–316 A.D.) also implemented an equally distributed land system

[1] *Corvee* refers to variants of a mandate that each household or adult male should contribute a certain number of days free manual work each year to the state

(占/课田). Peasants were allowed to own unclaimed land through cultivation. Each male laborer could claim up to 70 *mu* of land, 50 of which were subject to the land tax. A household tax was also levied, similar to that in the Three Kingdoms Period.

Like the above two periods, the Northern Wei (386–557 A.D.) also tried to ensure that every peasant had a piece of land to cultivate (均田). Each male peasant at or over 15 years of age could get two types of farmland. The first type was 40 *mu* of food or head land, which would be returned to the government upon the person's death. The second type was 20 *mu* of land for silk worms, which was privately owned and could be inherited within the household. Taxes in this period were called *Zu* and *Diao* (租调制). This system differed from prior systems with the same name in that each couple (husband and wife, or household) paid 2 *dan* of grain as rent (租) on government land as well as 1 *pi* of cloth and 8 *liang* of silk as tax on private land (调) (*dan*, *pi*, and *liang* were measurements in ancient China). Four unmarried adult males (at or above age 15) or eight servants/maids, or 20 cows would pay the same amount of rent and tax as a couple.

The early Tang Dynasty (618–780 A.D.) implemented the *Zu–Yong–Diao* (租庸调) system to collect its major revenues. *Zu* (租) and *Diao* (调) were similar to their counterparts in the Northern Wei Period. If a peasant did not want to, or could not perform his assigned *corvee*, he could pay with extra cloth or silk, called *Yong* (庸), as a substitute. This mechanism increased the flexibility of the tax system. Other revenues were from the household tax and land taxes. During the Tang Dynasty, households were classified into different classes according to their assets. The more assets a household owned, the higher a class they would be designated into, with the household tax, to be paid in cash, corresponding to the household's class designation. The land tax was a fixed amount of tax on unit farmland (2 *sheng* per *mu* of land), and it was sometimes calculated by a households' class designation.

Analysis From the above analysis, we identify a path dependence in that the tax system of the Western Jin Period was similar to (or inherited from) that of the Three Kingdoms Period. They both taxed farmlands at a fixed amount per unit of farmland and taxed households by the amount of asset ownership.

The Sui and early Tang Dynasties also followed a similar path from the Northern Wei Period in using analogous tax systems called the *Zu–Diao* or *Zu–Yong–Diao* system, which was actually a head tax with the amount of tax levy not related to owned assets. With further analysis, however, we do find that the head tax was closely related to the land systems. Since the government tried to ensure that every household/peasant had a minimum piece of land to cultivate for livelihood, the head tax system and the land system worked together to make the tax levy relatively equally distributed. In this sense, *Zu*, *Yong*, and *Diao* all fell under the head tax, whose levy and tax burden was still positively related to the amount of assets owned.

5.1.1.2 Property Taxation Since the Late Tang Dynasty

During the late Tang, Song, Yuan, Ming, and Qing Dynasties (780–1911 A.D.), the tax system reverted to a greater dependence on the land tax. In the late-Tang

Dynasty (780–907 A.D.), many peasants lost their farmland, which was then increasingly concentrated under the control of big landowners. With millions of poor peasants with no land to live on, the levy of *Zu*, *Yong*, and *Diao* was regressive and very inequitable; it caused bitter resentment among civilians, and the whole society encountered instability. In the year 780, Prime Minister Yang Yan abolished the old tax system and instituted a new "*Two-tax System,*" under which government revenue was mainly garnered through a household tax and a land tax. The household tax was levied according to household class designation: the more assets a household had, the higher a class the household would be assigned to, and the more household tax would be levied. The land tax was a fixed amount of levy on per unit farmland and was paid twice a year after the summer and autumn harvests. Both of these two new taxes, though under the old names, targeted big households that owned large tracts of land.

The Song Dynasty (960–1279 A.D.) levied a fixed amount, per–unit land tax. Like that in the late Tang Dynasty, this land tax was paid twice a year in summer and autumn. By the middle of the Song Dynasty, farmlands were again becoming highly concentrated in the hands of big landowners. Many of these landowners colluded with local officials to conceal the true amount of their land size in order to avoid the land tax, which not only slashed government revenue but also caused anger among the peasantry and the poor.

With support from the emperor, Chancellor *Wang Anshi* began, in 1068, a reform of the land administration and the tax systems. He commanded local governments to precisely measure farmlands of every property owner (方田) and to classify farmlands into five grades. The owners then would pay the land tax according to the size and the grade of their farmland (均税). During the Song Dynasty, a commodity economy gradually emerged and became especially developed by the middle of the dynasty. For example, in the year 997 (early in the Song Dynasty), land taxes accounted for 65 % of the total revenue; while in the year 1078, land tax was only 30 % of the total revenue, the other 70 % was from a commercial (sales) tax (Sun 2003, p. 213).

The main revenue source of the Yuan Dynasty (1271–1368 A.D.), founded by the Mongolians, was the land tax; in the northern part of the country, the head tax was also an important revenue source. Compared to earlier dynasties, the problem of wealth and land concentration (into the hands of Mongolian nobles) was much worse; the tax system was chaotic, with no uniform rules.

The Ming Dynasty (1368–1644 A.D.) had in its early years compiled very reliable registers of households (户口) and farmlands (鱼鳞图册); these official records proved to be an invaluable base for improving tax administration. However, by the middle Ming dynasty, highly unequal distribution of farmland became problematic just like in earlier dynasties. This repeated cycle from good governance in the early years to poor governance in the later years of each dynasty had turned out to be a persistent pattern that applied to every Chinese (probably foreign also) dynasty. In the middle Ming dynasty, big landowners colluded with local officials in concealing the true size of their farmlands to avoid the land tax. As a counter measure, in the year 1581, Prime Minister Zhang Juzheng implemented the *Yitiaobian*

(一条鞭法) policy that required local governments to strictly measure farmlands, which doubled the amount of taxable farmlands. The new policy also abolished *corvee* and merged it into the land tax to be paid in silver.

In the early part of the Qing Dynasty (1636–1911 A.D.), population growth exceeded the opening-up of farmland. As a result, farmland concentration to high officials and big owners was a worsening problem that heavily burdened poor peasants and forced them to abandon their homes. To solidify the still unstable dynasty, Emperor Kangxi implemented the policy of *Tandingrumu* (摊丁入亩) in 1716 which took the amount of the year 1710 head tax as the base and merged it into the land tax. The regressive head tax was then abolished; the land tax was assigned a new name, "land-head silver" (地丁银), and was a much more equitable tax. By 1725, the land-head silver made up 86 % of the total government revenue; it stayed at 71 % until 1753 (Sun 2003, p. 328).

Analysis The above analysis reveals that in the early period of every dynasty, the tax system, especially the land tax, tended to be more equitable. By the middle period of almost every dynasty, the privileged classes began to take control of large amounts of farmland and then tried to evade the land tax, thus eroding the revenue base of the government and causing huge income gaps. It was in this period that a reformer would emerge to overhaul land administration and the property tax in an effort to equalize tax burden between big land owners and petty peasants and tie the tax to a household's assets. The reform would bring some benefits, but by the late period of every dynasty, there would be no possibility for reforms under the existing regime to fundamentally improve the tax system. At that point in time, a dynasty was doomed to ruin. A new cycle started. It is thus no exaggeration to say that the decay and deterioration of tax administration in each dynasty was the root cause for its death; a new dynasty started with a relatively more equitable tax system to win support for the new government.

5.1.2 Summary of Findings

Table 5.1 provides a summary of the property taxes in Chinese history that were used by different dynasties in chronological order. To sum up, the property tax had long been an important, often the dominant revenue source for the Chinese governments in history. The status of it as mainstay of government revenue was from its stability; different dynasties in Chinese history used methods of tax levy calculation that reduced volatility in government revenue, but increased risk for land owners. The tax scheme shows variation among dynasties and the early, middle, and later years of each dynasty. As a general rule, the more equal and efficient the property tax was, the more prosperous the dynasty tended to be. In other words, an equal and efficient property tax system was an important underlying element of a prosperous dynasty. Thus, we conclude that the real property tax has deep roots in Chinese history.

Table 5.1: Summary of property taxes in Chinese history, by dynasty in chronological order

Dynasty	Main Revenue Sources	Rate Structure
Qin (221 B.C.–206 B.C.) Han (206 B.C.–220)	Land tax	Flat Proportional
Three Kingdoms (220–280) Western Jin (265–316)	Land tax and Household tax	Flat Regressive-Proportional
Northern Wei (386–557)	Head tax (*Zu-Diao*)	Regressive-Proportional
Early Tang (618–780)	Head tax(*Zu-Yong-Diao*) Land tax Household tax	Regressive-Proportional Flat Regressive-Proportional
Late Tang (780–907)	Land tax Household tax	Flat Regressive
Song (960–1279) Yuan (1271–1368) Ming (1368–1644)	Land tax	Flat
Qing (1636–1912)	Land tax (*Land-head Silver*)	Flat

5.2 Property Taxation in Ancient China and the Modern Real Property Tax

In this section, we compare and contrast property taxation in Chinese history as discussed in Sect. 5.1 with the modern real property tax as having been used in the United States. The term "modern" refers specifically to the contemporary or current period, and is not a broad definition as used in historical studies. For the convenience of this discussion, we refer to ancient Chinese versions of the tax, generically as a "land tax" and reserve the term "real property tax" for the modern US version of the tax. The comparison is made between the US and China because on the one hand, we know more about these two countries, and on the other hand, these two countries bear closer similarity than other countries in terms of the size of their population, land area, and total volume of economy.

5.2.1 Tax Base and Rate Structure

With regard to the tax base and rate structure, the land tax in Chinese history bears some similarities to the modern real property tax, as illustrated in Table 5.2. The tax was levied against the amount of land owned or the volume of yield from the land, which was a major property of the agrarian society. The tax was paid mainly with grain, sometimes cash. The rate structure of the land tax can be summarized into several categories. The first was a flat rate of land yield, such as, in the Spring and Autumn Period, the Warring States Period, and the Han Dynasty. The second was a fixed amount of tax per unit of land owned according to the designated class based on the quality (thereby, amount of yield) of farmland, such as in dynasties other than those just listed. The third was in the form of a head tax. For example,

Table 5.2 The base and rate structure of Chinese land taxes by dynasty

Dynasty	Type of Tax	Details
Qin (221 B.C.–206 B.C.)	Land Tax	Average output per unit × Tax rate × # of units Or Fixed amount tax per unit on farm land
Han (206 B.C.–220)	Land Tax	Average output per unit × Tax rate(1/10,1/15,1/30) × # of units
Three Kingdoms (220–280) Western Jin (265–316)	Land Tax	Fixed amount tax per unit of farm land
	Household Tax	By amount of household assets
Northern Wei (386–557)	Head Tax (*Zu-Diao*)	Head tax
Early Tang (618–780)	Head Tax (*Zu-Yong-Diao*)	Head tax
	Land Tax	Fixed amount tax per unit on farm land
	Household Tax	By amount of household assets
Late Tang (780–907)	Land Tax	Fixed amount tax per unit on farm land
	Household Tax	By amount of household assets
Song (960–1279)	Land Tax	Fixed amount tax per unit on farm land
Yuan (1271–1368)		
Ming (1368–1644)		Fixed amount per unit of farm land (corvees merged by Yitiaobian Policy)
Qing (1636–1912)	Land Tax (*Land-head Silver*)	Fixed amount per unit of farm land (head tax merged by Tandingrumu Policy)

the tax in the *Zu–Diao* or the *Zu–Yong–Diao* system was a version of a head tax. Since the distribution of farmland was more equal among peasants in the Northern Wei Period and the early Tang Dynasty, the *Zu–Diao* and *Zu–Yong–Diao* systems were more likely to be a property tax than just a head tax. The last one was in the form of a household tax, which, from the Three Kingdoms Period to the late Tang Dynasty, was levied according to the class designation (by their amount of assets) of a household. Whether the land tax was levied in proportion to the amount of land ownership or as a flat rate of land yield or as a flat-rate, semi-head tax, the tax levy was based on the gross yield from the land. In this sense, the land tax in Chinese history and the modern real property tax are close in the above two features.

5.2.2 *Elasticity and Stability*

Studies by Chinese economic historians (like Liang 2008) have laid the groundwork for quantitative examinations of historical records with regard to the amount of revenues from the land tax. Judging from accessible records, we observe a pretty stable collection of the land tax, i.e., revenue for governments, except in years of extreme catastrophes, natural disasters, and bloody wars. One explanation for the stable revenue from this tax was the use of flat taxes, instead of an ad valorem structure, especially since the Tang Dynasty. Uncertainty or fluctuation of revenue for the government from the above mentioned exceptional years was reduced at the cost of landowners who had to bear all the extra burden in those disaster years though they could also have pocketed more yield from the land in years of good harvests.

All in all, the land tax generated stable revenues to finance government operations in Chinese history. Table 5.3, with examples of the Qing Dynasty (1636–1911 A.D.), illustrates this point. The "land-head silver" (name of the land tax) generated a total of 21.3 million ounces of silver in 1652, the 8th year after the Manchurians took power and settled in Beijing. In 1903, the 8th year before its fall, the total collection reached 35.4 million ounces. The 66 % increase was mainly from the availability of more land for the tax base and also from higher productivity growth. Though the share of land tax in annual total revenue fell from 88 % in 1652 to a mere 28 % in 1903, when the composition of the national economy had changed drastically, land tax remained as one of the most important sources throughout the over 200 years rule of the dynasty.

5.2.3 *Control of the Tax and Use of the Revenues*

On other important aspects, however, the ancient Chinese versions of the land tax were very different from the modern real property tax. In all of the dynasties of ancient China, finance was highly centralized. Under the rule of ancient Chinese dynasties, the land tax as the major revenue source was controlled completely by the central government—it was a central, not local tax. Localities were mere representatives of the center to levy and collect the tax. The distribution of revenues was also at the will of the center.

The extent that the land tax could be interpreted as a benefit tax also depends on what services the government in general, and local governments in particular, provided. A cursory look at that aspect shows that government services in ancient China at the local level were the maintenance of public order, operation of the judiciary (law suits), and disaster relief, all financed with general tax revenue. Other key services like education and construction of local roads were either a private concern, as education, or financed with extra tax levies plus mandatory labor. Thus, the ancient land tax in China differs from the modern real property tax in its use and control.

In Ancient China, local public services were "local provision with central financing." It is reasonable to assume that regions with higher productivity, thereby more revenue from the land tax, had more local expenses as a ratio of total tax collections; these areas thus would have been able to provide more and better services than less wealthy areas or those with lower productivity. In this perspective, the land tax may also be taken as a limited benefit tax.

Table 5.3 Major taxes, collection and ratio in total revenue, selected years (in million ounces of silver). (Source: Sun 2003, pp. 328 and 346)

Year		Land-head silver		Salt levy		Customs duties		Lijuan(厘捐)		Total
Dynasty year	Western calendar	Amount	Percent	Amount	Percent	Amount	Percent	Amount	Percent	
顺治9年	1652	*21.3*	88	2.1	9	1	4	Not levied		24.3
康熙24年	1685	*27.3*	88	2.8	9	1.2	4			31.2
雍正3年	1725	*30.1*	84	4.4	12	1.4	4			35.9
乾隆18年	1753	*29.4*	72	7.0	17	4.3	11			40.7
乾隆31年	1766	*29.9*	62	5.7	12	5.4	11			48.6
嘉庆17年	1812	*29.6*	74	5.8	14	4.8	12			40.1
道光21年	1841	*29.4*	71	7.5	18	4.4	11			41.3
光绪11年	1885	*30.7*	40	7.4	10	15.9	21	14.3	19	77.1
光绪27年	1901	*29.6*	34	13.5	15	24.7	28	16.0	18	88.2
光绪29年	1903	*35.4*	28	12.5	10	55.4	44	16.0	15	124.9

Another important social institution which was closely related to taxation in Ancient China was the restrictive, exhaustive household registration system with which government prevented landowners, peasants, and their households from free migration, tied them to a permanent jurisdiction, and levied taxes and mandatory labor through this registration. Migration was deemed social disaster and usually occurred in periods of land concentration, war, or natural disasters.

5.3 Traces of the Real Property Tax in Chinese History

In this subsection, we narrow our focus down to the times when the property tax in Chinese history was specifically levied on residential property. The earliest example that we can find dates back to the Tang dynasty (618–907 A.D.); subsequent dynasties also used this tax occasionally. After 1912, the Republic of China levied this tax for a short period of time in two major cities. After 1949, the People's Republic of China issued two official documents on this tax.

5.3.1 Rise of the Residential Property Tax in China

The property tax on residential housing started in the middle of the Tang dynasty (618–907 A.D.); it was called the *Jianjia* (间架verbatim "number and structure of rooms") Tax. At that time, *Fan Zhen* (藩镇), which was the layer between the central government and localities, was endowed with sweeping administrative and military powers that weakened control by the center and resulted in a rebellion by governors of two *Fan Zhen*. Although the rebellion was put down in the end, the Tang Dynasty was not able to reverse the trend of decline. Out of the need to raise enough revenue, the central government decided, at the proposal and direction of Chancellor Zhao Zhan (赵赞), to tax residential housing in its capital. The central idea was that wealth was concentrated in the hands of rich businessmen, since much of their assets were in urban housing property; thus, a housing tax on the rich would be able to generate the urgently needed revenue. The policy was to classify houses into three classes, with differential tax levy for each of the designated property classes. The higher the property class, the more tax would be levied.[2] The tax was put into effect in the year 783 and levied on all property owners, which infuriated residents in the capital city. In October, of the same year another rebellion erupted; the rebels occupied the capital and announced repeal of the tax. After the rebellion was suppressed, the emperor abolished the *Jianjia* tax in January of the next year. Thus, the very first housing tax in Chinese history existed for less than a year.

The next-half century (907–960 A.D., the Five Dynasties and Ten Kingdoms Period) saw frequent changes in dynasties and kingdoms. Property tax on residential housing was again a favorite of emperors. Historical literature shows that the

[2] 间架税:"屋二架为间,上间钱二千,中间一千,下间五百";"匿一间,仗六十,告者赏钱五万"。.

five dynasties all issued special pardons for housing property from taxation in their capital city and other major cities in which the residential property tax was levied. According to historical records, the tax in the Later Jin Dynasty was calculated monthly and collected twice a year, in spring and autumn. During the Later Tang Dynasty, the emperor once levied in advance 5 months' worth of this tax.

The Song Dynasty (960–1279 A.D.) levied five taxes that included a *Wu* (屋, room) tax in major cities, although this was not a major revenue source. Major revenue sources were grain from the land and cloth or silk. There are records of the emperor pardoning the housing property tax in two cities for one year and, in another city, for half a year in the year 1008. During the later years of the dynasty, this property tax was even spread once to rural areas. Records show that housing property was classified into ten classes and that the tax was calculated according to the class.

During the early years of the Qing Dynasty (1636–1911 A.D.), *Fang Juan* (房捐,housing tax) was levied once in some regions, but it was abolished by three strong emperors (*Kangxi*康熙, *Yongzheng*雍正, and *Qianlong*乾隆). In the early period of the Republic of China (1912–1949 A.D.)[3], *Fang Juan* (housing tax) was also levied for a short period in Beijing and Shanghai.

Soon after the founding of the People's Republic of China in October 1949, the central government issued in August 1951, a "Provisional Regulation on Urban Real Property Tax", which provided that the real property levy was to be based on a "standard" housing price at the rate of 1 %, to be collected once a year, and that all cities that levied this tax should create a Housing Property Assessment Committee to conduct housing value appraisal, once each year. That is to say, the so-called "standard" price was then market price because in the early 1950s, private ownership was not yet abolished in China; the 1 % rate was reasonable and annual collection was similar to the practice of real property tax in the US. As was true with many other policies in that period, this provision was not in effect long enough to contribute much to government revenue, because the tax system in the 1950s went through frequent changes and socialism, or public ownership of housing property was soon to dominate until the early 1980s when China changed its policy orientation toward opening up and reform.

The State Council's (year 1986) #90 document, "Provisional Regulation on the Real Property Tax," was an updated version of the 1951 policy. Under the new provisions, owner occupied residential housing was exempted from the tax; thus, only commercial and rental housing was subject to the tax. Tax levy currently ranges from 70 to 90 % of the (1950s) original value of each parcel (to allow for depreciation), with the specific base to be determined by provincial governments—the central government allows variation in different provinces. Property with no earlier assessed value as base is to be assessed by local tax authorities with reference to that of similar parcels—detailed assessment is to be done at the local level. The tax rate is 1.2 %—still in the conventional range. In sum, the 1986 policy kept the core elements of the 1951 version and the practices remain similar to modern real property tax. However, since the base of the tax is very small, total collection in the

[3] After 1949, the Republic of China continued in Taiwan.

Table 5.4 List of residential property taxes in Chinese history by dynasty

Dynasty/period	Features	Background
Tang (618–907)	Tax residential and commercial housing in Chang'an city according to its size by fixed amount per room	Started in year 783 for raising revenue; repealed in year 784 due to strong opposition
Five dynasties & ten kingdoms (907–960)	Calculated monthly & paid twice a year	Frequent wars & changes of dynasty
Song (960–1279)	Extended to rural area; levy by ten classes; exempted in some years	
Qing (1636–1911)	Only levied in some areas; repealed later	
Republic of China in mainland (1912–1949)	Levied in Beijing and Shanghai for a very short period	
People's Republic of China (1949–present)	1 % of assessed value, annual collection	In effect in early 1950s, short lived
	1.2 % of assessed value on commercial housing, annual collection	Implemented since 1986; not a main revenue source

year 2010 from this tax accounted only for 1.08 % of total revenue of all levels of government.[4] Table 5.4 offers a summary of the above description.

5.3.2 China's Early Residential Property Tax vs. Modern Real Property Tax

The residential property tax used in China from the ancient times to the 1980s bears some similar features with the modern real property tax. They are both property taxes with real property, housing, as the base for levying the tax. The *Jianjia tax* in the Tang Dynasty was a specific rate tax, a fixed amount per room that was regressive. The *Wu tax* in the Song Dynasty was once calculated by the designated classes of property, which was progressive. The real property tax since the founding of the People's Republic of China has been levied on the basis of house value, which is proportional. To sum up, the more property a household owns or the higher the housing value is, the more real property tax the household should pay. Thus, the overall burden tends to be heavier on the wealthy than on the low income.

The above differences between the Chinese version property tax and the modern real property tax are also striking. First, the housing tax in China so far has never been a major revenue source for government: the Tang dynasty only resorted to it as a temporary tool to alleviate fiscal difficulty, in vain; the five dynasties took it as a petty tax; and it was a supplemental revenue source during the Song dynasty. After 1912, the Republic of China and the People's Republic of China both used it sporadically and irregularly and collection from this tax did not compose any substantive

[4] http://www.stats.gov.cn/tjsj/ndsj/2011/indexch.htm.

share of total government revenues. Thus, we can say little about the elasticity of this tax or the stability of its revenue. Related to the limited collection of this tax in China, housing tax revenue can only be taken as a very limited benefit tax because resources thus collected have not been able to finance a regular, key service that lasts long. From the perspective of local governments, the residential property tax revenue was not high enough to be a benefit tax. It was even impossible for local residents to participate in the decision-making process in the feudal society. As for the connection between this tax and regional public service and public participation in policy making, it was out of the question completely in the feudal society and rare even in the two recent Republics. Needless to say, the role of any tax changes with its socioeconomic environment. We should not expect to see modern features from the ancient roots of this tax.

5.4 Why China's Ancient Property Tax Did Not Evolve into A Modern Property Tax?

Why did the property tax in ancient China not continue, develop, and evolve into a modern property tax? There were profound reasons for this lack of evolution embedded in the political, economic, and social processes throughout the history of China. While an in-depth study should be done by economic historians, we conduct some brief analyses here about factors necessary for the development of a modern real property tax.

5.4.1 Stable Property Ownership

We believe that as long as one owns or uses property, a tax can be levied according to the property value, no matter whether this property (or land) right is public or private. A stable property right system is an important factor affecting the formation of a real property tax. During the period of the Republic of China, fighting among warlords, World War II, and the Chinese civil war happened one after the other; China was in political turmoil. At that time, although the national government and some local governments both had their own property right systems, regime change and frequent wars did not lead to the development of stable property rights.

After the establishment of the People's Republic of China in 1949, several changes were seen in the definition of the property ownership of land in the new constitution (Table 5.5). The constitution (see "the Chinese People's Political Consultative Conference Common Program" (1949) and "the Constitution of the People's Republic of China" (1954)) at first confirmed farmers' ownership of rural land. In 1982, the constitution (see "the Constitution of the People's Republic of China" (1982)) made clear that both urban and rural land belongs to the state. Therefore, the unstable status of property rights in the last century has been an important factor negatively affecting the smooth transition from a historical property tax to a modern real property tax.

Table 5.5 Changes of property ownership of land after 1949

Constitution	Date of adoption
1949 (Common Program)	The first plenary session of the Chinese People's Political Consultative Conference, September 29, 1949
1954	The first plenary session of the 1st National People's Congress, September 20, 1954
1975	The first plenary session of the 4th National People's Congress, January 17, 1975
1978	The first plenary session of the 5th National People's Congress, March 5, 1978
1982	The fifth session of the 5th National People's Congress, December 4, 1982

5.4.2 Smooth Transition of the Society and Economy

The establishment and perfection of the modern tax system can be seen in the process of social and economic transformation. Since the end of the feudal society, China's social and economic transformation has occurred in a tortuous environment. Thanks to the division of labor and specialization, the Northern Song Dynasty obtained a rapid development of the commodity economy. In 1078 A.D., at the heyday of this dynasty, industrial and commercial tax revenue accounted for 70 % of total government revenue (Sun 2003, p. 213). The Southern Song Dynasty expanded trade from inland to overseas, starting a large-scale sea trade. However, in the Ming and Qing dynasties, rulers implemented a ban on maritime trade, and adopted a series of policies that restrained farmers. Thus, during the Ming and Qing dynasties, the commodity economy was suppressed. During the mid-Qing Dynasty (during the reign of Emperor Qianlong) in China, the industrial revolution that was initially started by the British had begun in Europe (from the 1760s to the mid-19th century) which brought the human civilization into the period of steam power. While Europe and the USA entered the modern industrial era, China's feudal dynasty failed to embrace the new age, and unable to keep up with the changes brought about by the industrial revolution—China did not develop into a society with a commodity economy and began to decline. A declining society could by no means compete with its advanced foreign counterparts; thus, the process of China's economic development slowed down and finally grounded to a halt. In this context, the establishment and use of a modern real property taxation system was suspended, and the ancient property tax system did not evolve into a modern property tax system.

5.4.3 Free migration in the Market Orientation

Under the conditions of a market economy, free migration is the impetus of social progress and development so that human capital can be best utilized and utility can be maximized. Because real property cannot move with its owners, a freely migrating population means increased frequencies of real property transaction. In the transaction process, the price of real property gradually forms, reflecting its market value.

From 1912 to1949, a high proportion of the Chinese population was uprooted due to continuous wars, which was not the type of free population flow that helps to form the market price. From 1949 to the 1980s, migration of the Chinese was tightly regulated, even restricted, under tight government planning. Under normal circumstances, the state restricted the flow of population between urban and rural areas and between different cities through the household registration management system. Two large-scale migrations happened before the 1980s. One was from 1958 to 1962, the period of the so-called "Great Leap Forward" and natural disasters; the other was from 1968 to 1980, the period in which educated youth (with middle and high school traning) were sent to the countryside and moved back to cities later. Since the 1980s, migration has occurred in the process of China implementing its opening-up and reform policies, mainly due to labor force movements from rural to urban areas and from the western and interior regions to the eastern and coastal region. Population flow in this period has displayed several key characteristics of market economy; however, it was still bound by the household registration system. There has been no unconditional free migration in China so far, a limitation that prevents the true market prices of real property from being revealed. This factor is significant in terms of inhibiting the establishment of a modern real property tax in China.

5.4.4 Strong Governance Capacity

Governance capacity refers to the ability of a government to coordinate and regulate the political, social, and economic aspects of society. Based on the above analyses of the Chinese dynasties in history, it is apparent that when the ruling capacity of the government was strong, the dynasty was prosperous; conversely, when the ruling capacity was weak, the dynasty would decline and even collapse. In our view, the capacity of a government to control the distribution of wealth, make appropriate property tax policy, obtain information of the distribution of real properties, and build strong collection measures is reflection of its ruling capacity in economic, fiscal, and tax policies.

Before the end of the Qing Dynasty, China was once a world leader in terms of economic and social development; but after the middle and late periods of the Qing Dynasty, China's economic and social standing gradually weakened in the world. There was no smooth transition from a feudal to a capitalist society and then to a modern society. During the period of the Republic of China, fighting among the warlords and the Anti-Japanese War prompted then government to use its limited resources to maintain unity and national independence. After that, for approximately half a century after the founding of the People's Republic of China, the Chinese government invested most of its resources in figuring out the route to national independence and in focusing on the country's development through a trial and error process. Throughout most of the 20th century, the Consecutive Chinese government lacked the resources to build fiscal capacity and improve the tax system. Not until the end of the 20th century and the early 21st century, during a time of greater political stability and economic recovery, did the government start to seriously consider the improvement of the property tax system.

Conclusion

In this chapter, we have reviewed the evolution of property taxation in Chinese history; in particular, we have traced the tax on housing property with regard to its rise, levy, and collection. In summary terms, we have found the following as pertinent to this study. First, property taxation has a long tradition in China. The practice of government levying tax, and owners paying a tax on property, is deeply rooted in the country's history (which probably is true in most countries' history as well, since the earliest property was land and yield from land and government, in the earliest forms, relied on this property tax for financing). The tax on housing property also has a long history in China, dating back over a 1000 years. Though it was not regularly used or has not provided mainstay revenue, real property tax is no stranger in China. Each dynasty since the 10th century, and government in each period since the 1910s, resorted to this tax, even only for short periods. These two findings may have provided some sense of assurance that the real property tax is not "foreign" to China. Policy makers should adequately tap this historical heritage in designing tax policies.

Second, the various land taxes in Chinese history, as property tax, could be called "efficient" since they had the largest possible tax base. The tax was the most important revenue source for ancient governments and revenue from this tax was relatively stable, especially so if we take into account the "fixed amount" rates that were designed to shift revenue risk of an ad valorem tax from government onto taxpayers. The ancient and more recent residential property tax in China shares some similarities with the modern local property tax in some important features, as with the rate structure, assessment, levy, and collection. An important implication here is that the modern real property tax would have been a natural development in any country's socioeconomic development as long as the political and state systems allowed its birth and growth. We can infer from our review in this chapter that the real property tax was born a long time ago out of a natural need for it, but it has not fully developed in China as it has in western countries.

Third, and related to the second finding, neither the land taxes nor the housing property tax in Chinese history were a benefit tax. In all dynasties (except periods since 1912), they were not controlled by local governments and the use of collected revenue was not closely connected to services that local governments provided. Because they were not a full benefit tax at the local level, we say there remains a distinct gap between these earlier forms of the tax in China and the modern version of the real property tax in western countries. Thus, a major task for the research community in China is to fully explore the design features of the real property tax in order to "modernize" the Chinese versions of the tax for its full exploitation in 21st century China. We firmly believe that the pilot LPT in Shanghai and Chongqing has provided a golden opportunity for the modernization enterprise of the tax in China, and that if properly designed and implemented, there is a bright prospect for the real property tax to fully function as a local benefit tax that serves financial as well as governance functions.

Chapter 6
Design Features of the Local Property Tax Pilots

6.1 Relevant National Laws and Local Administrative Rules

China introduced the real property tax in urban areas in January 2011. The new policy was announced on January 27 and went into effect the next day, presumably to stem any possible distortionary housing market behavior. As has been the case with almost all major policy initiatives, the Chinese government launched this potentially politically loaded tax reform first as a pilot project in order to test the political acceptability of the tax, its technical soundness, as well as any administrative aspects. Rumor goes that multiple metropolitans were on the initial list of pilots, including Shanghai, Chongqing, Beijing, and Shenzhen; but the final pilots included only the first two. In the following sections, we briefly review China's national laws and local administrative rules with regard to the real property tax.

6.1.1 *China's Interim Rules on Real Property Tax* (中国房产税暂行条例)

The real property tax has been widely adopted around the world, especially by local governments. Tracing policy development of the Chinese government in the past three decades, we find that China promulgated in 1986 an "Interim Regulation on the Real Estate Tax" and thereby began to levy a "real estate tax" in all urban areas. The tax base, according to that document included housing, or real estate, owned by enterprises and business owners; residential properties were not included in the tax base. Thus, the "real estate tax" levied in China from 1986 to January 2011 was a different tax from the one we discuss in the following section.

Y. Hou et al., *The Property Tax in China*, Development and Governance,
DOI 10.1007/978-3-319-10049-4_6

6.1.2 Shanghai's Rules on Levying the Real Property Tax (上海开征房产税细则及暂行办法)

The policies with regard to the two pilot taxes were mainly made by the two metro governments, though input from the central government formed the underlying guidelines of the metro government rules. As local policies, details of the two taxes show many local considerations that are far from uniform. In the following, we present some of the major features of the two sets of policies as the general background to our discussion.

The official policy document in Shanghai was the "Interim regulation of Shanghai Municipal Government on the pilot real property tax on certain categories of residential housing." It was promulgated on January 27, 2011 to become effective the very next day. The tax was levied in all 18 urban districts of the city.

6.1.3 Chongqing's Rules (重庆开征房产税细则及暂行办法)

Chongqing's official policy document was the "Decree No. 247" of the Chongqing Municipal Government. As in Shanghai, the document was promulgated on January 27, 2011 and was to become effective the next day. In contrast to Shanghai's rules, the Chongqing version of the tax is applicable only in the nine main urban districts, not in the exterior rural counties under the jurisdiction of the metro government.

6.2 Policy Details of the Shanghai Pilot Local Property Tax

6.2.1 Eligibility

Eligibility of the tax, the *base*, differentiates registered permanent residents from nonregistered permanent residents into two separate categories. For the first category, the tax applies to new purchases (either apartment or single-family house) that will be the second (or more) owned by the family. For the second category, the tax applies to all new purchases whether it is the first or second by the household or individual. That is, registered residents enjoy a more favorable tax status: They will pay the tax only if they have already owned a unit before the effective date of the policy, whereas nonregistered residents will have to pay the tax for their very first unit. The statutory incidence of the tax falls on owners of property.

6.2.2 *Tax Rate and Exemption*

All taxable real property forms the tax base which will be *assessed* for tax levy. The assessed value changes over time. At the beginning of the pilot, a taxable property will be assessed at 70 % of its market transaction price (per square meter, and hereafter). The *tax rate* is temporarily set at 0.6 % of the assessed value. The rate will be 0.4 % if the transaction price of a property is lower than or equal to twice the average price for new construction in the previous year.

An *exemption* is provided. For registered permanent residents who have a newly purchased apartment or house as their second housing unit (or more), 60 m^2 per family member will be deducted from the tax base - the total floor space owned by the family including the new purchase. This exemption offers an extra perk for registered residents. These seemingly discriminatory clauses (they are indeed discriminatory) may be interpreted as measure to control the high population growth rate of the mega city and to curb a widespread help speculation in the housing market.

6.3 Policy Details of the Chongqing Pilot Local Property Tax

6.3.1 *Eligibility*

The Chongqing real property tax will be levied on three categories of residential property: (1) single family villas; (2) new purchases of luxury housing, either apartments or single-family houses; and (3) ordinary property purchased as a second housing unit (or more) by individuals or households who are *simultaneously* neither permanent residents, nor investors nor job-holders in the city. For the second category, "new" is defined as transactions made after the effective date of the tax and "luxury" is set as the market price per square meter over twice the average price of new construction in the nine central urban districts in the last 2 years. The statutory incidence falls on the property owner. The basis of tax *assessment* is the transaction price of the property.

6.3.2 *Tax Rate and Exemption*

For the first two categories, the tax is set at three *progressive rates* by the unit price (per square meter) of the transaction. The lowest rate is 0.5 % if the price is lower than triple the average price of newly constructed property in the nine main urban districts in the last 2 years. The medium rate is 1 % for houses with their price ranging from triple up to four times the average price of newly or apartments constructed property in the nine main urban districts in the last 2 years. The top rate is 1.2 % with properties priced at and above four times the average price of newly constructed property in the nine main urban districts over the last 2 years. Beside the three categories mentioned above, for ordinary housing units owned by a household (or individual) who is *simultaneously* neither a permanent resident, nor an investor nor a jobholder in the city, the applicable rate is the lowest, 0.5 %. On this last element, Chongqing drastically differs from Shanghai; Chongqing applies the lowest tax rate in order to attract immigrant purchasers whereas Shanghai tries to repel immigrants in an effort to mitigate the mounting population pressure in the central areas of the City.

Probably to partly mitigate the shock on owners of luxury property, an exemption is provided, but for only one apartment or house for each family. For purchases made before January 28, 2011 of single family villas, the exempted floor space is 180 m^2. For new purchases (made on or after January 28, 2011), the exempted area is 100 m^2. There are no exemptions for the third category properties, those purchased for investment on the booming housing market.

6.4 Comparisons Between Pilot Local Property Tax in the Two Metropolitans

There are similarities and differences between the tax policies of Shanghai and Chongqing. The two policies both impose the tax on a narrow tax base at a relatively low rate. The tax in Shanghai applies only to new purchases of a second house or apartment (or more), no matter how much the transaction price is, which means that only a very small part of the housing stock will be taxed. The assessment rate is set at 70 % of the market price and every family has a deduction of 60 m^2 per family member, which amounts to effectively 180 m^2 given that the city's average household size is 2.6 by the 2010 Census. In view of the current living standards in China, this amount of exemption is very large. Also, the tax rate, 0.6 or 0.4 %, is not high.

The tax in Chongqing applies only to luxury properties (owned by the rich) with a 100 or 180 m^2 exemption per family, and ordinary properties owned by nonimmigrant investors, which means that registered resident owners of ordinary property do not have to pay the tax, which is why local people have often called their real property tax the *luxurious housing tax*. Thus, it is obvious that the local property taxes (LPTs) as designed by the two metropolitans are not expected to generate sizeable amounts of revenue. We can probably conclude that the pilot tax policies are designed more as a signal that will help cool down the housing market rather than meet any other policy goals.

6.5 Tracing the Links Between the Pilot Local Property Tax and the Ancient Property Tax

Even though neither the Shanghai nor the Chongqing authorities mention that their pilot LPT has any connections with the ancient land tax or the earlier real property taxes in Chinese history, or whether they learned anything in designing their policies from those earlier taxes, it is worthwhile to explore whether such connections somehow exist. Such a historical exploration carries significance. As analyzed in the previous chapter, China has a long history of levying a property tax, the land tax in ancient times, and also some variants of a housing tax since the 10th century. China also, in two periods since 1949, tried to implement a real property tax in urban centers that is similar in technical details to a modern real property tax. So, it is reasonable to assume that route dependence, which is established in the academic literature for the design and implementation of public policies as a natural phenomenon, may have also been true in this case.

6.5.1 Two Pilots vs. Ancient Land Taxes

We can identify similarities as well as differences between the two LPT pilots and the land taxes in Chinese history. Among similarities, both can be treated as broadly defined property taxes; both fall under ad valorem taxes, with tax levy closely related to the amount of assets owned; and neither link the tax levy/revenue closely with local public services.

Differences between the two are also striking. We focus on two points here. First, the tax base of LPT pilots is small because the policy targets luxury housing and investment-related ownership; raising revenue is not the main purpose. The ancient land tax, household tax, and head tax, in contrast, had a very broad tax base with few exemptions for the purpose of raising sufficient revenue to finance the government. It can be argued that the pilot LPT is less efficient than the ancient property taxes in that the wealthy can avoid the LPT by changing their investment instruments, which, however, is part of the purposes of the pilot tax. We believe that as the pilots continue, the tax base will become larger, and thereby the efficiency of the tax will be raised.

From the equity perspective, the pilot LPT taxes only newly purchased housing units (Shanghai) or luxury housing units (Chongqing), which creates inequitable treatment among owners, at least before the policy changes to cover all property. In contrast, the ancient property taxes, especially those in the early years of each dynasty, tended to treat all property owners more equitably.

Table 6.1 Comparison between property tax in China and modern LPT

Features of modern LPT	Ancient land tax	Ancient residential property tax	Current pilot LPT
Broad tax base	Yes	Yes	No
Ad valorem rate structure	Approx. Yes	Approx. Yes	Yes
Tax revenue inelastic	Yes	Yes	Yes
Revenues belong to localities	No	No	Yes
Using tax through public choice	No	No	No
As main revenue of localities	Yes	No	No
A benefit tax	No	No	No

6.5.2 Two Pilots vs. Ancient Housing Taxes

Comparing the pilot LPT with the residential property tax in Chinese history, we find some similarities. Both are ad valorem taxes with the levy related to the value of the housing property. Since neither generates large amounts of revenue, they do not show a close link to any services provided at the local or central levels; also, public participation has, so far, never been high.

Among the differences between the two, we mention three here. First, the tax base of the pilot LPT is narrow even in comparison with residential property in ancient China. From the limited historical literature, we do not see exemptions from the housing property tax in periods when the tax was levied. In contrast, the LPT pilots in Shanghai and Chongqing allow large exemptions. This difference is derived from the design purpose of the two pilots. The pilot LPT is also designed to suppress housing prices, which is why it grants generous tax exemptions and a high threshold. Its counterparts in Chinese history were designed to raise revenue for the government, which would not have allowed large exemptions or a high starting threshold. The pilot LPT is a local tax. Its counterpart in the Tang Dynasty was a central tax. We did not find historical records on which level the government controlled and used revenues from the housing taxes.

6.5.3 Antecedents of Pilot Local Property Tax Features in Their Predecessors

Table 6.1 shows the degree of similarities between different types of real property tax in China and the modern LPT. We take seven features of the modern LPT as the bases of references to compare the two. When we compare the pilot LPT to the ancient land tax, we find that four aspects out of the seven are similar. When we compare the pilot LPT to the ancient residential property tax, there are five out of the seven aspects that are similar. The similarities among the different types of real property tax in China are the "inelastic" nature of the revenue; none of them uses the tax revenue "through public choice" and none is a "benefit tax."

Chapter 7
Progress of LPT in Two Pilot Cities

7.1 Overall Implementation of the Pilots

To ensure smooth implementation of the new real property tax, the application of appropriate techniques and the design of practicable procedures are of great importance. Through several rounds of field work in the two cities and interviews with residents and officials, we found that both the local tax bureaus in Shanghai and Chongqing have done their best in collecting the taxes that were levied, but the cost of implementation has been very high.

7.1.1 Identification of Real Property Taxpayers

The first task for the local tax bureaus before levying the tax is to identify property owners who are subject to the tax. In Shanghai, they are mainly owners of newly purchased secondary, or more, housing units. The local tax bureau should possess adequate updated information about property ownership or have easy access to such information that includes marriage status from the Department of Civil Affairs, household registration, and residency from the Department of Public Safety (Police), and the housing status of each household from the Department of Housing Management. The various departments of the metro government share relevant information to ensure the smooth implementation of the tax. Beginning January 28, 2011, all new purchases in Shanghai must apply for their recognition of the levy or exemption of the real property tax before proceeding with property registration. The procedure is illustrated in Fig. 7.1. With this requirement in place, the local tax bureau can easily identify eligible taxpayers.

7.1.2 Tax Preservation Measures

After initial identification of taxpayers, there must also be control measures in order to collect the full tax levy on time. The Shanghai Local Tax Bureau takes a series

Y. Hou et al., *The Property Tax in China*, Development and Governance,
DOI 10.1007/978-3-319-10049-4_7

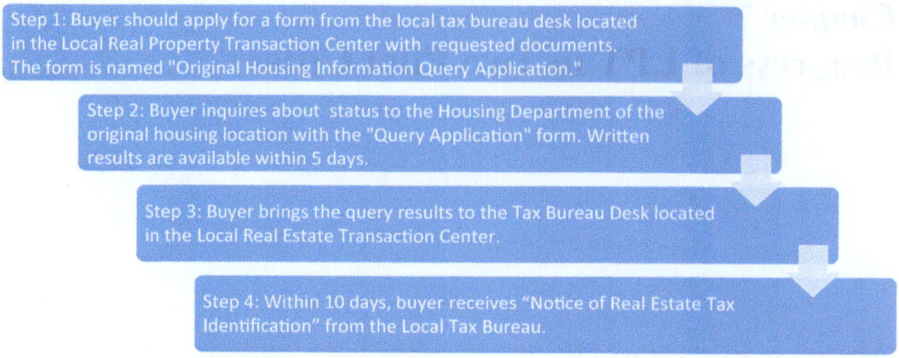

Fig. 7.1 Procedure of tax eligibility recognition or exemption from the real property tax in Shanghai. (Source: Open documents of district tax administration offices, Shanghai)

of tax preservation measures to collect this tax. After property owners are registered for their possession, the local tax bureau will send notice to taxpayers of the amount of tax levy every year. The government requires that all eligible taxpayers should file and pay, by themselves with valid identity proof, the property tax before December 31. Late payments or payments short of the levy will be charged a penalty of 0.05 % of the overdue amount per day from January 1 of the next year. If the property owner still does not pay the tax (plus penalty), the property will be forbidden from transaction and will be recorded in the citywide "Shanghai (Personal) Credibility Information System," which will adversely affect the property owner's personal credit and chance of getting loans from commercial banks. The local tax bureau, using real estate assessment techniques, has created and maintains a "Housing Stock Trading Price Comparison System," with which the bureau can issue levies based on market transactions to properties that report apparently low transaction prices without due reasons. With the above measures in place, voluntary filing among/by eligible property owners reached 80 %, and the final collection rate amounted to 90 % in 2012.

The Chongqing Local Tax Bureau has adopted tax preservation measures similar to those of Shanghai. The window for tax payment is from October 1 to October 31. To ensure timely and full collection, the bureau has also created and uses a "Housing Stock Trading Price Comparison System", with which the bureau assesses all eligible residential properties in stock and uses the assessed value as the base for tax levy. Properties that report apparently low transaction prices without due reasons will be levied on the basis of their market price.

As provided in the Chongqing official document, by August 31, the local tax bureau shall notify eligible property owners, via direct delivery, mail, or public notice, of the properties' precise location, assessment criteria, tax levy, and tax due date. If the owner does not pay the full levy on time, the bureau will specify a deadline; in addition, a penalty of 0.05 % of the overdue amount will be charged per day. The tax bureau is authorized to periodically publish the names of tax offenders at the local tax offices or on public media. Names of property owners who still do not pay their overdue tax will be recorded in the personal credit system. Further, the local tax bureau can notify banks and other financial institutions in which the owner keeps accounts, and request the institutions to withhold the tax plus penalty. Property owners who want to travel abroad are required to pay their tax and penalty or provide guarantee before their departure; otherwise, the local tax bureau has the authority to notify the Border Control Administration that can restrain the tax offenders from leaving the country. Finally, the local tax bureau can also transfer the overdue tax list to the local Departments of Land and Real Estate that can impose restrictions on the transaction of involved properties until the overdue tax plus penalty is paid off.

7.2 Amount of Tax Collected

As of the date of this writing, the amount of real property taxes collected in Shanghai and Chongqing in the first year of the pilot still has not been officially published. But we can obtain a rough estimate from different media reports.

7.2.1 Tax Collected in Shanghai

In a report of Mayor Han Zheng of Shanghai at the 28th session of the 13th Municipal People's Congress, the Shanghai Local Tax Bureau by late June 2011 issued 38,007 notices of "Real Property Tax Exemption" and 7,858 (about 2 %) notices of tax eligibility. The average amount of tax levy per property was 4,504 RMB.[1] According to another report, by the end of year 2011 a total of 20,000 properties had been identified as eligible for the real property tax.[2] Therefore, an estimate of the tax revenue is RMB 90 million, which is a negligible amount compared to the city's total budget revenue, to land transfer fees and to revenues from the real estate tax on commercial and residential properties (see Table 7.1 for details).

7.2.2 Tax Collected in Chongqing

In early 2011, Mayor Huang Qifan of Chongqing roughly estimated that revenue from the real property tax would be RMB 150 million in Chongqing,[3] which is also negligible in comparison to the city's total budget revenue, to its real estate tax revenue on commercial and residential real property, and to land transfer fees. See Table 7.2 for details.

---

[1] Source: http://sh.sina.com.cn/news/s/2011-07-27/0834190608_4.html.

[2] Source: http://newspaper.jfdaily.com/xwcb/html/2012-05/13/content_802639.htm.

[3] Source: http://news.xinhuanet.com/house/2011-01/27/c_121033370.htm.

Table 7.1 Estimated year 2011 revenue of the pilot local property tax in Shanghai in comparison with a few other key measures (in millions of RMB yuan)

Type of revenue	Amount
Real property tax on residential property (the pilot)	90
Municipal real estate tax on residential and business property[a]	2210
Real estate tax on residential and commercial property[b]	7370
Land transfer fees[c]	46,130
General budget revenue[d]	342,980

[a] This revenue belongs to the provincial level budget
[b] This revenue belongs to the consolidated budget of the provincial and the lower levels
[c] This revenue belongs to the budget of provincial level. Chinese governments use a multiple budget system consisting of general budget, fund budget, and budget of stated-owned assets. Land transfer fees is included in the fund budget
[d] This does not include tax rebates and subsidies from the central government, revenues from local government issued bonds, and fund budget revenue
Source: http://www.czj.sh.gov.cn/zwgk/czsj/czyjsqk/yjsczbg/201201/t20120116_129630.html

Table 7.2 Estimation of pilot local property tax in Chongqing (in millions of RMB yuan)

Type of revenue	Amount
Real property tax (on residential property)[a]	150
Real estate tax on residential and business property[b]	730
Real estate tax on residential and commercial property[c]	1610
Land transfer fees[d]	80,150
General budget revenue[e]	148,820

[a] This is the estimation made public in early 2011 by Mr. Huang Qifan, mayor of Chongqing
[b] This revenue belongs to the budget of provincial level. And this number comes from the estimation of budget in early 2011. (Source: http://cqcz.cq.gov.cn/zwgk/news_detail.aspx?id=38862)
[c] This revenue belongs to the consolidated budget of the provincial and the lower levels. And this number is estimated on the premise that this year's revenue has a 15 % increase over the last year. (Source: http://cqcz.cq.gov.cn/zwgk/news_detail.aspx?id=47438)
[d] This revenue belongs to the provincial-level budget
[e] This does not include tax rebates and subsidies from the central government, revenue from bonds issued by local government, and fund budget revenue. (Source: http://cqcz.cq.gov.cn/zwgk/news_detail.aspx?id=48709)

7.3 Real Property Market after Adoption of Pilot Tax

The short-term goal of the pilot local property tax in Shanghai and Chongqing is multifold: to curb real estate speculation, to guide residents towards rational housing consumption, and to help restrain the soaring housing price. Has the pilot real property tax achieved its design purposes? Let us start with the trend of housing prices.

7.3.1 Price Trend of Real Property

There is not much officially published data on real estate prices. We analyze the trend of housing prices based on the "Index of Real Estate Price in 100 Cities" from

Fig. 7.2 Average housing price and growth rate in Shanghai

the *China Real Estate Price Index System*.[4] From the average prices of sampled newly constructed property sales, we can identify the price trend of Shanghai in Fig. 7.2. From June 2010 to November 2012, the average price first rose and then fell. In September 2010, the average price was RMB 23,113 yuan/m^2. In July 2011, the average price went up to RMB 23,856 yuan/m^2. During this 11–month period, the average monthly price growth was 0.32 %; then the price showed a decline. In May 2012, the price fell to 22,991 yuan/m^2. Within this 11–month period the price was in decline at an average monthly rate of 0.37 %. After that, the price reversed back to gradual growth until the end of year 2012.

At the time of the levy of the real property tax in Chongqing, the average price also went through an increase and then decline (see Fig. 7.3). In August 2010, average price of sampled new constructions sold in Chongqing was RMB 6323 yuan/m^2. In May 2011, the average price rose to RMB 6750 yuan/m^2. During this period, the average growth rate of price per month was 0.73 %. Since May of 2011, the price showed a trend of decreases. In May 2012, the price fell to 6369 yuan/m^2. Within this period, the average monthly rate of decline was 0.48 %. Compared to the price changes in Shanghai, the range of changes is larger in Chongqing. Afterwords, the price in Chongqing again showed a rising trend until the end of year 2012.

Although the overall housing prices dropped after the implementation of the real property tax, we cannot jump to the conclusion that the drop in price can be totally attributed to the tax. In fact, the housing prices countrywide showed the same trend

[4] The China Real Estate Price Index System (CREPIS) reflects the price trend in China's major cities. This index consists of a series of indexes constructed with multiple methods. The index was originally developed by the Development Research Center of the State Council and the China Real Estate Development Group in 1994. The CREPIS publishes a price index of newly constructed housing, second-hand housing, and rental housing. In 2010, this system started a program called the "Index of Real Estate Price in 100 Cities" and publishes average prices in selected cities on the first day of each month.

Fig. 7.3 Average housing price and growth rate in Chongqing

Fig. 7.4 Average housing price and growth rate in 100 Chinese cities

of fluctuation as in Shanghai and Chongqing due to macro control measures by the central government as well as to effects of the economic downturn. From 2010 to 2012, the average housing price in the selected 100 cities displayed the same trend of rise followed by a drop, and the turning point emerged in the middle of year 2011 (see Fig. 7.4). In August 2010, the average price of sampled newly constructed housing sold in those 100 cities was RMB 8,305 yuan/m^2. In August 2011, the average price rose to RMB 8,880 yuan/m^2. During that period, the average monthly growth rate was 0.56 %; Then the price showed a trend of decline. In May 2012, the price fell to 8,684 yuan/m^2. Within this period, the average monthly rate of decline was 0.25 %. This trend shows that residents and real estate investors did not have an optimistic expectation of the real estate market. As parts of the nationwide real estate

Fig. 7.5 Average housing price and growth rate in Beijing

market, fluctuations in Shanghai and Chongqing should have reflected the same trend in housing prices even if there had not been the effect of their pilot real property taxes. Since June 2012, the price grew steadily again until the end of the year.

As further evidences the real estate market in Beijing showed the same trends as that in Shanghai, Chongqing, and the whole country in those two years (see Fig. 7.5). Housing prices were at their lowest point in August 2010, RMB 21,734 yuan/m^2, and the price peaked in September 2011, at 23,008 yuan/m^2, with average monthly growth rate of 0.44 %. In May 2012, the price dropped to 22,416 yuan/m^2. The average monthly rate of decline was 0.33 % from the prior turning point (September 2011) until May, 2012. Just like what happened nationwide, the price rose again from June 2012 to the end of the year.

7.3.2 Analysis

As shown above, housing prices are closely related and responsive to central and local governments' monetary, fiscal, and administrative macro control policies. The central government implemented tight monetary policies from 2010 through 2012. For example, since October 19, 2010, China's central bank raised the benchmark deposit and the lending interest rate five times; the central bank also raised the reserve requirement ratio 12 times since January 2010.

In a serious effort to curb the soaring housing price, the State Council of China adopted a series of measures to cool down the real estate market. On January 7, 2010, the State Council issued a "Notice on Promoting Stable and Healthy Development of the Real Estate Market" which provided that "down-payment for new purchases must not be lower than 40 % of the total price for families that apply for their second or more housing loans from financial institutions."

Four months later (April 17, 2010), the State Council issued another "Notice on Firmly Curbing the Rapid Rise of Real Estate Prices in Some Cities" which put into effect "more rigid differentiated housing loan policies," raised the down-payment requirement to 50 % for families that apply for a second (or more) housing loans from financial institutions, and stipulated that interest rates for such loans must not be lower than 1.1 times the benchmark interest rate. Further, the document provided that down payments and interest rates should be raised even higher for a third, or more, housing loan. For people who are not registered local residents (under the household registration system) and cannot provide evidence of paying taxes and social insurance contributions at the locality of the intended purchase (that is, these are potential "speculators"), loans from the banks for the purchase shall not be approved. Moreover, local governments can take temporary measures if necessary to limit the number of housing units that each resident is allowed to buy.

On January 26, 2011, the State Council issued a third "Notice on Issues about Further Controlling the Real Estate Market" which stipulated that for selling housing properties that have been less than five years since the last transaction, the total revenue of sale will be subject to the business tax. Down payment must be at least 60 % and loan rates must not be lower than 1.1 times the benchmark interest rate for families who apply for a second housing loan from financial institutions."

From the end of January 2011, the Shanghai Municipal Government implemented a policy that limited residents' real property purchases. Residents who are registered in the local registration system and already own one apartment or house, and residents who are not registered in the local registration system, do not own an apartment or house, but who can provide evidence of paying taxes and social insurance contribution for more than one year during the previous two years, can buy (only) one (more) apartment or house. Residents who are registered in the local registration system and already own two apartments or houses cannot buy any more apartments or houses in Shanghai. The same policy applies to residents who already own one or more apartments or houses but are not registered in the local registration system as well as residents who are not registered in the local registration system and cannot provide evidence of paying tax or social insurance contribution for more than one year in the previous two years.

The above list of restrictive measures by the central and municipal governments indicate that the pilot real property taxes were most probably NOT the main cause for the drop of housing price in Shanghai or Chongqing. Last but not the least, the decline in housing price was related to pro-cyclical effects of the real estate market.

7.4 Reflections

Actually, there are two goals of the local property tax pilots. The first is to readjust the real estate market and the second is to accumulate experience for future expansion of this tax to the whole country. After the government imposed comprehensive control measures of monetary, fiscal, and administrative policies, the housing price showed a tendency to decline. The real property tax, at least to some extent, may have contributed to the short–term dip in housing prices. During the first 20 months of the pilot taxes (January 2011–October 2012), related government departments cooperated with each other by sharing information and making full use of technical measures. Although there has only been very limited revenue collected from the pilot property taxes, the two metro governments have gained valuable experience, which will be shared with other cities. What is most important is that residents in other cities have also learned about real property taxes and hold some expectations of this tax. In sum, the real property tax pilots have achieved their goals under the above perspectives.

When will the real property tax be expanded nationwide? What will be the main features of this tax in China in the future? Will the tax assume a narrow tax base and be levied at low rates? Or will the base of this tax be enlarged to cover all housing property? Answers to these questions are still unknown. For the schemes of real property tax, there have been two extremes. On one side, the real property tax in America is an example. On the other side, the pilot real property taxes in China can be an illustration. In America, almost all owners of residential property are subject to this tax. The rate of this tax in most American states is higher than the two pilots in China, and the American property tax allows smaller exemptions than the Chinese pilots. US local governments rely heavily on revenues from the real property tax for their operation in providing basic public services. Furthermore, the tax rate is related to and may change each year according to the expenditures of local governments in America's decentralized system. In Shanghai and Chongqing, only a small portion of residential properties are now subject to this tax. This tax has lower tax rates and larger exemptions than its counterpart in America. Therefore, local governments harvest only negligible revenue from this tax as of this writing. Instead of raising revenue for the government, the pilot real property taxes bear the task of controlling real estate price. As a start (to be technically reasonable, politically acceptable, and administratively feasible), we can predict that when real property tax is adopted in other cities, it will still have the characteristics of a narrow base and low rates as it has been in Shanghai and Chongqing. We also conclude that this tax in China will apply mainly to newly purchased housing. In terms of tax administration, technical issues are not the main difficulties in its expansion. As for the timing of expansion, it is not predictable from a technical standpoint. However, it is very obvious that there is still a long way to go before the full launch of a comprehensive model of the real property tax that is specifically designed for and fits well in China's context.

Chapter 8
Public Feedback—Survey and Public Media Findings

It has been nearly 2 years (as of this writing) since the beginning of the pilot local property tax (LPT) in Shanghai and Chongqing. People throughout the country, if not from paying the tax itself, have begun to get at least some sense of this tax from the media. In the course of the pilot, different groups of the general public had different opinions about the tax. To identify the perceptions and attitude of the general public toward the tax, our research group designed two questionnaires. One is designed for urban residents who are purchasers and owners of residential property, and potential payers of the LPT. The other questionnaire is designed for officials who supposedly know more about policy issues than other private citizens and will be in policy making and implementation positions once the LPT is widely adopted. The residents' questionnaire consists of three parts: initial understanding of the LPT, attitudes toward the LPT pilots in Shanghai and Chongqing, and suggestions for improvement of this tax reform. The officials questionnaire is mainly concerned with officials' attitudes toward the relationship between the LPT and local governance.

Our first objective in conducting the survey was to ascertain the understanding (perception) of and attitudes toward the pilot tax among ordinary citizens and government officials. Another objective was to collect public input and advice on how to improve the LPT as has been piloted in the two metropolitans. Additionally, we wanted to capture the opinions of officials regarding the relationship between an LPT and local governance in China.

We conducted surveys in a 3-month window (from May 30 to August 31, 2012) among the two groups separately, though in some cases an individual identified him/herself as both a resident and an official. The timing of the survey was about 18 months after the pilot LPT began in the two metropolitans, which was enough time for media coverage of the LPT to inform the general public. The duration of the survey was also long enough to sample and capture a very wide range of respondents, and thereby, opinions. The residents' survey was conducted mainly online through an automatic, blind survey instrument. Given that Internet access and use has long been extremely popular in the country, this method best guaranteed the collection of true public opinions. This last point is especially appropriate since our survey window was 3 months long. The officials' survey was conducted on multiple occasions, depending on when/where we had permission, on trainees of finance-related

Y. Hou et al., *The Property Tax in China,* Development and Governance,
DOI 10.1007/978-3-319-10049-4_8

classes. This was not the best way to collect random opinions among officials because the participants in each training class were typically from very similar, if not the same, professions; however, given that we did not have government support or endorsement for this project and that our funding was very limited, this was the best we could have done. A few training classes responded to both the residents' and the officials' questionnaires. Most of our respondents were from the eastern and the interior regions of China, with very few from the western region, a distribution that is representative of the overall development of the real estate market. We collected 568 valid responses to the residents' questionnaire and 159 valid responses to the officials' questionnaire. The sizes were large enough to allow empirical analyses to arrive at some reliable, though preliminary conclusions. The two survey instruments are provided in the appendixes at the end of this monograph.

8.1 Household Survey

8.1.1 Sample Distribution

In this section, we present the distribution of our respondents in terms of occupation, education, age, family structure, and housing ownership and floor space. These categories are the basis for analyzing the results of the survey.

Most of the respondents are from financial institutions, government-supported entities, state-owned enterprises, and government agencies, as shown in Fig. 8.1. Those from financial institutions account for 41 % of the total. Those from government, government-supported entities, and state-owned enterprises account for 17, 18, and 17 %, respectively. Respondents who identify themselves as being in the private sector represent only 3 % of the total.

Most of the respondents are well educated, have easy access to information, and can effectively obtain and process information they need in a timely manner. They also are able to express their opinions about issues of concern and interest to them. Most respondents are from ages 22–50, which is the major and the largest group of

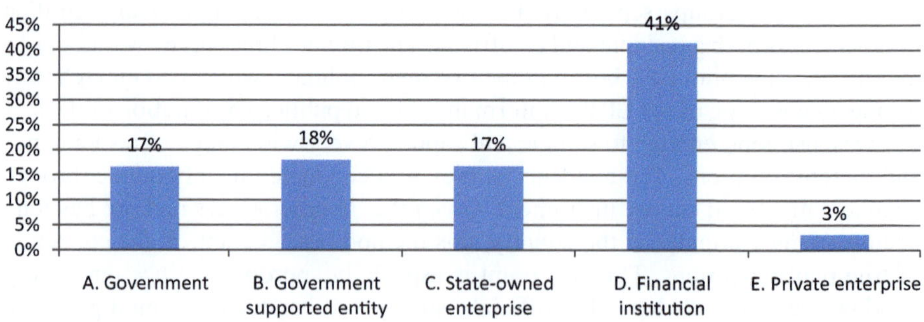

Fig. 8.1 Distribution of respondent occupation

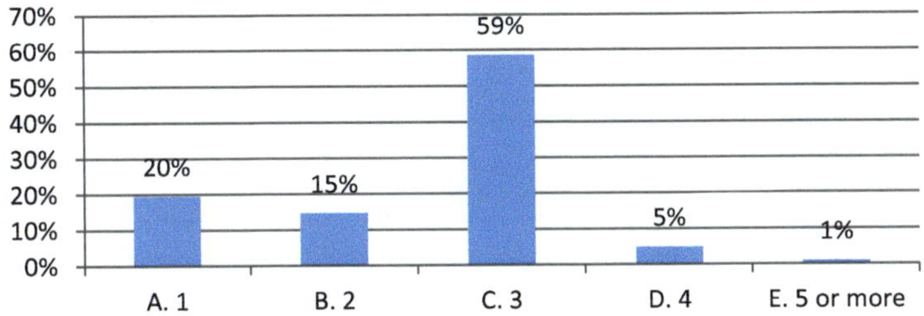

Fig. 8.2 Distribution of respondent household structure

the urban population who purchase and own housing property. Within this range, respondents aged 31–40 account for the biggest share, 41 %; they are potentially the strongest voice with regard to the real estate market. Those from 22 to 30 years make up 27 %; they are the group in urgent need of housing because of impending marriage. Those from ages 41–50 make up 26 %; this is the group that has its career and therefore needs to purchase bigger and better residences. Those from 51 to 60 years account for only 6 % of the total; those in this group probably have already somehow obtained (if not bought) their primary, even secondary, residence, and are not in much need of extra housing property.

Family structure is the key to housing needs. Among our respondents, 59 % are families with three members, which is the average of the mean from the 2010 Decennial Population Survey. Two parents with one child has been the national standard household structure of a core family in China, which is reflected in the amount of housing needed. Another 15 % are families with two members—couples with no children or couples with grown-up children who have assumed separate residence. Another 20 % are families with only one member; presumably, these are either singles or those who have divorced without a child or have lost their spouse. Additionally, only 5 % are families with four members and 1 % of the families have five or more members. The former cases are families with two children or one child and one grandparent; the latter cases are coresidents from three generations. Details are provided in Fig. 8.2.

Among responses to the question about how many housing units (a "housing unit" is a single-family house, a townhouse, or an apartment) the family owns (has the right of ownership), 46 % of the respondents said that they own one unit; 28 % own two units, and 9 % own three or more units. That is, about half of the urban residents already own their primary residence, and over a quarter also own a second home. One out of nine households has more than enough housing for residential needs, which implies investment activity since the more units one owns, the more likely it is that the owner is an investor in real estate and rents out the extra units. At the same time, 16 % do not yet have a residence of their own; they are now renting and will need to buy sooner or later.

Regarding the average floor space per housing unit owned, 40 % of the respondents reported that their average floor space is between 80 and 120 m^2. In a populous country like China, and given the average family size of three members, this is

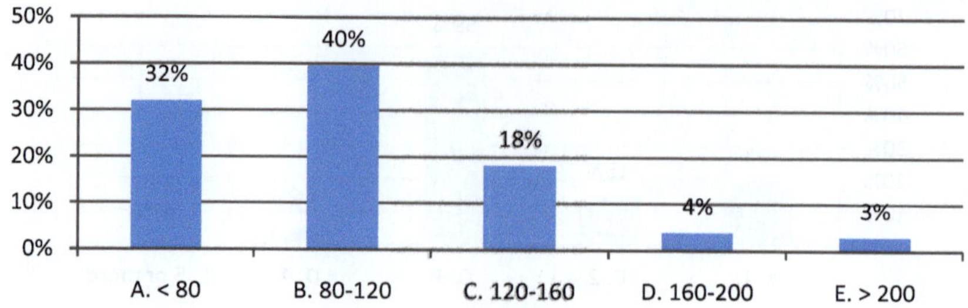

Fig. 8.3 Average floor space of housing units owned (in m^2)

already a comfortable living condition. Another 18 % reported an average between 120 and 160 m^2, and 7 % had more than 160 m^2. These are very high living standards already. Altogether, at least 65 % enjoy very good living conditions spacewise. Meanwhile, 32 % said their floor space is below 80 m^2, which is a group that will purchase larger residences in the future in order to improve their condition or to catch up with their peers. Details are provided in Fig. 8.3.

8.1.2 Citizens' Understanding of the Pilot LPT

Whether the respondents really understand the practices of the pilot LPT greatly affects their attitudes toward the tax. To ascertain their knowledge of the LPT in the two metropolitans, we included several questions in the questionnaire in this regard.

To our question of whether they had heard of the real property tax, 95 % of the respondents gave a postive answer; only 5 % indicated that they had not heard of the tax. This result shows that news of the pilot LPT in Shanghai and Chongqing had been widely spread and reached ordinary citizens across at least the eastern and the interior regions of the country. But whether the type of real property tax in their minds is the same as in the pilot real property tax is unknown.

At this initial level of knowledge about the property tax, attitudes of the respondents toward the LPT were more negative than positive, as shown in Fig. 8.4: only 35 % supported the tax, 44 % opposed the tax, and the rest did not care very much. Reasons for the indifference are not clear. The opposition reflects the expected mentality against any extra tax burden.

We included in the questionnaire another three questions to further reveal the level of initial understanding of the LPT by respondents. These questions were on eligibility of the tax, base for calculating tax payment, and frequency of the tax—one time or annual.

On how wide or narrow the eligibility of LPT should be (Fig. 8.5), 43 % chose the option that only newly purchased units and the second or more units should be eligible. That is, a relatively high proportion of respondents believed that previously owned units and the first or primary residence should not be taxed. The underlying distinctions in their minds were between new and prior purchases and between

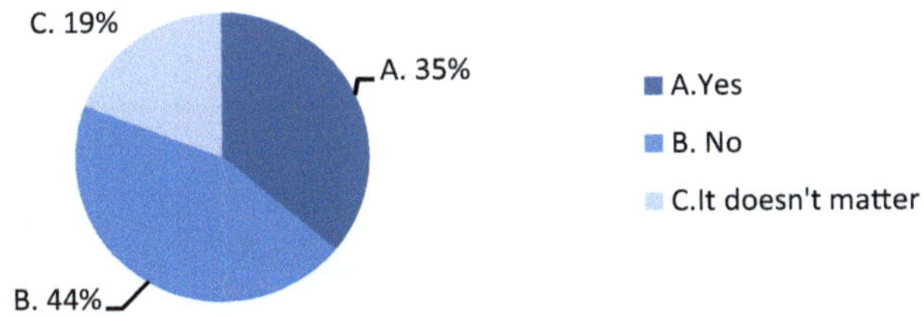

Fig.8.4 Public attitudes toward the LPT based on prior knowledge

primary and secondary residences. Both can be taken as a line between the wealthy and the nonwealthy, because new purchases are those on the high end of housing prices; thus, these owners by default are wealthy. By the same logic, those owning secondary homes possess the financial means besides their need for new purchases.

The second highest option (selected by 41 % of respondents) is that the second or more units, including prior purchases, should be subject to LPT. Here the underlying line is drawn between the primary residence and every extra unit; that is, only the primary residence should be exempted. This is the widest eligibility according to the respondents. Another 8 % answered that only newly purchased units should be subject to LPT. From these three replies, it is apparent that even though most respondents had heard of LPT, less than half of them understood the details of LPT in Shanghai and Chongqing. The fourth choice, that all real property should be eligible for the tax with no exemptions, was our embedded ideal answer, and 5 % chose it. Though this is by far the smallest share among the four options, 1 out of 20 still chose it.

Of the three options on the calculation of LPT payments, 41 % thought that the formula should be "floor space multiplied by unit price multiplied by a flat tax per square meter;" 37 % preferred the formula of "assessed value multiplied by a flat tax rate;" and 18 % chose "number of units multiplied by a flat tax per unit." Though this was a more technically sophisticated topic and the provided options were not exhaustive, over two fifths of respondents still chose to link size with unit price.

On the frequency of LPT levy and payment, 34 % of the respondents preferred it to be a one-time levy to be paid by the purchaser; 13 % preferred a one-time levy to be paid by the seller. Whether paid by purchaser or seller, these two answers showed

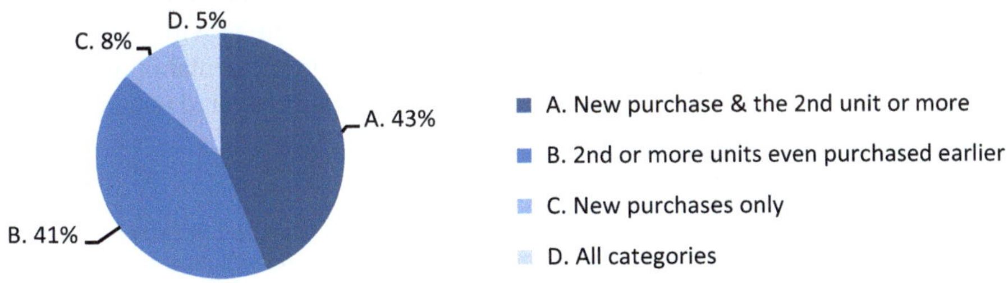

Fig. 8.5 Eligibility of the pilot LPT according to respondents understanding

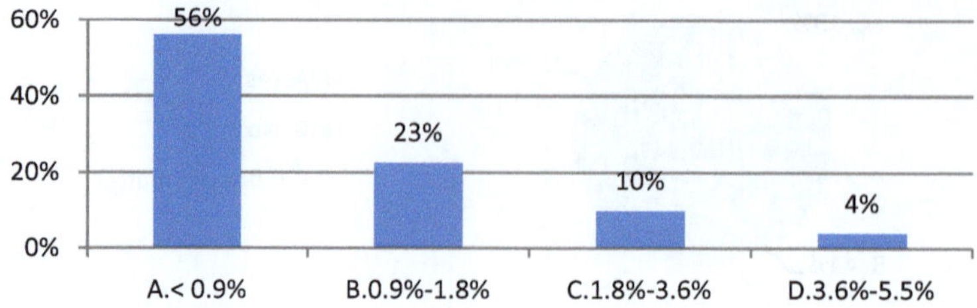

Fig. 8.6 LPT affordability each year according to respondents

a popular preference for the tax to be a one-time levy for every property sale, which may have been linked by the respondents to the current practice of levying a transaction tax on real property purchases. Nevertheless, almost half of the respondents (49 %) chose the option that the property tax should be paid once each year by the owner. That is, even though the LPT so far has been piloted in only two metropolitans, one half of the sampled citizens have already hit right upon the future direction of the real property tax and its frequency of levy and payment.

To further explore the basis for their prior knowledge about the LPT, we asked, "Do you think you will be a taxpayer if LPT is levied in the city where you reside?" Forty-three percent thought they will be LPT payers, and 55 % did not think that they will be. Then we asked, "How much LPT can you afford to pay if the tax is levied once a year?" As shown in Fig. 8.6, about 56 % put their affordable range at no more than 500 yuan, 23 % in the range 500–1000 yuan, and 10 % between 1000 and 2000 yuan, which, if converted into ratios of the national average urban household annual income (from the *China Statistical Year Book 2011*), is no more than 0.9, 0.9–1.8, 1.8–3.6 and 3.6–5.5%, respectively.[1] That is, a predominant proportion put their affordable tax payment at a rather low level.

8.1.3 Respondent Attitudes Toward Pilot LPT in Shanghai and Chongqing

Given that the pilot LPT in Shanghai and Chongqing had been in effect for only 15 months by the time of our survey, it is reasonable to assume that our respondents at that time did not know the details of the LPT. Therefore, at this point in the questionnaire (that is, in the middle of the survey, online as well as with the training classes), we clarified, citing specific examples of some implementation details of the policy as used in Shanghai and Chongqing. These details covered tax eligibility,

[1] The average urban annual income per capita in China is 19,109.4 yuan, and the average number of urban household member is 2.88. Thus, the national average urban household annual income is calculated as 55,035.07 (19,109.4×2.88) yuan. Source: *China Statistical Year Book 2011*, http://www.stats.gov.cn/tjsj/ndsj/2011/indexch.htm, 10–5.

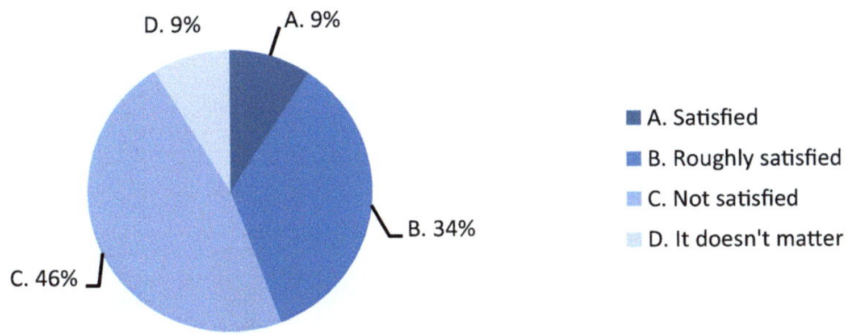

Fig. 8.7 Attitude toward LPT in Shanghai

tax rates, and frequency of levy/payment, etc. Then, the survey continued in an effort to capture any change in respondents' attitudes toward LPT.

8.1.3.1 Attitudes Toward Pilot LPT in Shanghai

To the question of their attitude toward the pilot LPT in Shanghai (Fig. 8.7), 9 % of respondents said they were satisfied; 34 % said they were somewhat satisfied; but a higher proportion (46 %) were not satisfied and another 9 % did not care. Then comparing the number of housing units owned by each respondent with his/her answer to this question, we found that the number of units owned is negatively related with the answer: the more units one owns, the more likely the person is to be dissatisfied with the Shanghai pilot LPT (36 % of respondents owned at least two residences).

The Shanghai LPT allows an exemption of 60 m^2 per household member from the tax. Concerning this floor space exemption, 19 % thought that the exempted area is too large; 31 % thought that it is too small; and 50 % thought this exemption quota is appropriate. We then compared housing ownership with answers to this question and found that with an increase in the number of housing units owned by the respondents, the percentage of respondents who chose "too large" and "appropriate" drops, while the percentage who chose "too small" rises.

In the fomula to calculate the Shanghai LPT, the assessment ratio is 70 % and the tax rate is 0.6 %. About the assessment ratio and tax rate, 58 % of the respondents thought that it would be better to lower them; 14 % maintained that they were too low and should be increased; and 26 % believed the current levels were appropriate. Similarly, we found a strong negative correlation between ownership and the desire to raise the two levels (Fig. 8.8): as the number of units one owns increases, a respondent was more likely to hold the opinion that the assessment ratio and tax rate should be lower, and vice versa. To sum up, 40 % of the respondents were satisfied or somewhat satisfied with the LPT in Shanghai. From the reply, we found that some respondents wish the LPT policy was more generous, while other respondents would have liked a higher tax rate and a broader tax base.

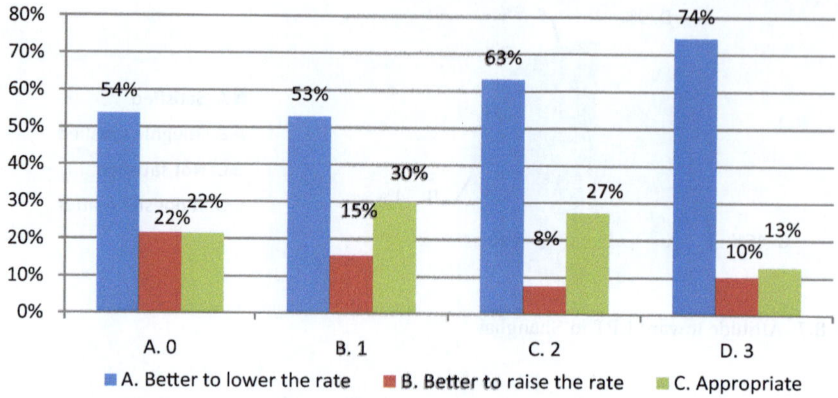

Fig. 8.8 House ownership vs. assessment ratio and tax rate

8.1.3.2 Attitudes Toward Pilot LPT in Chongqing

In response to our inquiry of their attitude toward the Chongqing LPT (Fig. 8.9), 12 % of the respondents said they were satisfied, 37 % said they were roughly satisfied, and 43 % were not satisfied. Another 8 % did not care. This is a distribution similar to the attitudes toward the LPT in Shanghai. Also similar is the negative relationship between the number of housing units owned by the respondents and the percentage of dissatisfaction. Thus, the results on the two different pilot LPTs are comparable and are reliable reflections of public perception.

The Chongqing LPT targets high-end, newly purchased housing, mainly single-family houses (or "villas" as they are called there), but also allows an exemption of 100 m^2 per household. When asked about their attitudes toward this exemption, 19 % of the respondents thought that the exemption is too large, 35 % thought it is too small, while 44 % regarded the exemption to be appropriate in size. Similar to their attitude to the LPT in Shanghai, the same relationship applied to the number of housing units owned and attitude to the size of the tax exemption: As the number of housing units owned increases, more of the respondents tended to think that the exemption is "too small," and vice versa.

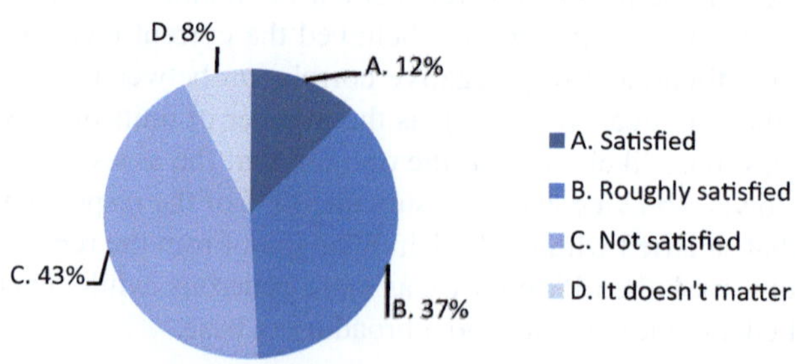

Fig. 8.9 Attitude toward the LPT in Chongqing

Another feature of the Chongqing LPT is that it applies only to new purchases; thus, even high-end housing (excluding single-family villas) bought before the effective date of the LPT (January 28, 2011) is exempted from the tax. Though such a practice has been common in policy enforcement, less than half (44 %) of the respondents supported this part of the policy whereas more than half (56 %) of the respondents were opposed to this part: they hold the view that all owners of upper-end property should be treated equally.

High-end housing in the Chongqing LPT refers to units with their market price per square meter more than or equal to twice the average price of the nine main central districts in the previous 2 years. These types of housing units are also called luxury housing. When the respondents were asked about their attitude toward the criteria of luxury housing in Chongqing, 23 % of them thought that the threshold (twice the average price) is too high, 30 % thought it is too low, and 47 % regarded it as appropriate.

Chongqing levies the LPT on detached (single-family) villas even if they were bought before the cutoff date (January 28, 2011). Among the respondents, 29 % were opposed to this policy, 60 % supported it, and the rest were indifferent. Again, the number of housing units owned by a respondent was positively related to his or her attitude toward this policy.

As we discussed before in this monograph, it was assumed among policy makers in China that the launch of the pilot LPT was somehow related to the rising housing prices on the market. In other words, the LPT was started on a trial basis as a potential policy tool to control the housing price. When the respondents were asked about whether LPT can be effective in suppressing housing prices, 38 % of them gave a positive answer, 44 % gave a negative answer, and the rest were not sure.

To sum up, one major difference in public perceptions of the two pilot LPTs is that the proportion of respondents who were satisfied or somewhat satisfied with the LPT in Chongqing is about 10 percentage points higher than with the Shanghai LPT. One key similarity across the two pilots is that some (mainly wealthy, owners of multiple units) respondents wished the LPT was more generous with exemptions, while other respondents (mainly middle and low income, owners of one unit) would have liked to see a higher tax rate and smaller exemptions.

8.1.4 Respondent Advice on Future Improvement of the LPT

As discussed above, among our respondents (as is also true among policy makers in China) some maintained the stance that all people who own real property should pay the tax. Some others held the view that the LPT could be used as a policy tool to influence and readjust consumer behavior to the real estate market and to narrow the income gap between the wealthy and the middle/low-income classes. Those with the second view insisted that only owners of two or more housing units should be paying the tax. In response to the question of who should be LPT taxpayers among property owners, ranked by the number of housing units owned (Fig. 8.10), 32 % of

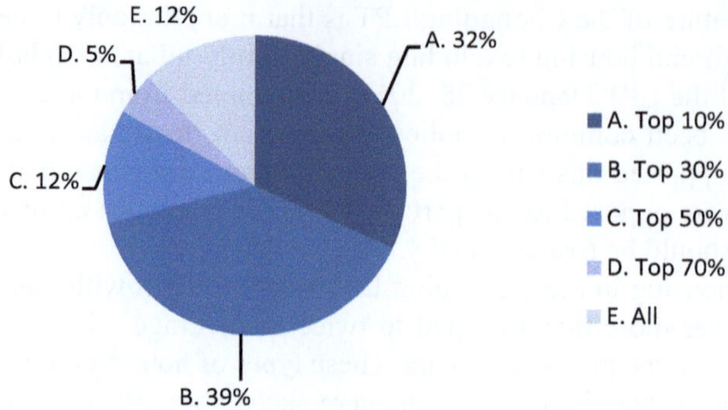

Fig.8.10 Who should pay the LPT among owners by number of units owned?

the respondents chose the top 10 and 39 % chose the top 30 %. Only 12 % thought all property owners should pay the tax whether they own just one unit or multiple units.

Both the Shanghai and the Chongqing LPT use "new purchase" (after the effective date of the tax) as the main eligibility criterion of the LPT. In the survey we asked a specific question on whether housing units bought before implementation of LPT should be taxed: 27 % held the opinion that all purchases, past and new, should be subject to LPT; 30 % insisted that only purchases made after LPT implementation should be taxed; and 43 % maintained that new purchases of ordinary housing (bought after LPT implementation) and all high-end housing, regardless of purchase date, should be taxed.

In the analysis we found that the attitude of an average respondent toward the tax tends to turn negative as the number of housing units one owns increases (Fig. 8.11); these people prefer to "let bygones be bygones" and blur the distinction between ordinary housing units and up-scale housing. That is, an average property owner

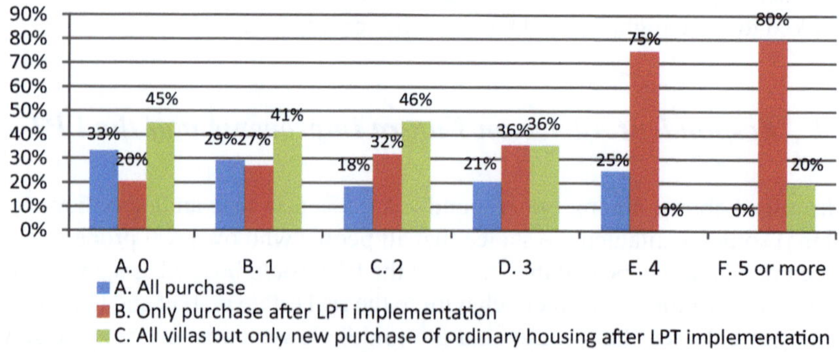

Fig. 8.11 Number of units owned vs. attitude toward goal of LPT

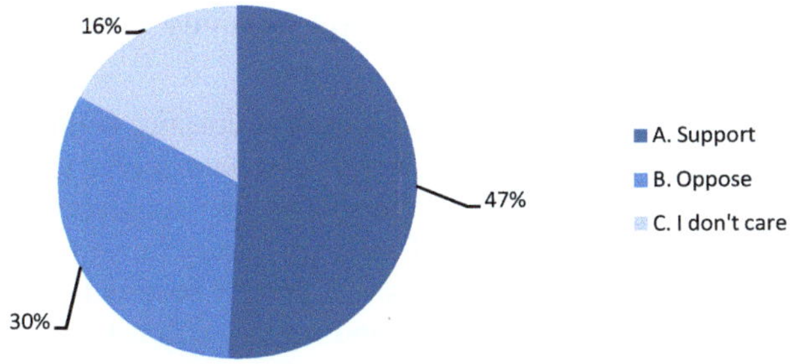

Fig. 8.12 Attitude toward LPT after the concept is clarified

on the margin does not want their housing property to be subject to the LPT if they are potential taxpayers. Thus, from the standpoint of political and administrative feasibility, an "incremental reform" would be more convenient in order to spread the LPT to the whole country.

Judging from the long-time practice of the LPT in developed countries, we know that some kind of and extent of exemption would be a convenient means to achieve feasibility, especially political feasibility (for acceptance by the general public), although any exemption compromises the efficiency of the tax. In this survey, we asked about the preferred size of floor space as a potential exemption, as compared with the current Shanghai or Chongqing LPT. (Shanghai exempts 60 m^2 per *member* for each household and Chongqing exempts 100 m^2 by *household* not per member.) The respondents chose from different models and sizes of floor space. For the Shanghai model of exemption by each household member, 7 % thought that the exempted floor space should be 40 m^2 or less per capita in each household; 20 % thought 40–60 m^2 per household member is proper; 44 % thought the per household member exemption should be more than 60 m^2. For the Chongqing model of exemption by the household, 7 % proposed 80 m^2 or less per household, 10 % chose 100–120 m^2, and 9 % preferred over 120 m^2 per household. From these responses, it is clear that more respondents prefer exemption by the number of household members, the Shanghai model, to exemption by household, the Chongqing model.

As for the acceptable range of the effective tax rate (the survey instrument provides a technial definition of the term), 55 % prefered less than 0.1 %, 27 % recommended 0.1–0.3 %, and 12 % chose 0.3–0.5 %. Only 6 % accepted a rate of more than 0.5 %.

After the practices of the Shanghai and Chongqing LPT were clarified, we asked the respondents again about their attitudes toward the LPT. Substantive changes were observable (Fig. 8.12): 47 % of them supported the LPT, a 12 percentage point increase from that before the clarification; 30 % opposed the tax, a 14 percentage point decrease from that before the clarification; and 16 % did not care.

8.2 Results of Government Officials' Survey

The ultimate goal of levying an LPT on residential housing is much more than to control the skyrocketing housing prices, it is also to help coerce local governments into becoming more responsible and accountable to their taxpayers. In the short run, Chinese governments may levy the LPT only on luxury housing units or nonprimary housing units. In the long run, however, the tax base will cover most, even all, housing units for reasons of efficiency and equity, with reasonable exemptions.

The ideal LPT is not only a means to raise own-source revenue for local governments, it also serves as an effective tool to improve local governance. Specifically, an ideal LPT should have the following characteristics. First, revenues from the LPT should belong to local governments at their full discretion and should be devoted to key public services closely related to people's daily lives. These include education, public safety, public health, recreation, and roads. Second, tax rates should be determined locally in accord with total local expenditure needs. As such, the rate varies across different localities. Third, the budget and budgeting process should be transparent so that local residents can evaluate the performance of local officials and government by comparing what they pay with what they gain from public expenditure. The selection or appointment of local officials should be based on their prior performance and future plans. Our survey of government officials' attitudes toward LPT is based on the above propositions.

8.2.1 Sample Distribution of Surveyed Officials

Among the known government departments, a quarter of the government officials that we surveyed are from the general offices, and significantly high proportions are from departments of finance (11 %), revenue service (11 %), and education (5 %). In terms of the administrative rank of the agency that the respondents work in (Fig. 8.13), 31 % are at the rank of ministry or province, 23 % are at the rank of department, 26 % at division, and 5 % at subdivision.[2]

As for the administrative rank of the individual respondents, there are no officials in our sample at the ministerial/provincial rank and very few are at the department rank. The largest proportions are at the ranks of division (43 %) and subdivision (34 %). This high concentration of the survey sample at the division and subdivision ranks offers an obvious downside as well as an apparent upside. The downside is lack of variation; the upside is that our sample comprises mostly those officials who are at the frontline of policy consultation, implementation, and enforcement. Given that it usually takes an entry-level person 5–10 years to be promoted to this rank, our sample can probably provide the most up-to-date and frontline information that is direct and first-hand.

[2] In the Chinese bureaucratic hierarchy, every government and its agencies are designated a rank. A provincial government's of the same rank as a ministry of the central government. Departments are under a ministry or province; divisions are under departments, and subdivisions under divisions.

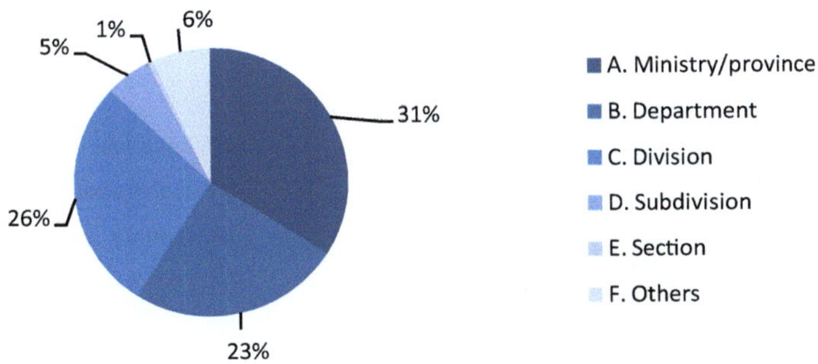

Fig. 8.13 Administrative rank of respondent's agency

8.2.2 Attitudes Toward LPT and Local Governance

From our proposition of the ideal LPT as a stable own-source revenue at full local discretion, we asked whether it is feasible for LPT to become a revenue source for localities. In response to this question, the positive and negative answers were split (41 and 42 %, respectively) and 13 % were not sure about the answer. In terms of the question of whether it is feasible for localities to determine their own LPT rate according to local needs, 22 % of the respondents gave a positive reply but a dominant 64 % gave a negative reply. The remaining 14 % did not know the answer.

Another proposition of ours is to devote LPT revenue to providing key public services such as public education, pulic health, public safety, local roads, and recreational facilities. Higher demand for these basic services will be closely connected to the LPT rate (on top of intergovernmental transfers), thus establishing the direct link between own-source revenue and the qualiy and quantity of services. Through the direct link, accountability for expendtitures will be clearer and officials' performance will be easier to track and evaluate. When asked about the above concept, 37 % of the respondents thought it was feasible to establish the link, 45 % held a negative view, and the remaining 18 % did not provide an answer.

If the LPT is implemented as discussed above to supplement the financing of basic services, residents of each locality will demand increased transparency. As for whether this idea can become a reality, a landslide 82 % said "Yes," only 11 % said "No," and 7 % did not have an answer. If the LPT is implemented as described above, local residents will also overtime require that the localities provide performance reports for each major program. As for this possibility, 78 % of the responses were positive, only 15 % gave a negative reply, and 7 % did not have an answer. Along with the above design of the property tax, we asked the respondents whether local residents would participate in decision making through various means such as public hearings. Seventy-two percent said "Yes," 17 % said "No," and 11 % did not have an answer.

The *Constitution of the People's Republic of China* provides that the local General Assembly of People's Representatives has the right to elect, appoint, or recall local officers. In compliance with the above provision, the number of candidates

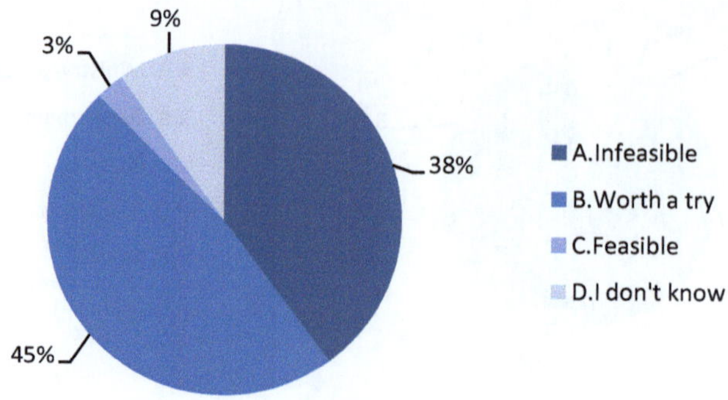

Fig. 8.14 Attitude of officials toward improving efficiency through LPT

for public offices can be increased in the process of election so that local residents can vote for their preferred candidates based on nominees' administrative plans. In regard to this proposition, 36 % of our respondents thought that it is possible, 43 % insisted that it is impossible for China's local governments, and 21 % did not have an answer.

Through implementing the LPT and other related budgting and administrative reforms, the efficiency of local governments can and will be improved. When asked whether this proposition was feasible (Fig. 8.14), 38 % of the respondents thought that the idea was impracticable, 45 % believed it was worth a try, and 3 % thought that it was feasible.

8.3 Regression Analyses of Survey Responses

In this chapter, we use the data (though very limited) collected from the surveys to conduct regression analyses based on the survey results presented in the previous two subsections. Before investigating the statistical effects of the respondents' opinions about the LPT pilots, we would like to note that most variables used in the analyses are not continuous (except individual income and household income), but categorical or ordinal (see survey instruments in Appendixes 8.2 and 8.3 for details). Thus, we need to be more careful in inferring policy implications from these regression results.

As indicated in the attached survey instruments, the answers to the survey questions were often binary, such as agree/disagree or yes/no, or ordered categories (ordinal responses). For example, in question #30 for residents' opinions about an appropriate effective tax rate, the provided answers to choose from are: "A. Less than 0.1 %; B. 0.1–0.3 %; C. 0.3–0.5 %; D. >0.5 %." For all these types of answers, we converted the responses into ordered categories from 1 to 4.

With these types of variables we have, the empirical models are *logit* and *ordered logit* regressions. When we need to use a dummy (0/1) variable as the dependent variable, we cannot use ordinary least squares (OLS) regression for at least two reasons. One is that OLS may predict a value outside the range 0 and 1, which does not make sense as a probability. The second reason is that a binary-dependent variable cannot satisfy the requirement of normal distribution, which is assumed in OLS. Alternatively, we need to have a *logistic* transformation for the binary dependent variable described as follows:[3]

$$\textbf{OLS}: \pi = \alpha + \boldsymbol{\beta X}$$

$$\textbf{Logit}: \log\left(\frac{\pi}{1-\pi}\right) = \alpha + \boldsymbol{\beta X},$$

where π is the dependent variable with a range between 0 and 1, $\boldsymbol{X}$ is the vector independent variables, and α and β are coefficients to be estimated. With the transformation, the range of the dependent variable $\log\left(\frac{\pi}{1-\pi}\right)$ changes to $(-\infty, +\infty)$ with π in [0, 1]. In the *logit* regression, maximum likelihood estimation (MLE) is used to estimate α and β. Therefore, *pseudo* R^2 rather than R^2 are reported in the regression results.

Ordered logit is an extension of the logistic regression model for dichotomous dependent variables, allowing for more than two (ordered) response categories. Examples of multiple ordered response categories include opinion surveys with responses ranging from "strongly agree" to "strongly disagree" and employment status (not employed, employed part time, or fully employed) (see Wooldridge 2009; Greene 2012).[4] In our survey samples, about half of the questions have this type of ordinal response.

In the survey questionnaires, most of the questions were about the opinions toward the LPT. As we know, the variables regarding opinions are usually endogenous. To address the endogeneity problem, in the statistical analysis we focus on how the personal characteristics of the respondents affect their views on each question. Specifically, the exogenous variables are individual rank and department rank for officials, and demographic characteristics and socialeconomic status for residents.

8.3.1 Opinion of Citizens Toward LPT

For ordinary citizens, we focus on three aspects of their opinion about the pilot LPT or their preferences on the property tax design: (1) Who is more active in

[3] *Probit* is another appropriate method. The regression results are very similar to those of *logit*.

[4] Wooldridge (2009), Chap, 17; Greene (2003), pp. 736–740.

supporting the LPT reform and why? (2) Which characteristics do citizens who propose a broader tax base or a higher tax rate possess, and what about the reverse? (3) When comparing the policy designs in Shanghai and Chongqing, which one do these citizens prefer and why?

8.3.1.1 Who Supports the LPT?

In terms of citizens' attitudes toward the LPT reform, we use personal characteristics to predict their attitudes. As indicated in Table 8.1, before we clarified the LPT reform in the survey questions, those who can accept a greater tax amount had a higher probability of supporting the LPT reform. We would like to note that the amount of acceptable tax payment here does not correlate with their individual or household income, since it reflects more of their acceptability (attitude toward) of this tax. Actually, in our data, the correlation coefficients between acceptable tax amounts and income (either individual or household) are close to 0. The other statistically significant variables are the number of owned housing units and the average size (floor space) of these units, with land classified as state-owned. These results are also reasonable because these respondents tend to be the losers of the LPT reform in that they will have to pay the tax.

After the detailed clarification of the LPT reform, however, the coefficients of the acceptable tax amount drop dramatically, and the coefficients of the number and average size of owned housing units on state-owned land changed to become insignificant. This may be because the respondents in the survey became more rational regarding the LPT reform after they had more knowledge and understanding of the LPT, while they tended to make judgments based more on their own characteristics before the clarification. Also, from the size of pseudo R^2 in these regressions, we can find that, even though they are consistently low, the R^2 before the clarification are much higher. It means that the respondents' personal characteristics can better explain their attitudes before the clarification of the policy. After that, these respondents were more rational, which is consistent with the above conclusion. Connecting these results to the reality in China for policy implications, we need to explain the policy in greater detail and its relevance to governance to help people accept and boost the LPT reform.

We also compared the attitudes of respondents in different sectors. Before the clarification of the LPT reform, respondents working in "government" and "government-supported entities" were significantly more supportive than those in "state-owned enterprises" and "financial institutions." However, after the clarification, the proportions of supportive respondents in all these four sectors markedly increased and the difference becomes statistically insignificant.

8.3.1.2 Who Is Proposing a Broader Tax Base or a Higher Tax Rate?

In the survey, after we introduced the policy details to respondents, they were asked to illustrate again their opinions regarding the tax base, the effective tax rate, and the

Table 8.1 *Ordered logit* regression: determinants of support for LPT. Dependent variable: the extent to support the LPT reform (ordered category)

	(1)	(2)	(3)	(4)
Variables	Before	Before	After	After
Payer=1 if potential payer	−0.1721	0.1544	−0.2261	−0.1323
	(0.2976)	(0.4045)	(0.3065)	(0.4083)
Bear: acceptable tax amount	*0.4502****	*0.4781****	*0.2566***	*0.2571***
	(0.1039)	*(0.1163)*	*(0.0996)*	*(0.1094)*
Interaction: payer*bear	−0.1420	0.0142	0.0286	0.1931
	(0.1426)	(0.1669)	(0.1495)	(0.1749)
Age		0.1643		0.1294
		(0.1143)		(0.1148)
Number of household members		0.1346		−0.0850
		(0.1144)		(0.1184)
Individual income		0.0378		0.0063
		(0.0327)		(0.0337)
Interaction: payer* individual income		−0.0230		−0.0264
		(0.0390)		(0.0395)
Household income		−0.0009		−0.0179
		(0.0185)		(0.0191)
Interaction: payer* household income		−0.0172		0.0069
		(0.0209)		(0.0199)
Number of owned housing units (on		*−0.2657***		−0.1555
state-owned land)		*(0.1254)*		(0.1213)
Average size of owned housing units		*−0.3067****		−0.1065
(on state-owned land)		*(0.1091)*		(0.1072)
Number of owned housing units (on		−0.1772		0.1636
collectively owned land)		(0.1933)		(0.2136)
Average market price of primary		−0.0163		0.0377
residence		(0.0441)		(0.0459)
Observations	546	488	519	464
Pseudo R^2	0.0338	0.0778	0.0148	0.0391

Standard errors in parentheses
*$p<0.10$; **$p<0.05$; ***$p<0.01$

extent (amount) of exemption. As shown in Table 8.2 also with ordered regressions, people with a higher acceptable tax payment propose a broader tax base, a higher effective tax rate, and a lower exemption. From the perspective of owned housing units, respondents with more housing units, larger average size, and higher market prices hope to have a narrower tax base, a lower effective tax rate, and expect more exemptions.

Due to more pressure in daily lives and smaller tax payment capacity, respondents with more household members prefer a lower effective tax rate and people with lower individual incomes suggest having more exemptions. Older people also support a broader tax base, possibly because they tend to be in the high-income group with a higher acceptable tax payment.

Some of the conclusions here are not very intuitive since, in reality, most respondents prefer a narrower tax base and a lower tax rate to pay a smaller amount

Table 8.2 *Ordered logit* regression: who are proposing broader tax base, higher effective tax rate, and higher exemption?

Variables	(1) Percentage of taxpayer	(2) Only new, between, or all	(3) Effective tax rate	(4) Exemption (SH)	(5) Exemption (CQ)
Payer=1 if potential payer	0.0768	−0.2220	−0.5970	−0.1093	−0.5947
	(0.3684)	(0.3826)	(0.4249)	(0.4997)	(0.7952)
Bear: acceptable tax amount	0.2213***	0.1728*	0.4732***	−0.3201***	−0.0243
	(0.0853)	(0.0893)	(0.0908)	(0.1047)	(0.1861)
Interaction: payer* bear	0.2426*	0.2193	0.2467*	−0.0835	−0.0347
	(0.1311)	(0.1449)	(0.1379)	(0.1684)	(0.2679)
Age	0.2000*	0.2499**	−0.0467	0.0162	0.4087
	(0.1077)	(0.1082)	(0.1190)	(0.1390)	(0.2612)
Number of household members	0.0188	0.0266	−0.2151*	0.0642	−0.2942
	(0.1053)	(0.1078)	(0.1130)	(0.1405)	(0.2271)
Individual income	0.0213	−0.0080	0.0190	−0.0703*	−0.0231
	(0.0307)	(0.0308)	(0.0294)	(0.0415)	(0.0752)
Payer* individual income	−0.0367	0.0089	−0.0290	0.1211**	0.0690
	(0.0360)	(0.0366)	(0.0372)	(0.0510)	(0.0872)
Household income	−0.0124	0.0024	0.0017	0.0458	0.0174
	(0.0182)	(0.0166)	(0.0177)	(0.0282)	(0.0436)
Payer* household income	0.0127	−0.0157	−0.0031	−0.0530*	−0.0264
	(0.0186)	(0.0183)	(0.0184)	(0.0287)	(0.0437)
Number of owned housing units (on state-owned land)	−0.1414	−0.2791**	−0.2223*	0.2325	0.4661*
	(0.1130)	(0.1168)	(0.1267)	(0.1567)	(0.2419)
Average size of owned housing units (on state-owned land)	−0.1487	−0.2384**	−0.0581	0.4026***	0.3137
	(0.0961)	(0.1021)	(0.1074)	(0.1415)	(0.2173)
Number of owned housing units (on collective land)	0.2299	−0.5024***	−0.0764	−0.0882	−0.0648
	(0.1851)	(0.1924)	(0.1882)	(0.2567)	(0.3051)
Average market price of primary residence	−0.0163	0.0183	−0.0123	0.1515***	0.0296
	(0.0415)	(0.0428)	(0.0455)	(0.0556)	(0.0901)
Observations	489	484	485	367	120
Pseudo R^2	0.0336	0.0521	0.0899	0.0885	0.0718

Standard errors in parentheses
$*p<0.10$; $**p<0.05$; $***p<0.01$

of tax. Therefore, we need to keep in mind that these conclusions are based on a comparative perspective, which means, with all other variables constant, how does a change of one independent variable affect an opinion. For instance, compared to respondents with a lower acceptable tax payment, people with a higher acceptable payment accept a *comparatively* higher property tax rate with all other characteristics constant.

8.3.1.3 Compare SH and CQ: Who is Satisfied with the Design in SH or CQ?

For the policy reform designs in Shanghai (SH) and Chongqing (CQ), what are the opinions of respondents toward the two models? Who are satisfied with the design in Shanghai or Chongqing? The regression results in Table 8.3 precisely reflect the characteristics of the pilot designs of LPT reform in Shanghai and Chongqing. For the pilot LPT design in Shanghai, not surprisingly, respondents with more household members tend to be more satisfied, while people with a higher average market price of their primary residence tend to be less satisfied. The reason is that in Shanghai's design, the exemption is household member based (60 m^2 per member). According to the Population Census in 2010, the per capita living space in cities of China was only 29.15 m^2; thus, "more members in the household" is really a bonus regarding the size of exemption according to this design. But Shanghai does impose a substantial penalty to housing units with higher prices in terms of the tax rate, which changes from 0.4 to 0.6 % (50 % penalty) once the price is higher than double the average price. It is highly likely that many respondents have housing units with a price beyond this threshold, which is why people with a higher housing price tend to be less satisfied.

In Table 8.3, the significant variables in the first two columns show that those who accept a larger amount of tax payment and favor a higher effective tax rate tend to be more satisfied with Shanghai's design. Older people also tend to show more satisfaction with this design. One possible explanation is that these respondents tend to be richer and live in a very decent condition with less stress from society. They mostly thought that the design in Shanghai is more consistent with their value judgments. In terms of economic incidences, on the other hand, we still need to think more thoughtfully as to why this happens.[5]

Similarly, for the design in Chongqing, respondents who proposed a broader tax base (including all old and newly purchased housing units regardless of the price or house type) are less satisfied with this design. It is consistent with the design because Chongqing poses a sharp discrimination between general housing units and those with higher prices or (luxurious) villas. With the change of R^2 from column

[5] The validity of survey data is another obstacle for us to have a reasonable and reliable inference for the regression results.

Table 8.3 Satisfaction with the LPT policy designs in Shanghai and Chongqing. Dependent variable: the extent of satisfaction with LPT designs (ordered category)

Variables	(1) Shanghai	(2) Shanghai	(3) Chongqing	(4) Chongqing
Percentage of people who should pay LPT		0.3798		0.1718
		(0.3354)		(0.3358)
Only new, new and part of old, or all be levied		0.1678		*−0.4092****
		(0.1282)		*(0.1267)*
Effective tax rate		*0.2275***		−0.0137
		(0.1056)		(0.1046)
Payer=1 if potential payer	−0.3250	−0.2791	0.2766	0.2199
	(0.3751)	(0.3828)	(0.3767)	(0.3834)
Bear: acceptable tax amount	*0.2891****	*0.2096***	0.0523	0.0655
	(0.0934)	*(0.0981)*	(0.0868)	(0.0918)
Interaction: payer* bear	−0.0938	−0.1347	−0.1366	−0.0834
	(0.1372)	(0.1428)	(0.1341)	(0.1379)
Age	*0.2209***	*0.1921**	−0.1442	−0.1249
	(0.1090)	*(0.1110)*	(0.1078)	(0.1104)
Number of household members	0.1801	*0.2029**	−0.0824	−0.0749
	(0.1113)	*(0.1139)*	(0.1069)	(0.1092)
Individual income	−0.0167	−0.0161	−0.0269	−0.0203
	(0.0311)	(0.0326)	(0.0291)	(0.0304)
Interaction: payer* individual income	0.0075	0.0063	0.0257	0.0218
	(0.0359)	(0.0373)	(0.0347)	(0.0358)
Household income	−0.0015	−0.0014	0.0098	0.0095
	(0.0175)	(0.0178)	(0.0163)	(0.0166)
Interaction: payer* household income	0.0023	0.0033	−0.0160	−0.0165
	(0.0182)	(0.0185)	(0.0173)	(0.0175)
Number of owned housing units (on state-owned land)	*−0.2631***	*−0.2294**	0.1216	0.0882
	(0.1193)	*(0.1222)*	(0.1122)	(0.1143)
Average area of owned housing units (on state-owned land)	−0.0445	−0.0403	0.0462	0.0100
	(0.1006)	(0.1024)	(0.0976)	(0.1001)
Number of owned housing units (on collective land)	−0.3247	−0.2973	0.2055	0.1410
	(0.1997)	(0.2025)	(0.1732)	(0.1778)
Average market price of primary residence	*−0.1197****	*−0.1235****	−0.0565	−0.0522
	(0.0427)	*(0.0433)*	(0.0423)	(0.0429)
Observations	491	477	492	479
PseudoR^2	0.0354	0.0450	0.0110	0.0202

When we control for the occupation of these residents, results are the same. And there are no differences in different industries for satisfaction of the two designs
Standard errors in parentheses
$^*p<0.10$; $^{**}p<0.05$; $^{***}p<0.01$

1 to 2 or 3 to 4, we also find that the inclusion of attitudes toward tax base and tax rate does help predict the satisfaction of policy designs in Shanghai and Chongqing. This reminds us that decision makers need to take citizens' consideration (public opinion) into account, combining it with general citizen (or local resident) characteristics when they design policy details.

8.3.2 Opinion of Government Officials on the Effects of LPT

In the survey for government officials, only ten questions were provided to increase the feasibility of the survey (Dillman 2000). Most of the questions were about the respondents' opinions, which are endogenous (see Appendix 8.1 for detail; only two others are exogenous: individual and department ranks). We mainly sought to investigate how the rank of the individuals and the rank of their department affect their opinions toward the different perspectives of the LPT reform. Finally, we tried to find out, in the respondents' view, how the different aspects of property tax will help to achieve the overall purpose of LPT reform—improvement of government efficiency and accountability.

In Table 8.4, all dependent variables are dummy variables except the last one, *efficiency*, which is an ordinal variable of values 1, 2, or 3, with higher values indicating more positive attitude. Correspondingly, all the first seven regressions are *logit* regressions while the final one is *ordered logit*. In all regressions, the department rank does not have significant effects on the attitude of respondents toward the LPT and local governance. These results make sense because the rank of the department where the respondent worked, in many cases, does not necessarily carry any information about the personalities or characteristics of the individuals working there. For example, a respondent with a low individual rank may work in a department with a very high department rank.

Individual rank, however, does have a significant effect on the attitude of respondents toward the LPT and local governance. Based on the regression results in Table 8.5, the higher the individual rank, the more positive attitude a respondent holds toward the possible consequences that property tax can be a main revenue source, can be used for designated categories of expenditure, can help to increase public participation and the feasibility of direct election, and finally, can support the property tax reform. The marginal effects are around 0.2, which indicates that the probability will increase by 20 % with each higher level of the individual rank.[6]

Regarding the overall effect of the LPT reform, we also investigated the determinants of "support" or "not support". The results in Table 8.6 identify those factors that the officials thought are important to achieve the goal of the LPT reform. Since these factors may be correlated with each other, only one is used as an independent variable in each regression in the first column (separate regressions). For those officials who believed that the property tax can be a stable main revenue source, can be spent on designated public services, and that the tax rate can be determined according to different local needs, the results indicate that the respondents tended to support the LPT reform and expected that this reform can improve the efficiency and accountability of local government. More importantly, those officials who insisted on the feasibility of local direct election tended to have more positive attitudes toward the LPT reform.

[6] It would be better if we can control other characteristics of these officials, however, we cannot identify the information exactly.

Table 8.4 Effects of *department rank* on respondent attitude toward LPT and local governance[a]

	(1)	(2)	(3)	(4)	(5)	(6)	(7)	(8)
Estimator	Logit	Logit	Logit	Logit	Logit	Logit	Logit	Ologit
Dependent variables	Rev	Rate	Exp	Trans	Perform	Public	Election	Efficiency
Department rank	0.0359	−0.0066	0.2744	−0.1709	0.1913	−0.2986	−0.0657	0.0189
	(0.1946)	(0.2267)	(0.2038)	(0.3257)	(0.2645)	(0.2538)	(0.1986)	(0.1904)
Observations	118	117	113	127	126	122	108	123
PseudoR^2	0.0002	0.0000	0.0119	0.0035	0.0050	0.0122	0.0007	0.0000

Standard errors in parentheses
$^{*}p<0.10$; $^{**}p<0.05$; $^{***}p<0.01$
[a] See Appendix 8.1 for definition of variables

Table 8.5 Effects of *individual rank* on respondent attitude toward LPT and local governance

	(1)	(2)	(3)	(4)	(5)	(6)	(7)	(8)
Estimator	Logit	Logit	Logit	Logit	Logit	Logit	Logit	Ologit
Dependent variables	Rev	Rate	Exp	Trans	Perform	Public	Election	Efficiency
Individual rank	0.8714**	0.0770	0.6596*	0.2258	0.7046	1.4506***	0.9208**	0.6513*
	(0.3613)	(0.3940)	(0.3647)	(0.6155)	(0.4853)	(0.5278)	(0.3919)	(0.3478)
Marginal effects	0.2178**	0.0148	0.1640*	0.0172	0.0754	0.1600***	0.2276**	0.1491*[a]
	(0.0903)	(0.0757)	(0.0906)	(0.0465)	(0.0500)	(0.0527)	(0.0966)	(0.0806)
Observations	107	104	101	108	109	105	93	107
PseudoR^2	0.0417	0.0003	0.0245	0.0021	0.0251	0.0960	0.0466	0.0220

For the *ordered logit* regression, the marginal effects are −0.1604* (0.0857), 0.1491* (0.0806), and 0.0112 (0.0095) for the three categories, respectively

Standard errors in parentheses

*$p<0.10$; **$p<0.05$; ***$p<0.01$

Table 8.6 Factors to achieve overall purpose of LPT reform in improving local governance. Dependent variable: attitudes toward the overall effect of LPT reform to increase efficiency of local governance

Variables	Separated regressions	Backward estimation (Ordered logit)					
		(1)	(2)	(3)	(4)	(5)	(6)
Local own source revenue	*0.9308***	0.8156	0.8282	0.8350	0.8651*	0.9551*	1.1288**
	(0.3690)	(0.5310)	(0.5235)	(0.5223)	(0.5133)	(0.5031)	(0.4810)
Feasibility for different rates according to expenditure	*1.3593****	0.7300	0.7590	0.7625	0.6762	0.6749	
	(0.4451)	(0.7056)	(0.6748)	(0.6748)	(0.6047)	(0.5979)	
LPT for public services	*0.7440***	0.0765					
	(0.3739)	(0.5453)					
More transparency for local governments	−0.1229	0.3658	0.3685	0.3164			
	(0.5895)	(1.0711)	(1.0709)	(1.0537)			
Requirement for performance report	−0.7850	−0.2237	−0.2099				
	(0.5480)	(0.8650)	(0.8609)				
Public participation in budgetary decision making	0.4513	0.9066	0.8872	0.8303	0.8550		
	(0.4917)	(0.9133)	(0.9001)	(0.8650)	(0.8616)		
Direct election for top local officials	*1.2888****	1.2022**	1.2191**	1.2369**	1.2806**	1.4122***	1.6389***
	(0.3933)	(0.5685)	(0.5557)	(0.5518)	(0.5336)	(0.5187)	(0.4824)
Observations		86	86	86	86	86	86
Pseudo R^2		0.1584	0.1583	0.1579	0.1572	0.1491	0.1397

Standard errors in parentheses
*$p<0.10$; **$p<0.05$; ***$p<0.01$

With statistical techniques, we also used *stepwise regression* to refine the important factors contributing to the LPT reform. The second part of Table 8.6 describes the regression results from *backward elimination*. In fact, we can get the same result as that in the sixth column when we use *forward selection*. In these officials' view, the property tax as a main revenue source of local governments and local direct elections are the two most important elements we need to have in order to achieve the goal of the LPT reform: to increase the overall efficiency of local government from several perspectives.

These conclusions are still preliminary due to the limitation of observations (sample size and representativeness) and the validity of the sample data. However, these results are consistent with the public choice theory that main revenue source is a prerequisite for LPT as a governance tool and that local direct election is necessary for residents to execute their preferences.

8.4 Summing Up: Main Findings

We sum up our main findings as the following four points:

1. *Close to half of the respondents supported the LPT in Shanghai and Chongqing.*

Although more than 90 % of them had heard of the pilot LPT in Shanghai and Chongqing, most of them were still not clear about the main points of the policy. After the definition and concept were clarified, 47 % of them supported the pilot LPT.

2. *The respondents were more satisfied with the Chongqing LPT than the Shanghai one.*

The percentage of "Satisfied" or "Roughly satisfied" answers in our survey for respondents' attitude toward the LPT in Chongqing was 49 %, while this percentage was 41 % in Shanghai. Specifically, the respondents who did not own housing units differed little in their attitudes toward the LPT in Shanghai and Chongqing. With the increase in the number of owned housing units, the percentage of respondents who were "satisfied" with the LPT in Shanghai tended to decrease while that of respondents for the Chongqing LPT tended to increase.

Therefore, respondent attitudes mainly differed among the respondents who own two or three housing units. Through analyzing these details, we can identify the reason why they had such different opinions (see Figs. 8.15, 8.16). Since the LPT policy in both metropolitans will not influence households who will buy a housing unit as their primary (first) residence, there is no obvious difference between the attitudes toward LPT in the two cities. According to the LPT policy in Shanghai, those respondents who already own two or three housing units have to pay taxes if they purchase another unit after January 28, 2011. But for the same group in Chongqing, the purchase of a second or third unit (not including luxury housing units) does not subject them to the tax as long as the price of the new purchase does not reach the

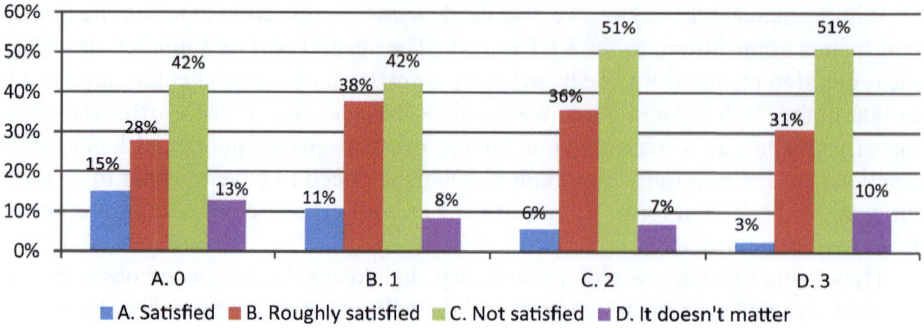

Fig. 8.15 Number of units owned vs. attitude toward LPT of Shanghai style

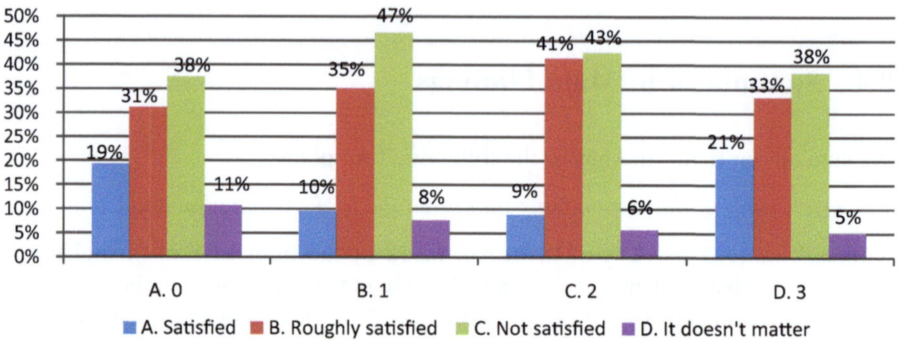

Fig. 8.16 Number of units owned vs. attitude toward LPT in Chongqing

threshold level (twice the average price). This is the reason why respondents who already owned two or three housing units preferred the LPT design in Chongqing.

3. *There is a positive correlation between the number of housing units owned and the degree of opposition to LPT.*

From the analysis, we found that there is a positive correlation between the number of owned housing units and the degree of opposition toward the LPT. We can see in Fig. 8.17 that 42 % of the respondents who did not own housing units supported the LPT and 34 % of them opposed it. On the other extreme, 21 % of the respondents who owned three housing units supported the LPT and 49 % of them opposed it. Generally, the larger the number of owned housing units, the higher the proportion of respondents who went against it.

As stated above, although many of the respondents had heard of the new tax, most of them were not really clear on the details. After the pilot LPT was clarified for them in the middle of the survey, their attitudes changed. The proportion of respondents supporting the LPT increased, while the proportion of those opposing the LPT decreased (Fig. 8.18). Take, for example, the respondents who own two

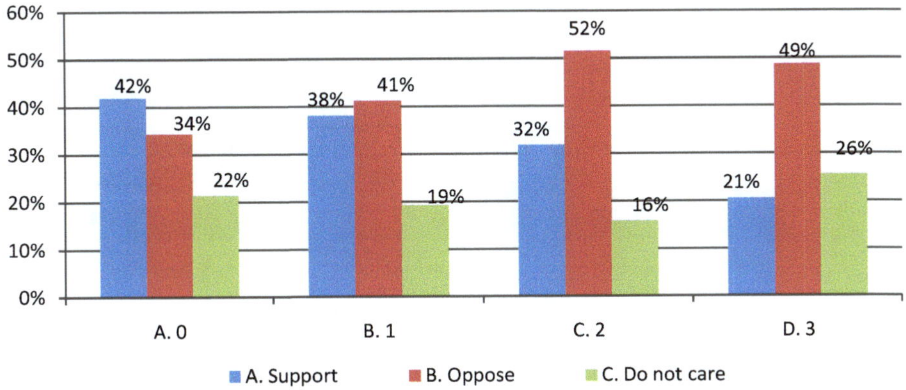

Fig. 8.17 Number of units owned vs. attitude toward LPT before policy clarification

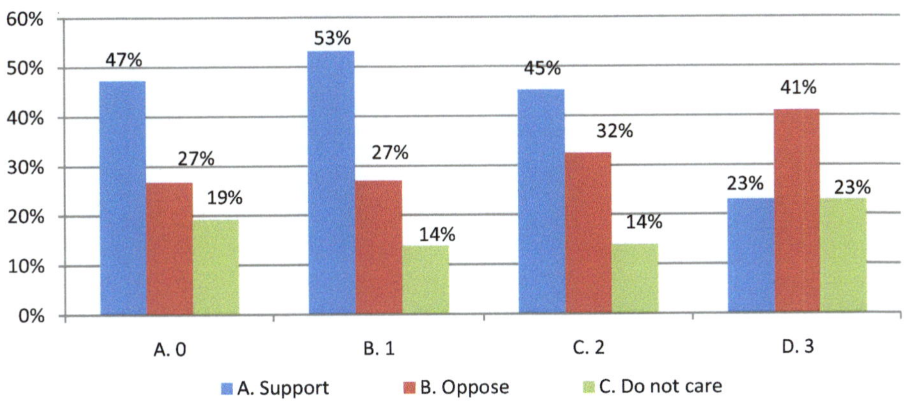

Fig. 8.18 Number of units owned vs. attitude toward LPT after policy clarification

housing units—the proportion of those supporting the LPT increased from 32 to 45 % and the proportion of those opposing the LPT dropped from 52 to 32 %.

4. *Forty-five percent of the surveyed officials thought that the LPT is worth trying in order to improve local governance.*

The LPT is not just a tool for raising revenue. If the LPT reform is accompanied with budgetary and administrative reforms, it could also be used as an effective tool to improve local governance. Forty-five percent of the surveyed officials thought that it is worth trying to improve local governance through the LPT reform. Lastly, we found that the higher their rank, the greater the proportion of those respondents who believed that it is feasible to realize this idea (Fig. 8.19).

All in all, our survey findings reveal a positive public perception of the pilot LPT reforms that have been implemented in Shanghai and Chongqing. Given that the

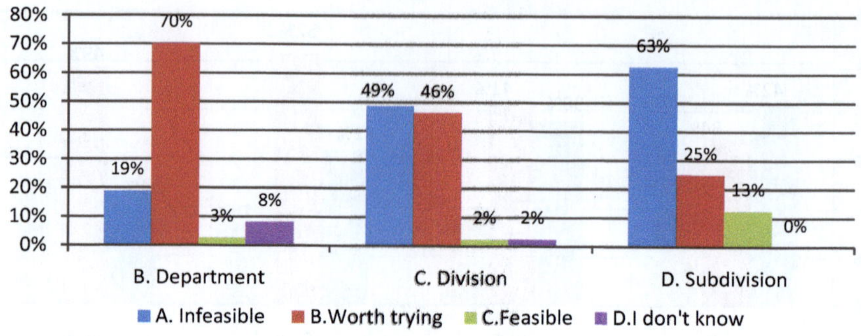

Fig. 8.19 Rank of affiliated agency and attitude toward LPT

pilot LPTs are still new, that our sample size is not very large, and that the survey instruments are yet to be perfected, the findings are still preliminary. Still, these findings are encouraging and can serve as a guide in refining policies. We hope they can be of practical use by the Chinese government as well as the research community.

Chapter 9
Simulation

The revelation of true preferences of the quality and quantity of key public services, the efficiency in providing these services by local governments, and the accountability of local officials to tax payers have long been a critical issue in the study of governance, political economy, public finance, and public administration. The real property tax as a local own-source revenue at the discretion of localities has served as the link among these issues in western countries, the USA being an example. Despite many advantages this revenue source has rendered, financing basic public services with the property tax has led to equity issues, which is why the financing responsibility in the USA has tended to move up, or centralize, to higher levels, education being a typical example.

In unitary countries with a long tradition of centralized administration and governance, this direct tax-service link is mostly missing. When central transfers are not used, reliance on local own-source revenue leads to extreme inequity, with service adequacy, efficiency, and accountability out of the question. At the other extreme, a heavy reliance on transfers, preference revelation, operational efficiency, and local accountability remains absent. How to build the tax-service link is a serious issue of democratic governance and financial administration. In this sense, the local property tax impacts both the revenue and expenditure sides of local public finance. How will a "chinking-in" (its introduction) of the local property tax (LPT) affect an existing integrated tax system and expenditure framework? How will a new LPT affect local governance, intergovernmental relations, and efficiency gains via public choice? These are the research questions for this chapter.

China's pilot introduction of the LPT in two metro areas (Shanghai and Chongqing, as discussed in previous three chapters) will soon be expanded nationwide, according to a Chinese Central Government announcement. This event provides us a valuable opportunity to estimate the potential impacts of levying the LPT and using its revenue locally. We view the Chinese LPT as an old fiscal institution being tested in a completely new political and socioeconomic environment.

This chapter investigates the potential effects of China's new LPT on local revenue and expenditure. The impacts are estimated for three types of localities: metropolitan districts, urban districts, and counties that are relatively more rural in comparison with their urban district counterparts. Estimates of the impacts of LPT on revenue are based

Y. Hou et al., *The Property Tax in China,* Development and Governance,
DOI 10.1007/978-3-319-10049-4_9

on socioeconomic conditions, eligibility and structure of LPT, as well as the gradual expansion of the LPT levy. Estimates of LPT impact on expenditure show, how the distribution of LPT collection in four main outlay programs (education, health, safety, and recreation/roads) may affect service level, operation, and local official accountability. Since actual data is rare on China's pilot LPT, this chapter uses publicly available, official 1994–2009 local government revenue and expenditure data and local sociodemographic data to run simulations on varying parameters of tax rate, coverage, and use.

This chapter makes both theoretical and policy contributions to the literature. Can the efficiency gain of public choice theory be achieved if a LPT is "chinked in"? How can the LPT be appropriately applied to an integrated tax system? Answers to these questions will add significantly to existing research; they can also be applied as guidance for China's ongoing reform. This chapter is organized as follows. Section 9.1 deliberates on sample selection and on the parameters used in the simulation. Section 9.2 discusses the four major outlay programs in the sampled localities in the sample period (1994–2009). Section 9.3 uses simulated revenue from the local real property tax for five propositions that we see as vital in establishing the link between taxation, service, and accountability. Lastly, the chapter concludes with Section 9.4.

9.1 Sample Selection

In this subsection we offer details on our sample selection and the choice and calculation of parameters for the simulation exercise. These form the basis of this empirical study. Since city-wide hedonic (micro) data are not yet publicly available for real property tax research in China, this was the most challenging and difficult part for us. We obtained all data from public sources and official documents. Even though many data details are far from ideal for such a study, we believe what we have done so far, represents the best that is doable to the date of this writing.

9.1.1 Metropolitan, Central City, City, and County

The unit of analysis in this study is the district or the county. In the Chinese administrative hierarchy, the district is a sub-division under the jurisdiction of a medium-sized (and larger) city; it is classified as an *urban* area with exclusively urban (no rural) residents in the Chinese household registration system. A county parallels a district in the hierarchy, but it has both urban and rural areas. The county seat is urban, but in some cases large established towns are also classified as urban and the rest of the county is mostly rural. Residents are classified as urban or rural by their location of residence in the household registration system. This study focuses on the urban districts, but also examines the urban-rural combination counties to form a contrast and to offer variation. Districts are selected from three types (by size) of cities as three sub-sets of data; counties are the fourth sub-set.

Metropolitan municipalities have provincial status, but they are different from provinces in that almost all of their jurisdictions are highly urbanized. Of the current four metros, Beijing, Tianjin, and Shanghai are in this category. The fourth one, Chongqing, is a little different since it was granted this status only recently (1997) and still has more than half of its jurisdictions over rural areas. On the other hand, Guangzhou, a mega-city in southern China, has many characteristics of those metropolitans though it is not of provincial status. Thus, in this study we treat Beijing, Tianjin, Shanghai, and Guangzhou as metropolitans. From each of these four metros, we select three urban districts.

We select another two sub-sets as our urban sample. The first is the central city group consisting of the 27 provincial capitals. The other is the group of prefecture level cities, one from each of the 27 provinces. They are medium-sized (in a Chinese sense) and economically developed. To avoid potential data endogeneity issues arising from sampling between the two subsets, our selection is based on two criteria—economy (development) and distance from provincial capital (location). For the first criterion, we compose a measure of the provincial average level of economic development from tax collections and per capita GDP (which, in fact, is gross provincial product). The provincial capital usually performs better on these measures than other cities in each province. On the location criterion, our sample cities need to be more than 150 miles away (2–3 h by car or by train) from the provincial capital. The purpose of using this measure is to avoid the possibility that some people may choose to live in these low-cost (in terms of housing price) areas and commute to work in the economically more developed provincial capitals. Details on the sampling methodology are provided in Appendix 9.1.

Finally, we compose a group of counties as our fourth subset. The reasons that counties are worth special attention are several fold. County seats are the merging points between urban and rural areas; most of them display strong similarities to cities while still carrying features of the countryside. The housing price in these county seats is much lower than in cities so that housing is much more affordable, which makes them attractive to rural residents who have assembled the financial means to possess an urban dwelling for access to services that are available only in urban centers. For the above reasons, county seats are a very important sub-sample for a study like this one. We choose one county from each city in the first three sub-samples. Obviously, a county under a metropolitan differs in substantive ways from one under a prefecture-level city in that the former is much more urban than the latter; still, these two share the basic half-city, half-country features that are common to counties. Thus, our total sample consists of 62 districts (12 metropolitan, 27 in provincial capitals, and 23 in other cities) and 61 counties.[1] The sample period is from 1995 to 2009.

[1] There are some changes in names or codes in districts or counties; to keep the consistency, we convert them into the most recent ones. In Wuhan of Hubei, there are no counties; two districts

9.1.2 Parameters Established for Simulation

Next, we discuss the parameters that we developed for the simulation and background parameters that are necessary for understanding the real property market as well as the base and levy of the local property tax.

1. Local Property Tax Base

We exhausted the publicly available data sources for data on urban area residential floor space, but could not find a usable micro-data set as the base for property tax levied in each of our sample areas. The closest that we could get to the real situation is to make an estimate based on provincial data and statistical inference. We found that, among the obtainable sources, the survey data from China's *Population Census* in 2000 and 2010 was the most precise and reasonable. The two Censuses provided the per capita residential living space (floor area) in each province, which then decomposed into cities, towns, and rural areas. With the corresponding Census population data, we calculated the total urban residential floor space. In the same way, we could also get the total space including all three areas. Thus, we made a case-by-case revision based on our judgment of whether the per capita data from the 2000 Census was reasonable in comparison with data from other available sources. Another problem with the data is that houses in towns and rural areas in many parts of China do not have market values since they are either not permitted for sale or have not been through a transaction. To circumvent this conundrum, we focused on the urban areas for the local property tax. Details are provided in Table 9.1; a list of the data sources is offered in Appendix 9.2.

The annual sales data of residences and the average market prices (per square meter) for commodity houses in each province from 1995 to 2010 are from *the China Statistical Yearbook* series. With these data, and based on the above two data sets in 2010 and 2000 as two reference points, we calculated the floor area for each province from 1995 to 2010. For all years, we revised the sales data according to the real change between years 2000 and 2010.[2] With revised sales data and stock living space in 2010 and 2000, the living space in each year can be calculated simply by adding sales data to living space in the previous year. Through using average housing prices for each province and year, we obtained an estimated total property value of urban residential housing. We assumed that the proportion of population in each district and county accounts for the corresponding proportional property values in the provinces.

---

were selected. In Hainan, Xizang, Qinghai, and Xinjiang, two counties were selected from prefectural cities because there are no urban districts.

[2] First of all, for each province we calculate the real changes of living space from 2000 to 2010 by $R_{2010} - R_{2000}$ (from Population Censuses), and sum up the sales data from 2001 to 2010 [sum(S_{2001}:S_{2010}), from *China Statistical Yearbook* series]. Then we can calculate revised sales data by the formula (take 2005 as example): revised $Sale_{2005} = S_{2005} * (R_{2010} - R_{2000}) / sum(S_{2001}:S_{2010})$. We made this calculation for each province and year. The same revision applies to sales data of villa and subsidized houses which we will do in the next step.

Table 9.1 Total and per capita living space in cities (years 2000 and 2010)

Codes	Provinces	Total 2000	Total 2010	Per capita 2000	Per capita 2010
	All	561,237	1,015,763	21.81	29.15
11	Beijing	15,960	35,845	19.57	27.81
12	Tianjin	8,388	16,900	17.20	25.51
13	Hebei	22,537	38,195	21.80	30.10
14	Shanxi	12,394	21,506	18.73	25.77
15	Neimenggu	9,366	18,143	17.78	24.86
21	Liaoning	31,932	52,673	18.31	25.76
22	Jilin	15,548	23,769	17.81	25.21
23	Heilongjiang	21,349	30,909	17.60	23.72
31	Shanghai	22,554	39,554	19.85	25.11
32	Jiangsu	44,876	87,143	26.68	33.86
33	Zhejiang	29,478	54,112	26.36	30.97
34	Anhui	15,017	31,468	19.37	29.42
35	Fujian	15,546	32,086	24.50	30.29
36	Jiangxi	10,744	20,166	21.91	29.76
37	Shandong	45,101	80,036	23.02	32.41
41	Henan	29,625	55,517	23.71	34.02
42	Hubei	33,906	51,154	23.50	33.22
43	Hunan	23,449	36,561	25.13	33.45
44	Guangdong	50,459	108,228	22.41	26.37
45	Guangxi	12,089	22,320	22.39	30.71
46	Hainan	2916	4981	19.90	25.42
50	Chongqing	13,363	22,570	22.75	29.77
51	Sichuan	26,347	43,233	24.30	30.70
52	Guizhou	7108	13,003	17.86	25.94
53	Yunnan	7842	17,080	20.13	31.27
54	Xizang	360	732	19.51	31.81
61	Shannxi	11,611	21,708	19.36	28.81
62	Gansu	6539	12,079	18.58	26.69
63	Qinghai	1791	3416	19.44	27.77
64	Ningxia	2303	5350	20.65	28.38
65	Xinjiang	7559	15,467	19.63	28.00

Data for total are calculated from population census in 2000 and 2010, respectively, in 10,000 m^2
Per capita data are from population census in 2000 and 2010, respectively, in m^2
Per capita data of Zhejiang in year 2000 was revised based on calculation from the 2010 population census data by deducting sales data after 2000
Per capita data in Guangdong seem too low intuitively, probably because the population denominator is high when migrant workers are included in its population

We would like to note that the estimated figures from this calculation method may have resulted in an overestimation of the tax base in counties because our calculation was based on the population ratio of each county in its province and a county's population includes rural residents, and because housing price is lower in counties than in urban districts (the average market price for each province is for urban sales only, without consideration of this rural-urban difference). However, the per capita living space in the urban areas of each county is higher than that in urban districts, which cancelled out some of this overestimation in calculating property values. Finally, the market values of houses in districts and counties we selected are estimated as local property tax bases for the sampled jurisdictions.

2. Effective Tax Rate

For a new local property tax in China, we are interested in whether there is a tax rate that is feasible in China's current socioeconomic context in which there are dramatic differences among provinces in social, economic, and demographic characteristics. For this reason, we calculated a tax rate for each province on the basis of their average per capita income and expense levels, as well as their mean housing prices.

First, the per capita average of total annual income in provinces was obtained from each year's *China Statistical Yearbook.*[3] The expenses for food, clothing, health care and health services, and transportation were deducted from total personal income. We call this calculated remainder *discretionary personal income.* With the comparison to income tax and consideration of other socioeconomic circumstances, we assumed that 10% of the above calculated discretionary personal income was the reasonable amount for potential property tax payment and that this 10% is a technically reasonable, politically acceptable, and administratively feasible amount for most households in current China.

The feasible effective property tax rate (ETR) for households in each province was calculated with the following formula:

$$ETR = \frac{\left[income - \left(food + clothing + health + trans\right)\right] * 10\%}{floor\ space * unit\ price}$$

where *floor space* and *unit price* denote per-capita living space and average housing price in cities of each province. Since we did not have data for city-only population in each province except for years 2000 and 2010,[4] we used the *interpolation* method with data in years 2000 and 2010 as a reference to calculate per capita data. We assumed that per capita living space had increased as proportional to a combined consideration of the changes in total stock and population. Here, we assumed an accelerated smooth increase for per capita living space.[5] According to the above formula, we calculated an average feasible effective property tax rate for each province from 1994 to 2010.

[3] All data used for calculation in this part are in per capita provincial average.

[4] The population of cities and townships are combined together in each year's *China Statistical Yearbook.*

[5] The formula is $(1+x)^{10}=S_{2010}/S_{2000}$, based on the per capita living space in 2000 and 2010, we can calculate x for each province. The rationale is that even though total available living space increases more quickly with new construction, the total urban population also increases pretty fast in the same period. Table 9.1 indicates that at the national level the total living space doubled while the per capita level increased only about 50%. Thus, we argue that this formula can generate the closest estimation to the real situation.

3. Exemption

To further refine our tax base in order to make it more acceptable to the general public, we designed an exemption. Though it is almost impossible for us to obtain detailed hedonic housing characteristics in our sampled areas, we found a good proxy for appropriate living standard for urban households, which is a "separate flushing toilet" in the housing unit. From the 2010 population census, we calculated the percentage of housing units that were not equipped with this gadget and used this ratio as the proportion of property values that may be exempted from the local property tax in each province. The national average of this ratio for cities in years 2000 and 2010 was 50 and 30 %, respectively, with large interprovince variation.

4. Background Parameters
a. Socioeconomic Status

For the socioeconomic status of households in cities and counties (including town), we looked at per capita *disposable personal income*. This measure rose drastically with China's rapid economic growth: nominal income quadrupled from RMB 1516 in year 1990 to RMB 6296 in year 2000, then increased another three times to RMB 19,109 in 2010.[6] Converted into the 1978 price level, these numbers are 198, 384, and 965, respectively, representing a 500 % growth. The substantive increase in personal income reduced the share spent on basic necessities, so the *Engel coefficient* in the above three benchmark years dropped from 54.2 to 39.4 % then further to 35.7 %. In the course of these high-rate increases, however, the distribution of income became more and more skewed, showing an increasing income disparity. Between the three geographic regions, the eastern provinces lead the country and the western provinces lag far behind the national average. Income disparity has become particularly large between individuals and households at any cross-section. The 2010 census contained a survey of over 65,000 households that were divided into seven groups by their income. The top 10 % is eight times higher than the bottom 10 %. Details are shown in Table 9.2.

Accompanying the economic growth were also big improvements in educational attainment. In high schools, the percentages of students who graduated and entered colleges were 27.3, 73.2, and 83.3 % in 1990, 2000 and 2010, respectively. People who held a college degree or higher, increased from 1.4 % in 1990 to 3.6 % in 2000 and 8.9 % in 2010. The education expenditure increased from less than 90 billion in 1992 to 1650 billion in 2009, of which about two thirds was from provincial and local governments while only 7 % was from the central government.[7]

The age structure in China also changed during this period. In Table 9.3, we find that in the past 20 years, the percentages of kids declined. In contrast, the percentage of people aged 65 or older continually increased. A study by the United Nations predicts that the senior ratio will rise further to 10.9 % in 2020.[8]

---

[6] Source: *China Statistical Yearbook 2011, Schedule 10–2*. The figures are in RMB or Yuan.

[7] Source: China Statistical Yearbook 2011, Schedule 10–1, 3–5, 20–38; China's Education Statistical Yearbook 2010, 4495.

[8] Source: http://wenku.baidu.com/view/ad979dfb0242a8956bece4b8.html

Table 9.2 Distribution of household disposable income in year 2010. (For more years of data, see details in Appendix 9.3) (Source: China Statistical Yearbook 2011, Schedule 10-7)

Household groups	Group	Amount in RMB
Poverty within lowest (5 %)	Households in poverty	4,739
Lowest (10 %)	Lowest income	5,948
Low (10 %)	Low income	9,285
Low-mid (20 %)	Lower-middle income	12,702
Mid (20 %)	Middle income	17,224
Mid-high (20 %)	Upper-middle income	23,189
High (10 %)	High income	31,044
Highest (10 %)	Highest income	51,432

The total number of households in the survey was 65,607
The grouping of surveyed households into quintiles was to rank the households by their disposable income and cut off into quintiles, with the first and the last quintiles further broken into two. These seven groups are given the group names shown in column 2. The bottom 5 % are households in poverty

Table 9.3 Demographic structure of population (in percentage). (Sources: The China Statistical Yearbook 2011 and the China Population Census 2010)

Age	1990	2000	2010	2010 (city)
0–14	27.7	22.9	16.6	12.2
15–64	66.7	70.1	74.5	80.1
65 and older	5.6	7.0	8.9	7.7

b. Household Residences

Before investigating the status of household residences, two types of households need to be distinguished. In China's registered permanent residence system, there are two different households: "family households" and "non-family households" (institutional households). Non-family households refer to those whose residences are registered in some institutions rather than individual families. In this chapter, the analyses are based on family households only, and in fact, local property tax will only be levied on these family households.

Regarding the size and structure of households in cities and counties, the numbers of people per household continually decreased from 3.50 in 1990 to 3.13 in 2000 and to 2.88 in 2010. However, during this period, the average number of employed people in each household did not change much. The numbers were 1.98, 1.68, and 1.49, respectively. This change of household structure resulted from the trend that the younger generation chose to live by themselves rather than with their parents.[9]

Household living space became bigger also. From Table 9.4, we find that floor area per household has increased with the time of construction during the recent 30

[9] Source: *China Statistical Yearbook 2011, 10–5.* The rural area has the same trend, but the number of people per household decreases more slightly. They are 4.80, 4.20, and 3.85 in the three years (from ibid, *10–18*).

Table 9.4 Household living space with time of construction, in square meters (m^2). (Source: Calculated from the China Population Census 2010)

Year built	Total			Cities		
	1980–1989	1990–1999	2000–2009	1980–1989	1990–1999	2000–2009
Per household	87.2	102.7	113.9	68.3	83.1	94.7
Per room	28.7	31.0	33.1	29.1	33.1	37.3

Table 9.5 Building structure in years 2000 and 2010. (Source: calculated from the China population census 2000 and 2010)

Structure	2000	2010	2010 (cities)
Reinforced concrete	14.5 %	22.8 %	41.3 %
Composite/mixed	NA	40.3 %	47.5 %
Masonry-timber	73.9 %	30.1 %	10.3 %
Other	6.8 %	6.8 %	0.9 %

years. The structures of houses tended to be more reinforced concrete rather than masonry-timber (Table 9.5). From year 2000 to 2010, the percentages of houses in masonry-timber structures decreased from 73.9 to 30.1 %, while houses in reinforced concrete structures increased from 14.5 to 22.8 % with a large jump to 41.3 % in cities. During this period, the new composite structure emerged rapidly and occupied about 40.3 % in 2010.

9.2 Trend of Outlay on Education, Health, Safety, Recreation and Roads

9.2.1 *Total Revenue at Local Level*

Total revenue consists of own-source revenue and intergovernmental transfers. Examining these two parts of our sample localities, we found that local own-source revenue increased by several fold for all local governments in China, urban districts, and the more rural counties, in our observed period (1994–2009) (see Figs. 9.1, 9.2 and 9.3). The increase was especially fast from 1998 to 2005, then exponentially in the most recent few years. The major difference lies with the amount of fiscal transfers that localities received from the center and their provincial government. Since the policy has been to redistribute toward the economically less developed counties, this non-own-source part more than doubled for counties from 1998 to 2009 in both capacity transfers and special/program transfers, the former a discretionary lump sum and the latter conditional for specific purposes. Over the same period, these two types of transfers also increased for districts in provincial capitals and prefectural cities, but at a lower rate. In contrast, transfers remained flat for metropolitan districts, with almost no increase. These indicate that the Chinese Government has

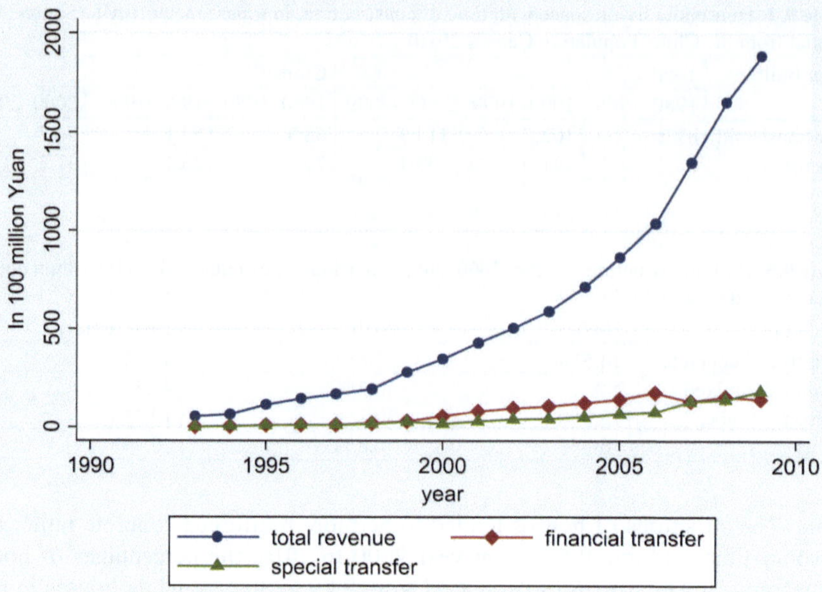

Fig. 9.1 Total revenue for metropolitan districts

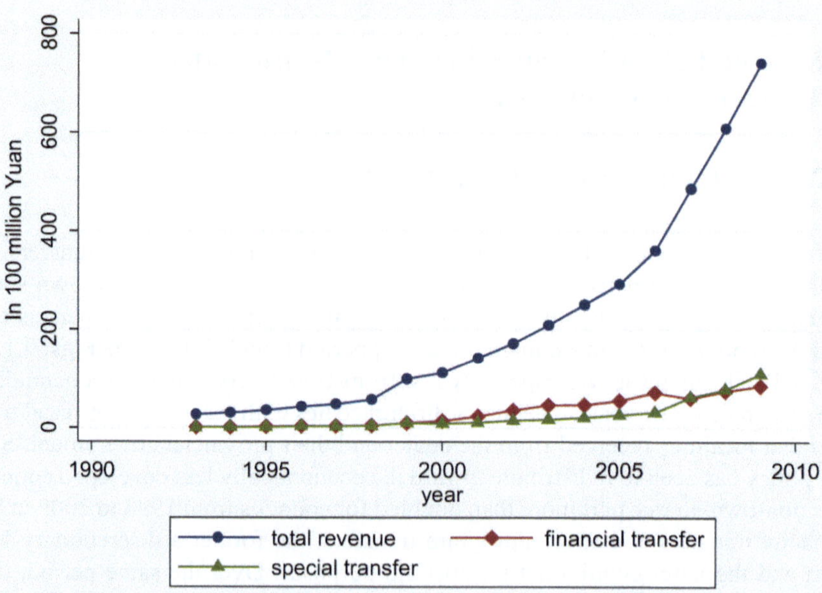

Fig. 9.2 Total revenue for urban districts

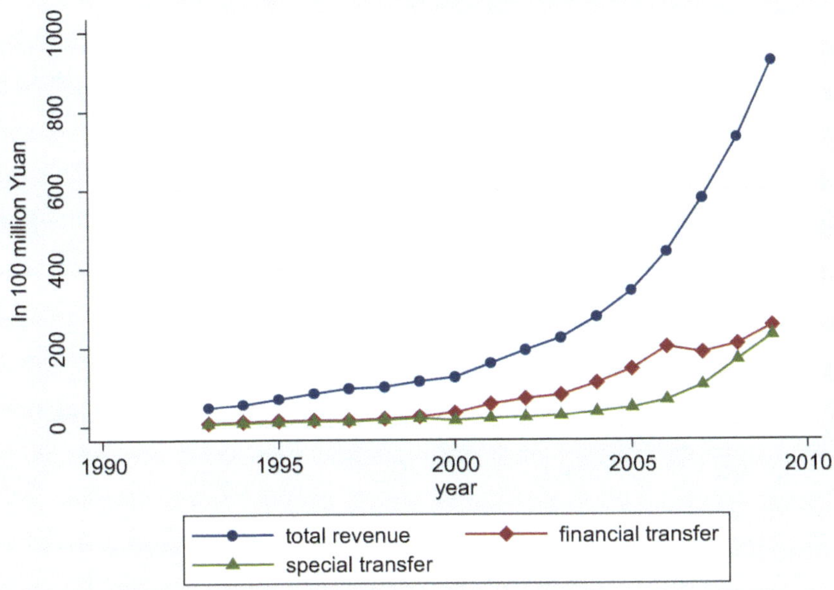

Fig. 9.3 Total revenue for counties

deliberately used transfers as a redistributive tool to reduce fiscal disparity between localities.

In per capita terms (Figs. 9.4, 9.5 and 9.6), the above differences remained, only becoming more apparent. While the total revenue of metropolitan districts was the highest at over RMB 9000, their transfers remained the lowest among their counterparts, showing even some decline from 2006 to 2009. For other urban districts, transfers showed some increases. Especially noteworthy is that from 2000 to 2006, lump sum transfers exceeded special transfers; then beginning in 2007, special transfers passed lump sum grants. In contrast, discretionary transfers for counties have dominated until now with special transfers following quickly in the past few years, such that the combined total transfer amounted to close to two-thirds of their total revenue. With such large transfers, their total revenue surpassed urban districts. The last point bears directly into our simulation results.

9.2.2 *Trends of Expenditure 1994–2007*

On total expenditure, we observed (in Figs. 9.7, 9.8 and 9.9) that metro districts are the highest, followed by counties, and then other urban districts, which reflects the amount of revenue available for each group. As for the amount spent on the four basic public services (data available till 2007), education took the largest share of

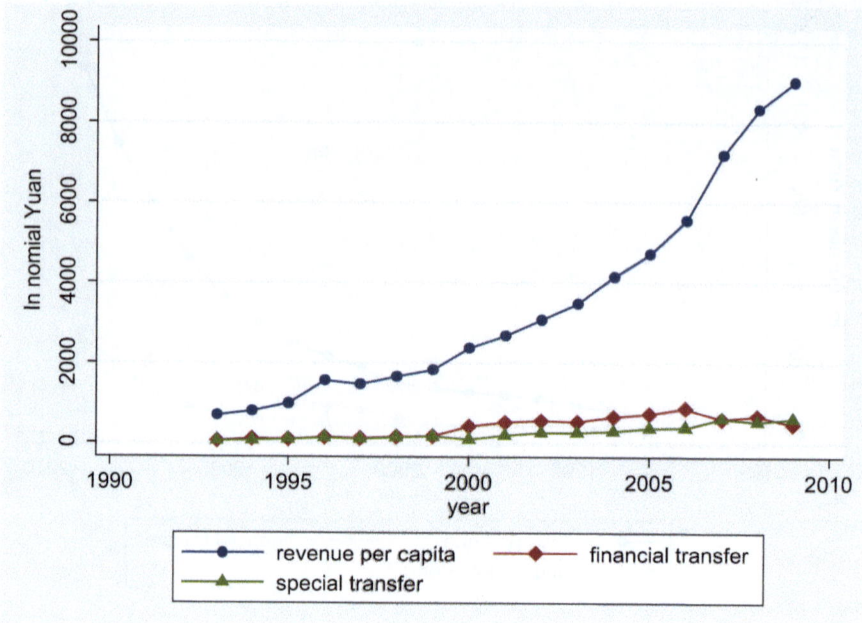

Fig. 9.4 Per capita revenue for metropolitan districts

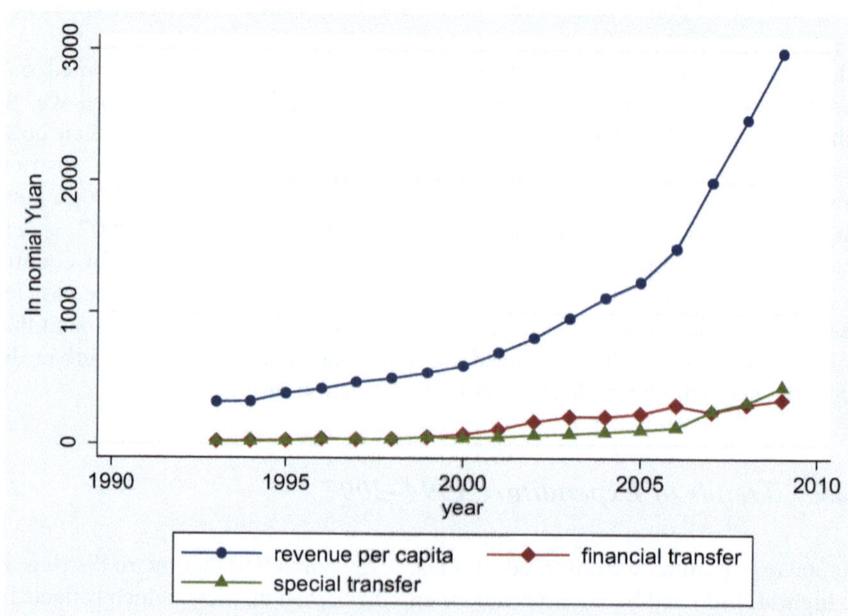

Fig. 9.5 Per capita revenue for urban districts

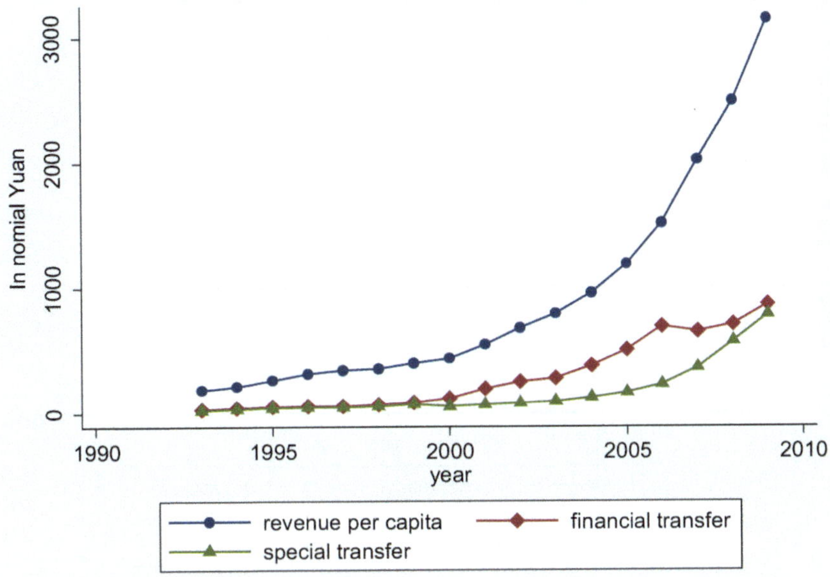

Fig. 9.6 Per capita revenue for counties

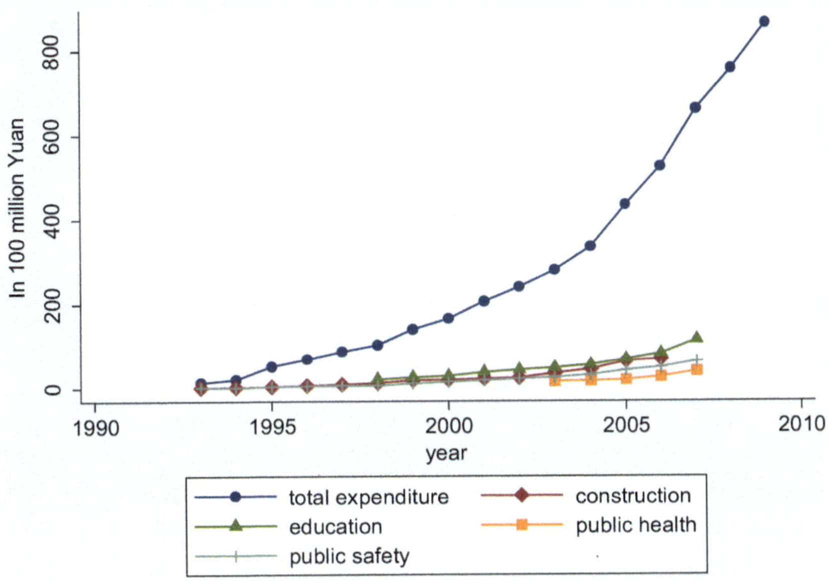

Fig. 9.7 Total expenditure for metropolitan districts

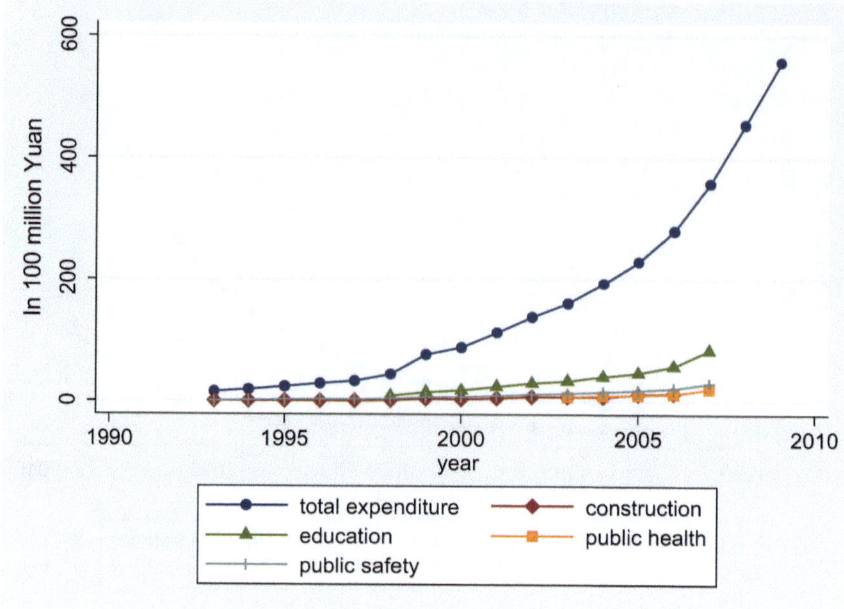

Fig. 9.8 Total expenditure for other urban districts

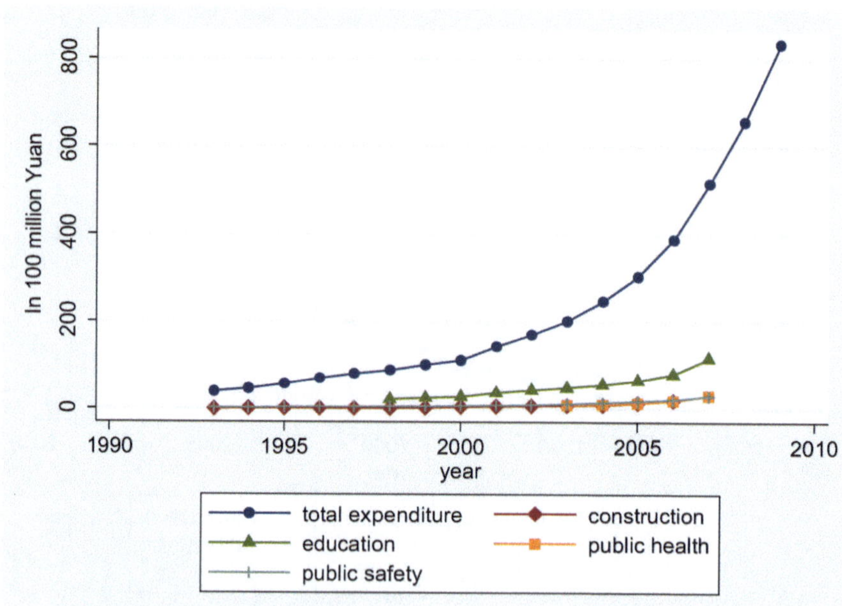

Fig. 9.9 Total expenditure for counties

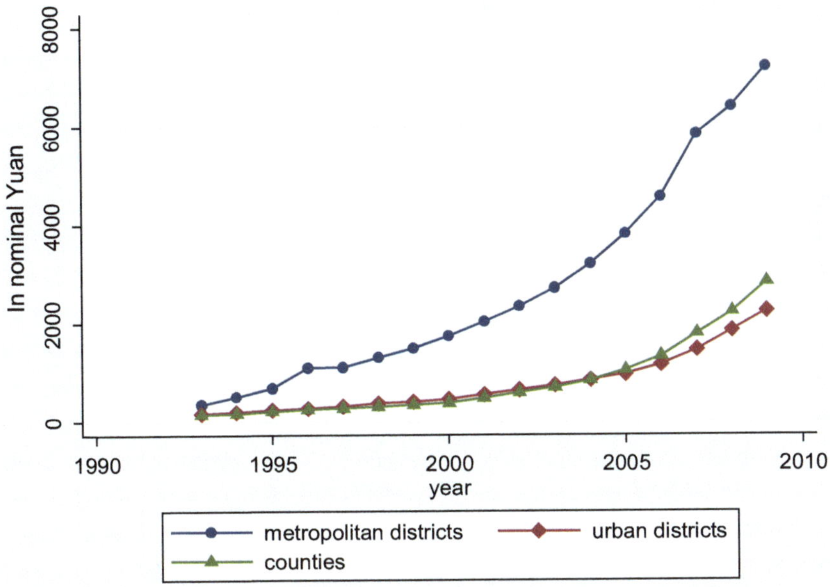

Fig. 9.10 Per capita expenditure for metropolitan, other urban districts, and counties

the four in all three groups and public health the smallest. In metro districts, local infrastructure outlay was second largest, followed by public safety. In other urban districts, public safety occupied the second place; whereas, in counties, outlay on local infrastructure took almost as low a share as public health. These truthfully reflect the provision of services in these different types of localities; again, our simulation results (increase ratios of LPT revenue to supplement local existing outlays) reflect on these past trends.

In per capita terms, metropolitan urban districts with the highest revenue recorded a public expenditure that is large at about RMB 7200 per person in 2009[10] and that of other urban districts and counties was about RMB 2200 and 2500, respectively (Fig. 9.10). With regard to outlay on the four basic service programs—education, public health, public safety, and construction (including roads and recreations)—they occupied the main part of expenditures. In each category, per capita expenditure in metropolitan districts was also the highest (Figs. 9.11–9.13). However, the per capita expenditure in construction for metropolitan urban districts was extremely high compared to the other two types of local governments. The amount in metropolitan districts was RMB 600 per capita, which is about ten

[10] This amount here is smaller than per capita revenue which is about 9000, because part of total expenditure is "upward transfer" (to higher level government) which is an established institution in China. The same applies to nonmetro urban districts and counties. However, the amount or proportion of "upward transfer" for nonmetro urban districts is smaller with counties as the smallest.

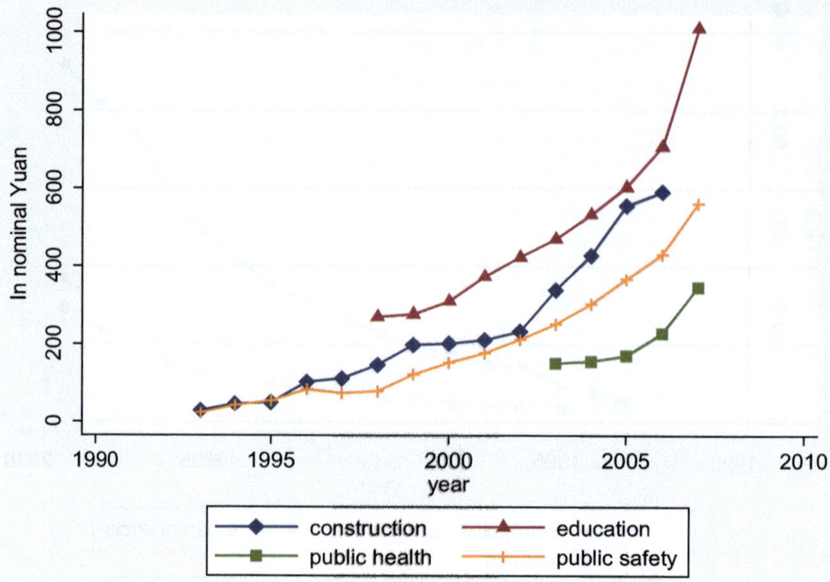

Fig. 9.11 Per capita expenditure in four categories for metropolitan districts

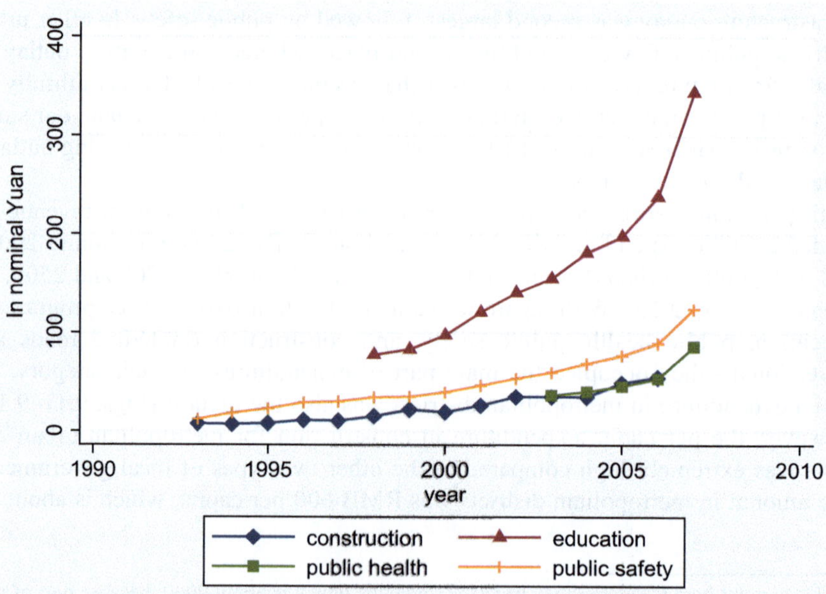

Fig. 9.12 Per capita expenditure in four categories for other urban districts

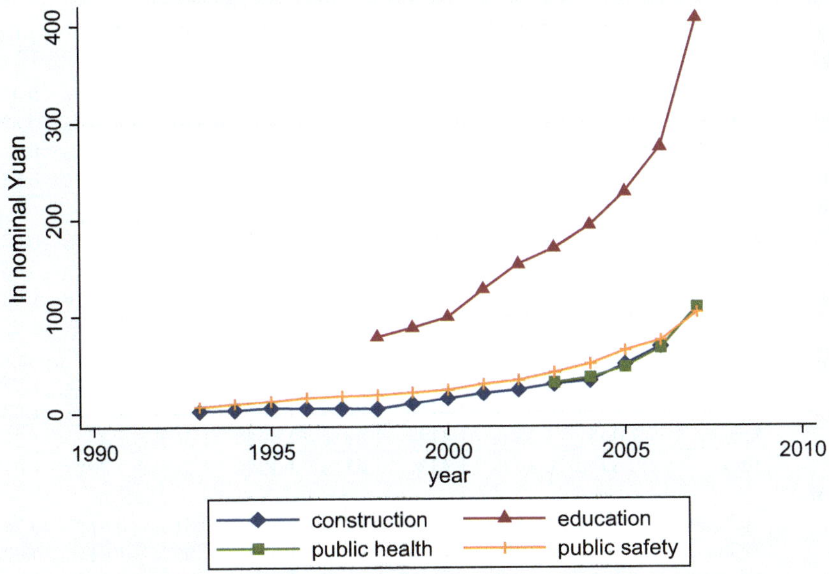

Fig. 9.13 Per capita expenditure in four categories for counties

times the amount in other urban districts and counties. This helps explain the better infrastructure in metropolitan districts. Per capita expenditure in public safety for metro-urban districts was also relatively large. In other urban districts and the counties, education is predominantly the most important part of public expenditure, especially for counties. As shown in Figs. 9.12, and 9.13, the amount of per capita expenditure in education was almost the sum of the other three groups.

9.3 Potential Effects of the LPT Revenue

9.3.1 Simulation Results

1. Effective Tax Rate and Household Tax Payments

Using the parameters that we developed above, and based on the background factors, we calculated the ETR of the real property tax at the provincial level for each sample year. Since we derived this rate backwardly from discretionary personal income, deducting basic necessity expenses (food, clothing, medical expenses, and transportation), and then multiplying by the selected parameter of 10 %, this rate demonstrates some embedded features. This calculated ETR tends to tip up in years

Table 9.6 Effective tax rate (ETR) of LPT for selected provinces and years

Code	Province	1995	2000	2005	2006	2007	2008	2009	2010
Municipalities									
11	Beijing	0.50 %	0.65 %	0.82 %	0.78 %	0.58 %	0.58 %	0.55 %	0.44 %
12	Tianjin	0.78 %	1.18 %	0.94 %	0.92 %	0.85 %	0.98 %	0.88 %	0.82 %
31	Shanghai	0.74 %	0.99 %	0.85 %	0.89 %	0.81 %	0.93 %	0.66 %	0.62 %
44	Guangdong	0.62 %	0.83 %	0.90 %	0.90 %	0.77 %	0.85 %	0.85 %	0.85 %
East									
32	Jiangsu	0.70 %	0.91 %	0.86 %	0.92 %	0.93 %	1.04 %	0.91 %	0.87 %
33	Zhejiang	0.97 %	1.12 %	0.91 %	0.89 %	0.84 %	0.84 %	0.69 %	0.65 %
37	Shandong	0.91 %	1.17 %	1.13 %	1.19 %	1.15 %	1.25 %	1.11 %	1.08 %
21	Liaoning	0.61 %	0.75 %	0.90 %	0.95 %	0.96 %	1.01 %	1.02 %	1.05 %
Interior									
41	Henan	1.60 %	0.94 %	1.19 %	1.18 %	1.16 %	1.26 %	1.16 %	1.07 %
43	Hunan	1.13 %	1.37 %	1.41 %	1.28 %	1.20 %	1.24 %	1.13 %	1.03 %
14	Shanxi	1.00 %	1.33 %	1.41 %	1.61 %	1.59 %	1.56 %	1.48 %	1.29 %
22	Jilin	0.69 %	0.99 %	1.33 %	1.43 %	1.32 %	1.35 %	1.20 %	1.07 %
West									
51	Sichuan	0.72 %	1.11 %	1.04 %	0.94 %	0.82 %	0.81 %	0.81 %	0.78 %
61	Shannxi	0.75 %	1.18 %	1.10 %	0.99 %	1.01 %	1.05 %	1.01 %	0.92 %
45	Guangxi	1.13 %	1.04 %	1.21 %	1.21 %	1.21 %	1.22 %	1.13 %	1.11 %
15	Neimenggu	0.71 %	1.59 %	1.86 %	1.78 %	1.64 %	1.60 %	1.46 %	1.39 %

when the provincial average housing price was low (before the recent housing price peak) or when income is high. The national average ETR has ranged from the lowest 0.84 % in 1995 to its peak at 1.3 % in 2003; afterwards, it gradually declined to 0.96 % in 2010. These numbers at least stay within the comparable range in comparison with those in the USA. This relatively low range helps make the tax acceptable to the general public. Table 9.6 displays the rates of selected provinces for selected years (See more details see the full version of Table 9.6 in Appendix 9.3).

Then, multiplying the ETR by the provincial average market housing price we arrived at the average household LPT payments for each of the sample years. For illustration, Table 9.7 (panels A and B) shows the example results. Panel A provides the per capita income and per capita LPT payment in the four metropolitans and some provinces selected as representatives of the eastern, interior, and western regions in years 1995, 2000, and 2005–2010. Panel B offers the LPT payment as a ratio of discretionary personal income. With deductions and exemptions included in the calculation, the final actual household tax payment ranges between 5 and 6.5 % for years 2006–2010, well within the acceptable range. This tax-income ratio would have been even lower at 4–6 % for years 1995, 2000, and 2005.[11]

2. Tax Revenue for Localities

Applying the effective tax rate to the tax base in each locality gives us the annual revenue from this source for each local government. Dividing this amount by the

[11] This ratio would have been the same whether we use per capita or per household figures.

Table 9.7A Average per capita income and property tax payment for selected provinces and years

Code	Province	1995		2000		2005		2010	
Municipalities		Income	Tax payment	Income	Tax payment	Income	Tax payment	Income	Tax payment
11	Beijing	6238	279	10416	576	19533	1174	33360	2118
12	Tianjin	4931	212	8165	462	13563	782	26942	1655
31	Shanghai	7196	326	11802	651	20603	1276	35739	2227
44	Guangdong	7445	358	9854	552	16250	905	26897	1574
East									
32	Jiangsu	4647	206	6841	371	13330	811	25115	1640
33	Zhejiang	6225	282	9334	520	17877	1034	30135	1869
37	Shandong	4265	202	6522	363	11608	711	21737	1338
21	Liaoning	3708	137	5389	260	9837	520	20015	1161
Interior									
41	Henan	3302	137	4784	256	9146	562	17142	1037
43	Hunan	4705	213	6261	340	10106	573	17657	1038
14	Shanxi	3307	143	4745	245	9539	582	16893	1112
22	Jilin	3176	125	4829	229	9123	495	16794	946
West									
51	Sichuan	4005	161	5926	307	9004	481	17129	950
61	Shannxi	3311	140	5149	276	8902	500	17065	975
45	Guangxi	4809	215	5882	321	10022	581	18742	1149
15	Neimenggu	2874	110	5151	278	9565	549	19014	1028

For each year, the first column is per capita income and the second column is per capita property tax payment

Property tax payments are calculated from *China Statistical Yearbook* series according to formula described in the paper

annual total outlay of each government equals the ratio of LPT revenue that could be generated each year. The full sample average of this ratio ranges from 11 to 19 %. Each year this ratio can be as high as 43–57 %, whereas the lowest dips to 1 %.[12] Thus, the LPT carries great potential as an extra revenue source that is reliable, since its tax base increases steadily with economic growth, and is very stable, since it is an inelastic tax. Table 9.8 showcases some examples. Full details are provided in Appendix 9.3.

From Table 9.8, we can identify the following: LPT revenue can be a large proportion of expenditure for metropolitan areas due to their higher property values, with an average of 17 %. Urban districts in a provincial capital have higher property values (market price being high) than prefectural urban districts. However, total public expenditures in provincial capitals are higher than that in prefectural cities; thus, provincial-capital districts show an average LPT tax-outlay ratio of 10 %, which is lower than that of prefectural urban districts (15 %). Among urban districts in these two types of cities, this ratio tends to be highest for the eastern region, lower for the interior, and the lowest for the western region. Of prefectural urban districts in the

[12] The lower ratios are mainly in western area, while the lowest ratios in eastern area are around 10 %.

Table 9.7B Average LPT payment as ratios of per capita income for selected provinces and years

Code	Province	1995	2000	2005	2006	2007	2008	2009	2010
Municipalities									
11	Beijing	4.5%	5.5%	6.0%	6.2%	6.3%	6.3%	6.4%	6.3%
12	Tianjin	4.3%	5.7%	5.8%	6.0%	6.0%	6.1%	6.1%	6.1%
31	Shanghai	4.5%	5.5%	6.2%	6.3%	6.0%	6.1%	6.2%	6.2%
44	Guangdong	4.8%	5.6%	5.6%	5.8%	5.6%	5.7%	5.8%	5.9%
East									
32	Jiangsu	4.4%	5.4%	6.1%	6.3%	6.4%	6.4%	6.4%	6.5%
33	Zhejiang	4.5%	5.6%	5.8%	5.9%	6.2%	6.2%	6.1%	6.2%
37	Shandong	4.7%	5.6%	6.1%	6.1%	6.1%	6.1%	6.1%	6.2%
21	Liaoning	3.7%	4.8%	5.3%	5.5%	5.6%	5.5%	5.5%	5.8%
Interior									
41	Henan	4.1%	5.4%	6.1%	6.2%	6.1%	6.1%	6.2%	6.0%
43	Hunan	4.5%	5.4%	5.7%	5.7%	5.9%	5.7%	5.8%	5.9%
14	Shanxi	4.3%	5.2%	6.1%	6.1%	6.1%	6.2%	6.3%	6.6%
22	Jilin	3.9%	4.7%	5.4%	5.7%	5.6%	5.6%	5.4%	5.6%
West									
51	Sichuan	4.0%	5.2%	5.3%	5.5%	5.4%	5.3%	5.5%	5.5%
61	Shannxi	4.2%	5.4%	5.6%	5.6%	5.6%	5.7%	5.7%	5.7%
45	Guangxi	4.5%	5.5%	5.8%	6.1%	6.1%	6.0%	6.2%	6.1%
15	Neimenggu	3.8%	5.4%	5.7%	5.8%	5.7%	5.6%	5.5%	5.4%

Table 9.8 LPT revenue as ratio of local expenditure for selected districts and counties in year 2009

Metropolitan districts		Region	Provincial urban districts		Prefectural urban districts		Counties under prefecture	
Code	Percent		Code	Percent	Code	Percent	Code	Percent
110102	9%	East	320102	14%	320302	49%	320322	20%
110105	19%		330102	10%	330302	22%	330322	11%
110108	17%		370102	11%	370602	13%	370682	23%
120101	12%		210102	11%	210202	12%	210224	8%
120102	28%	Interior	410102	10%	410302	7%	410322	7%
120104	27%		430102	3%	430412	3%	430422	11%
310101	13%		140106	14%	140502	13%	140522	8%
310104	17%		220102	18%	220502	23%	220523	8%
310110	25%	West	510104	2%	510302	12%	510322	10%
440103	11%		610102	8%	610302	12%	610322	10%
440104	15%		450102	8%	450302	8%	450322	7%
440106	11%		150102	9%	150402	9%	150422	8%

For each type of area, the first column is code for each district or county and the second column is ratio

eastern region, for example, high property values lead to higher property tax revenue as ratios of public expenditure than in the interior and the western regions, where a large part of their total expenditure is from intergovernmental transfers. These ratios

Table 9.9 Predicted LPT revenue as percentage of local expenditure for selected samples in year 2020

Metropolitan districts		Region	Provincial urban districts		Prefectural urban districts		Counties under prefecture	
Code	Percent		Code	Percent	Code	Percent	Code	Percent
110102	7%	East	320102	13%	320302	54%	320322	27%
110105	27%		330102	10%	330302	23%	330322	11%
110108	17%		370102	12%	370602	12%	370682	25%
120101	12%		210102	10%	210202	17%	210224	8%
120102	24%	Interior	410102	8%	410302	7%	410322	8%
120104	32%		430102	3%	430412	4%	430422	14%
310101	11%		140106	16%	140502	14%	140522	7%
310104	18%		220102	15%	220502	25%	220523	11%
310110	28%	West	510104	3%	510302	15%	510322	12%
440103	10%		610102	9%	610302	15%	610322	13%
440104	15%		450102	9%	450302	8%	450322	8%
440106	10%		150102	11%	150402	11%	150422	7%

For each type of area, the first column is code for each district or county and the second column is ratio

for county governments tend to be lower than those in urban districts in each of the three regions (for explanation, see earlier text).

We made linear predictions of the growth of the LPT revenue and total local government expenditure each year till year 2020, and converted LPT collection as a ratio of local expenditure. Results are shown in Table 9.9. The predicted values show that the LPT revenue will remain a quite high ratio of total local expenditure; thus, it will remain a steady revenue source for localities. Even though the predictions are a little simplistic, since they are estimates derived with the ordinary least squares (OLS) time trend rather than alternative, more sophisticated methods, they are useable as an implication for future directions (for the full version of Table 9.9, see Appendix 9.3).

3. LPT Revenue for Basic Services

Supposing that local governments use this extra revenue exclusively on four basic public services valued by most residents—education, public health, public safety, and local roads and parks—this revenue can do a lot to change the outlay structure, assuming that existing central and provincial fiscal (capacity as well as special/program) transfers (capacity as well as special/program) for these programs remain and do not shrink. Preliminary results show that if used completely on education, total education outlay in the sample from 1998 to 2007 could have increased, on average, by as much as 52–76% (Details are in Appendix 9.3). Supposing further that these new tax collections are split into four equal parts, and are spent on the previously mentioned four basic programs (25% of LPT revenue for each), they would provide fast improvements to the service quality in localities. Tables 9.10–9.13 showcase some representative examples.

Table 9.10 Twenty-five percent LPT revenue as ratio of education expenditure for selected districts and counties in year 2007

Metropolitan districts		Region	Provincial urban districts		Prefectural urban districts		Counties under prefecture	
Code	Percent		Code	Percent	Code	Percent	Code	Percent
110102	20%	East	320102	15%	320302	47%	320322	21%
110105	22%		330102	13%	330302	29%	330322	16%
110108	28%		370102	16%	370602	13%	370682	20%
120101	12%		210102	13%	210202	16%	210224	9%
120102	12%	Interior	410102	15%	410302	11%	410322	8%
120104	27%		430102	4%	430412	7%	430422	16%
310101	18%		140106	17%	140502	16%	140522	8%
310104	30%		220102	17%	220502	38%	220523	15%
310110	41%	West	510104	4%	510302	22%	510322	13%
440103	15%		610102	8%	610302	8%	610322	9%
440104	17%		450102	13%	450302	9%	450322	7%
440106	14%		150102	8%	150402	12%	150422	8%

For each type of area, the first column is the code for each district or county and the second column is ratio

Table 9.11 Twenty-five percent LPT revenue as ratio of public health expenditure for selected districts and counties in year 2007

Metropolitan districts		Region	Provincial urban districts		Prefectural urban districts		Counties under prefecture	
Code	Percent		Code	Percent	Code	Percent	Code	Percent
110102	31%	East	320102	59%	320302	482%	320322	99%
110105	65%		330102	60%	330302	70%	330322	51%
110108	80%		370102	67%	370602	70%	370682	89%
120101	53%		210102	47%	210202	70%	210224	38%
120102	54%	Interior	410102	53%	410302	34%	410322	46%
120104	102%		430102	22%	430412	19%	430422	65%
310101	86%		140106	48%	140502	56%	140522	36%
310104	97%		220102	54%	220502	114%	220523	57%
310110	138%	West	510104	20%	510302	42%	510322	39%
440103	43%		610102	31%	610302	48%	610322	57%
440104	55%		450102	55%	450302	57%	450322	36%
440106	41%		150102	55%	150402	59%	150422	52%

For each type of area, the first column is code for each district or county and the second column is ratio

As shown in Table 9.10, a quarter of LPT revenue in year 2010 dedicated to education could increase current-year outlays by 12 % for counties and provincial capital districts, 19 % for prefecture city districts, and 21 % for metropolitan districts, respectively. From Table 9.11 we see that a quarter of the LPT revenue dedicated to public health substantially increases local outlay on this program, from about 50 % for counties and provincial districts to 70 % for metropolitan districts

Table 9.12 Twenty-five percent LPT revenue as ratio of public safety expenditure for selected districts and counties in year 2007

Metropolitan districts		Region	Provincial urban districts		Prefectural urban districts		Counties under prefecture	
Code	Percent		Code	Percent	Code	Percent	Code	Percent
110102	54%	East	320102	40%	320302	144%	320322	128%
110105	40%		330102	36%	330302	37%	330322	38%
110108	63%		370102	25%	370602	53%	370682	92%
120101	35%		210102	27%	210202	38%	210224	27%
120102	34%	Interior	410102	30%	410302	31%	410322	38%
120104	51%		430102	17%	430412	11%	430422	61%
310101	32%		140106	79%	140502	95%	140522	39%
310104	57%		220102	101%	220502	60%	220523	51%
310110	64%	West	510104	6%	510302	32%	510322	66%
440103	18%		610102	14%	610302	102%	610322	85%
440104	19%		450102	19%	450302	20%	450322	25%
440106	13%		150102	101%	150402	40%	150422	65%

For each type of area, the first column is the code for each district or county and the second column is ratio

Table 9.13 Twenty-five percent LPT revenue as ratio of general service expenditure including roads and recreations for selected districts and counties in year 2007

Metropolitan		Region	Provincial urban districts		Prefectural urban districts		Counties under prefecture	
Code	Percent		Code	Percent	Code	Percent	Code	Percent
110102	13%	East	320102	16%	320302	47%	320322	38%
110105	46%		330102	37%	330302	32%	330322	13%
110108	55%		370102	18%	370602	23%	370682	36%
120101	25%		210102	15%	210202	20%	210224	7%
120102	37%	Interior	410102	8%	410302	5%	410322	8%
120104	60%		430102	7%	430412	4%	430422	14%
310101	46%		140106	27%	140502	17%	140522	10%
310104	65%		220102	30%	220502	28%	220523	21%
310110	89%	West	510104	3%	510302	21%	510322	19%
440103	20%		610102	14%	610302	15%	610322	21%
440104	32%		450102	6%	450302	8%	450322	10%
440106	17%		150102	15%	150402	18%	150422	16%

and to over 90% for prefectural districts. An equal percentage of LPT revenue for public safety would increase the program outlay by 40% for metropolitan and provincial districts and by close to 60% for prefectural districts and counties, as can be seen in Table 9.12. The same proportion of LPT revenue for local public service facilities could also increase this program outlay by 16% for provincial districts, 18% for counties, 20% for prefectural districts, and as high as 42% for metropolitan districts (Table 9.13) (for a full version of Tables 9.10–9.13, see Appendix 9.3).

9.3.2 Extending the Simulation Results

Next we extend the simulation results to the main propositions of this study: the local property tax as a formal institution that directly links local government own-source revenue to public service, efficiency in the provision of services, and accountability of local governments in tax administration and service provision. We elaborate on this extension with the following five propositions.

Proposition #1: LPT Revenue at Full Local Discretion (FLD) Advances in political science and economics in the past few decades have provided solid evidence that local governments are the closest among the several layers of government to service recipients (Shah 2007). With this proximity, local governments have the easiest access to real-time, fullest possible information among all government levels about the tastes, preferences, and demands of local residents; thus, they can best overcome the principal-agent information asymmetry problem and minimize transaction (and other) costs in providing basic public services.

Here, we argue for proposition #1 that given these advantages, local governments are best situated among the several government levels to keep full control of the local property tax so as to fully employ the potential of this tax as a fiscal institution for the above listed purposes. This is the basis for the other several propositions that follow. We define "full control" as "full local discretion" (FLD) with three typical features. First, the locality decides on the use or nonuse of LPT as a revenue source. Then, the locality makes its own decisions on the eligibility of the tax, the scope and extent of exemptions, and the tax rate structure—how high or low the rate should be. Finally, the locality also decides for itself on the use of the revenue collected. In developed western countries these FLD practices are routine, but they are new in many transitional economies including China.

The three decisions mentioned above should be made through administrative or political procedures since we take LPT as a formal institution. In the Chinese case for which we did the simulation in the above subsections, a district or county can adjust the distribution of LPT revenue among the four major types of public services. They may decide to spend 25 % of LPT revenue on each of the four functions. Alternatively, some districts may like to change the ratio, for example, spending a higher ratio on education at the cost of construction, whereas some others may introduce the opposite changes.

Full local discretion over this new revenue source changes intergovernmental relations in the government system. The new stable own-source revenue lays the financial foundation, and thereby directly adds to local autonomy, which gives stronger local voice than in a system where every decision on local affairs is made by higher level governments. However, it is not a zero-sum game. Higher levels can still maintain their necessary room for policy control through grant formulas or grant types. Assuming that the existing programs of intergovernmental transfers will stay and do not shrink in size, any increases in the amount and types of transfers will be in the hands of the center and the province: a locality will need to follow policy directions from above in order to receive more transfers.

Proposition #2: Full Local Discretion Plus Public Choice (PC) Local discretion over the property tax, however, is not a free lunch to local officials; nor should it be.

The new tax and extra revenue both put local officials into direct contact with local residents, i.e., real property owners as tax payers and service recipients. Property owners naturally dislike new taxes on their assets, but they care for the value of their property, which is a function of service quality in the local area; these two sides will balance. Residents care more for the key, basic public services that meet their daily needs, even if all their needs are not met. With local discretion, residents will exert public (political) pressure to increase outlay on some, or all, of these four services. The demand varies with the composition, economic status, and demographic characteristics of localities.

Given that districts and counties in China are large in both population and area, preferences are to a large extent heterogeneous, with slim odds of becoming homogeneous in the short term. Thus, the short-term predictable change will be a substantive increase in public oversight on the local government: taxpayers will scrutinize the amount, use, and outcome of their tax payments. Therefore, the new tax means an additional burden to the residents, but also gives them new leverage and a weapon against corruption and inaction by local officials and inefficiency of the local government in general. To the local government and officials, discretion with extra revenue will provide the resources that they desperately need to increase the four listed services and improve their quality; the extent of the increase and the improvement is up to the collective choice.

Proposition #3: Public Choice Plus Direct Election (DE) Public choice is not guaranteed without a formal mechanism to express and aggregate the preferences of tax payers. This institution is direct election of major officials at the local level, which is something that has been proven effective and acceptable with the lowest social and political costs. Local direct election changes the accountability route, from officials reporting to their appointers in higher level governments to officials reporting to their voters. In this case the voters are property owners and local residents. Direct election installs a new appointment and removal procedure of local officials whose accountability link to tax payers becomes strongest and most direct in comparison to the old route. Changes in the reporting and accountability structure add local voice in bargaining with higher levels government.

Proposition #4: Direct Election Plus Free Migration (FM) Since the feudal society, it has long been tradition in China to tie citizens to a fixed location for tight control. From 1953 to the early 1980s, the dual urban and rural household registration system again played that role, leading to a huge gap between rural and urban residents in living standards, social status, and public service provision. Since the mid-1980s, household registration has loosened gradually, but even until now, the residence registration system is still not eliminated. Even among urban residents, migration from a small city to a provincial capital or from all other city types to the metropolitans is still not free. But within the same metropolitan or within and among provincial capitals, migration is possible. Thus, it is reasonable to assume that even under today's tight residence registration, limited free migration is possible once districts in the same (type of) city adopt the LPT and supplement their own-source outlay on the key public services. Coupled with the direct election of major local officials, positive competition between similar and neighboring districts will play a role in promoting the efficiency of tax administration, revenue collection, and the effective use of tax revenue in service level and quality. We can further assume that as China's reform moves ahead toward complete free migration, competition of this kind will exert strong pressure on local governments and officials for efficiency and accountability.

Proposition #5: Transparent Budgeting As Integrating Device To put all the above propositions to work necessitates an integrating mechanism. This mechanism is modern public budgeting as an administrative instrument for efficiency and effectiveness and a tool for democratic governance in accountability. Public budgeting was invented in Western Europe at the turn of the 19th century, but traces of it date back to 13th century England. The Magna Carta established the contractual relationship between the King and the Lords on taxes under which the latter would pay the former. The key is transparency so that all parties involved clearly know in advance their liabilities and rights, which makes financial planning possible and provides certainty.

Public budgeting again proved an effective administrative instrument and governance tool at the turn of the 20th century when the USA introduced it from Europe to cure numerous diseases then rampant in the country: inefficiency, corruption, absence of fiscal discipline by politicians, and inadequate accountability by public officials. First, public budgeting entails some essential features that include the comprehensive listing of revenues and expenditures, prior authorization and specification of all taxes and outlays, publicity of the decision making process, and the final document that must be published each year in a timely manner. All these features help ensure that the preferences of residents/tax payers are fully considered in the taxing and spending decisions. Second, taxpayers participate in making the budgetary decisions so that the choices embedded in the adopted budget are those of the people. Most importantly, local directly elected officials are held accountable to the voters for the efficient use of the revenues equitably levied, cost-efficiently collected, and most effectively spent to achieve the policy goals that have been set by the people and placed into the annual local government budget.

Will public budgeting, as described above, work in the Chinese context? How will it work in practice if it can in theory? Whereas full details of implementation can be laid out only after more exploration and years of practice, initial introduction of public budgeting in China has already produced encouraging results that point to transparency, increases in efficiency, and it adds to people's voice. These indicate that public budgeting has potential to serve as the integrating device in materializing the several propositions advocated in this study.

The working mechanism of public budgeting toward this end can be described in Fig. 9.14, which illustrates the relationship between the five propositions and how a levy on local property will contribute to transparent budgeting.

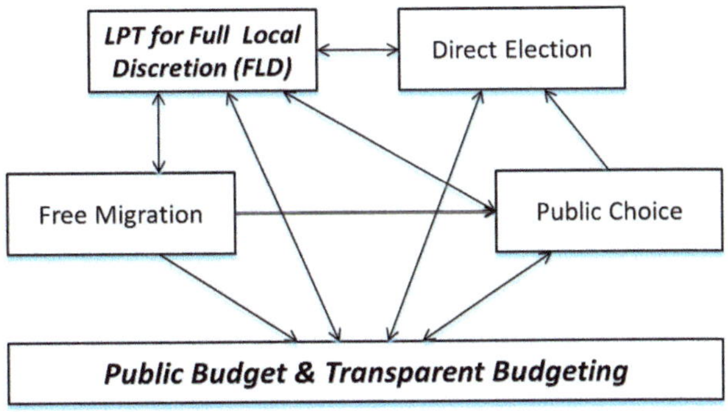

Fig. 9.14 Working mechanism of the five propositions

Conclusion

In this chapter we have exploited publicly available data to run simulations on a proposed financial reform in China—to levy and collect a local real property tax and allow local governments to keep this revenue as supplements to existing outlays on key public services. Though the simulation is still very preliminary and the results rough, we can already derive some interesting and potentially remarkable inferences. A brief summary follows.

LPT can be designed to improve on equity and reduce disparity with a technically reasonable and politically acceptable ETR, at around 1 %, that considers the burden on average residents, their expense on necessities, and the market housing price. Applying this ETR to the average household residence with a mean number of household members leads to a reasonable tax payment on home owners (at around 6 % of their annual household income), but sizeable revenue for local governments. Using this extra revenue to supplement outlays on key basic services will generate remarkable increases in the level and quality of services and contribute from 10 to 40 % to local expenditure. Furthermore, linking the adoption of LPT to local autonomy, public participation in budgetary decision making, and accountability of local officials, and coupling this with free migration of the population and direct election of officials, the landscape of local governance in China could be fundamentally changed. These are doable through the use of public budgeting as an integrating device. This is a modest proposal, but a gigantic step in cleaning up (even if not eradicating) many rampant problems and hitting multiple birds with one stone.

Though this chapter is mainly a simulation, it also bears potential theoretical contributions to theories of public finance and public administration. On public finance, the conceptual derivations done in the chapter presume that fiscal federalism may work even in a political and state system that does not have conventional free and open elections; thus, the principles of fiscal federalism are universal and generic. These principles can work as catalysts to promote transparency, local autonomy, and democracy in a country like China. On public administration, our conceptual work suggests that public finance as a technical dimension of overall government administration can work toward improving operational efficiency, policy effectiveness, and accountability of elected officials.

Chapter 10
Towards Local Property Tax as an Institution

Up to now, we have deliberated on the various aspects of the local property tax (LPT) in theories of public finance and on the practice of this tax in two pilot metropolitans in China. In this brief final chapter we summarize our key points as policy recommendations for the Chinese government to consider in its next round of policy formulation and implementation. In a nutshell, we believe that the LPT should be installed not merely as a tax to increase government revenue or as a means to control housing price; it should be fully employed as a fiscal and budgetary institution that will contribute to mitigating multifarious socioeconomic problems in the processes of high economic growth, fast urbanization, and widening income disparity, which have been increasingly apparent in China in the past two decades.

10.1 Embracing the Full Functions of LPT

It is not right—rather it is fundamentally wrong—to take the local property tax merely as an extra source of revenue for local governments; this tax should be introduced and used as a measure to further promote comprehensive reforms of the Chinese society. Any compromise on this high bar will dampen the potential effects of the LPT as an institution and cost the country a chance in its process of modernization.

To levy and collect a recurring (annual) tax on housing property as a tax on the stock of accumulated fixed assets is an inherent component of a modern taxation system; it is as natural and necessary as the income tax. As the country's economy reaches the medium level of development in which an increasingly large portion of the population owns real property, the quantity and quality of housing ownership will vary considerably. Such a tax plays multiple roles. Every citizen is statutorily liable to pay this tax for housing property he or she owns. Every public and private entity that owns and operates housing property should also be subject to this tax.

Devoting revenue from this tax to basic public services links citizen tax payments directly to the benefits that local residents receive and enjoy, which ties the local government as close as possible to the population it serves. This mechanism

Y. Hou et al., *The Property Tax in China*, Development and Governance,
DOI 10.1007/978-3-319-10049-4_10

raises economic efficiency, citizen satisfaction, and resource allocation efficiency. For these purposes, the property tax should be designated as a local tax, placed at the discretion of local governments under the constant supervision of citizens with taxing and spending decisions made through the public budgeting process. This mechanism reshapes intergovernmental relations by relieving the central and provincial governments of responsibilities that they do not have the informational advantage to handle, thereby holding local governments and officials accountable for affairs and duties that they can best handle and should deliver well.

10.2 Bottlenecks in Adopting LPT

There currently exist no insurmountable hurdles in China to install the LPT as a fiscal and budgetary institution. Relatively speaking, all technical issues are not difficult to solve and the ruling party has appeared ready to charge forward. However, some deep-rooted problems remain as potential bottlenecks. These need to be addressed.

The first and foremost is lack of transparency both on the government's and the citizens' sides. For governments, it is crucial for the budgeting process to be open and public, to make the budget document public, and to make the budget execution outcome public. It has been interesting that in recent years the central government has taken a lead in budget transparency, while other levels lag behind, especially the local level. Now is the time that local governments should make themselves open and transparent. On the part of citizens, it should be a statutory requirement that all real property ownership information be made public, with full and free access through some standardized process. Transparency is the information infrastructure for building trust between the government and its citizens. Without transparency, none of the other parts of the LPT institution are possible.

The second is the mentality that the tax burden is too heavy and that the society has become more inequitable. We have discussed earlier in this monograph the positive and negative sides of LPT's political acceptability. This widespread mentality leads to a subtle social issue: the rich complain about the LPT as a Robin Hood policy and the middle class, especially the lower middle class, vehemently resist the LPT as a new tax on their meager assets. This issue has made the policy makers hesitant in deciding between a narrow or wide base (eligibility) for the LPT. The narrow base was used to start the levy only on some property holders: owners of luxury houses or investors of multiple housing units, as seen in the narrow base design of the Chongqing and Shanghai pilots, respectively. Conversely, the broad base will cover all housing property, which is the most economically efficient in theory and the most fair to all property owners. The broad base will also generate adequate revenue for the LPT to be a major local revenue source. In other words, the narrow base sounds more acceptable politically in the short run but will cause complications in tax administration; the broad base sounds less acceptable in the short run

Table 10.1 Current taxes related to real estate

	Household (residential)	Enterprise (commercial)
Stocks	None	Property tax,[a] urban land use tax, and cultivated land use tax
Flow/transaction	Individual income tax, business tax, land value-added tax, deed tax, stamp tax, and urban maintenance and construction tax (and added educational expenses)	Corporate income tax, business tax, land value-added tax, deed tax, stamp tax, and urban maintenance and construction tax (and added educational expenses)

[a] This property tax is levied according to the "Provisional Tax Regulations of the People's Republic of China" (State Council document [1986] no. 90)

but will render the tax the most operable in every aspect. Sooner or later, the broad base will need to be the mode one way or another.

Then, the real issue is how long or short the transition will be from the narrow to the broad tax base. Our stance on this issue is that the sooner the broad base model, which may includes a per capita floor space exemption (for example, the average per capita housing size), is used, the better. Adoption of the broad base will need to be compatible with the design and completion of local government accountability and governance aspects, which we have discussed in earlier chapters.

10.3 The Link Between "New" Property Tax and Existing Tax System

With the introduction of a real property tax, a government must face the problem of how to link the "new" property tax to the existing "old" tax system. Will the new tax lead to an increased overall tax burden on residents? Obviously, we need to pay attention to this critically sensitive issue.

In the current tax system, the following taxes that have been levied are related to real estate: property tax, land value-added tax, urban land use tax, cultivated land usage tax, business tax, city maintenance and construction tax (and added educational expenses), deed tax, stamp tax, corporate income tax, and personal income tax. We can classify these taxes into four categories based on two dimensions: whether a tax is targeted on the stock or the flow or transaction of assets, and whether the taxpayer is a person and/or an enterprise. As shown in Table 10.1, the current tax system does not include a tax on the stock of personal housing ownership.

Going through the details of current tax policies concerning real estate, we find that four taxes are on the flow or transaction of assets—business tax, personal income tax, land value-added tax, and urban maintenance and construction tax (plus added educational expenses), and these can be exempted under certain conditions as listed in Table 10.2. The taxes that cannot be exempted, to a large extent, reflect regulatory interventions by the government on the real estate market. Tax exemptions

Table 10.2 Exemption provisions of the personal income tax, business tax, and land value-added tax

Individual income tax	This is exempted for individuals who transfer a house that had been used for more than 5 years and was their only house
	Notice on Personal Income Tax on Housing Transfer (State Administration of Taxation (200) no. 108)
Business tax	For individuals who sell a house that was bought less than 5 years ago, the business (sales) tax should be paid in full; for individuals who sell a luxury house that was bought more than 5 years ago, the business (sales) tax should be paid according to the difference between the sales revenue and the purchase price; for individuals who sell a normal house that was bought more than 5 years ago, the business (sales) tax is exempt
	Notice on Adjusting the Business Tax Policy on Housing Transfers (Ministry of Finance (2011) no. 12)
Land value-added tax	For individuals who sell their houses because of job relocation or for improving their living conditions, the land value-added tax is exempted after getting the approval of tax authorities, if they had lived in those houses for 5 or more years; if they had lived in those houses for 3 or more but less than 5 years, the land value-added tax is halved; if they had lived in those houses for less than 3 years, the land value-added tax is levied in accordance with the normal regulations
	Detailed Rules for the Implementation Method of Land VAT Provisional Regulations of the People's Republic of China (Ministry of Finance (1995) no. 6)

are policy adjustments made on occassions as the intent of the government changes. Therefore, with regard to residents, introduction of the real property tax as we have discussed in this monograph probably does not generate the need to integrate the current real estate tax.

From the perspective of enterprises, there has been a tax on the stock of real property: property tax, urban land use tax, and land usage tax. The levy of a new property tax overlaps with the above three taxes. In this regard, it is necessary to integrate these taxes with the new real property tax. A feasible approach towards integration is to incorporate the "old" property tax, urban land use tax, and land usage tax into the new property tax. But there does not seem to be the need for readjustment of taxes related to real estate in flow or during transaction held by enterprises.

It is our hope that levying the LPT in China will tie the costs to the benefits of public service investment in every local jurisdiction and that levying this tax will not increase the overall tax burden of the average citizen. Thus, the introduction and adoption of the LPT should proceed as integration and optimization of the overall tax system—the add-on of the real property tax requires a reduction of the taxes in the flow and transfer stages of asset acquisition.

Levying the real property tax will inevitably be accompanied by an adjustment of intergovernmental fiscal relations. With the increase of local own-source revenue from the real property tax, local governments will gradually have more abundant revenue, and the original revenue allocation among different levels of government will eventually be broken. This also means that the distribution of taxes on flows/transactions and income taxes will change between central and local governments. Other taxes on flows/transactions and income taxes may be moved up and collected at a higher level of government.

10.4 Prospects of Institutionalizing Local Property Tax in China

At the end of 2012, the ruling party of China set the goal of the country's socio-economic development for the next ten years as doubling the country's economy (GDP) and per capita personal income and substantially raising the urbanization ratio. These two new specific goals have placed the local property tax onto a more urgent track for quick, rather than slow, adoption. As we see it, trials of broad base local property taxes will be implemented in many more localities in the next few years and the time for full adoption of the broad base model is not far.

Appendixes

Appendix 4.1 Excerpts of Official Documents of Chinese Government(s) as Illustration of the Policy Process on Adopting the Local Property Tax

Official language in documents	Source
实施城镇建设税费改革，条件具备时对不动产开征统一规范的物业税，相应取消有关收费。	《中共中央关于完善社会主义市场经济体制若干问题的决定》（2003年10月14日）
稳步推行物业税	《中共中央关于制定国民经济和社会发展第十一个五年规划的建议》（2005年10月11日）
研究推进房地产税制改革	《2009年国务院政府工作报告》2009年3月5日
深化房地产税制改革，研究开征物业税	《国务院批转发展改革委关于2009年深化经济体制改革工作意见的通知》【国发〔2009〕26号】（2009年5月19日）
制定物业税税基评估技术标准，建立物业税税基评估系统，积极推进深圳开征物业税试点工作。	《深圳市综合配套改革三年（2009~2011年）实施方案》（2009年7月11日）
研究推进房地产税改革	《中共中央关于制定国民经济和社会发展第十二个五年规划的建议》（2010年10月18日）
对部分个人住房征收房产税改革于2011年1月28日起在上海和重庆两市开始试点	上海市人民政府关于印发《上海市开展对部分个人住房征收房产税试点的暂行办法》的通知【沪府发〔2011〕3号】和重庆市人民政府令第247号
加快建设城镇住房信息系统，改革房地产税收制度，促进房地产市场长期平稳健康发展。	《国务院政府工作报告》2012年3月5日
想在这个基础上进一步研究推进房产税改革的方案，适当扩大试点范围，积极稳妥地加以推进。	财政部部长谢旭人就“当前的财政政策和财政工作”回答中外记者的提问（2012年3月6日）

Y. Hou et al., *Local Property Tax in China,* Development and Governance,
DOI 10.1007/978-3-319-10049-4

Appendix 8.1 Definition of Variables Used in Regression Analyses

Variables	Definition
Rev	Local own-source revenue
Rate	Feasibility for different rates according to expenditure
Exp	LPT for public services
Trans	More transparency for local governments
Perform	Requirement for performance report
Public	Public participation in budgetary decision making
Election	Direct election for local officials
Efficiency	The overall effect of LPT reform to increase efficiency of local government

Appendix 8.2 Survey Instrument for Residents

Questionnaire on Pilot Local Property Tax in China

Background Chinese governments began piloting the local property tax (LPT) in Shanghai and Chongqing since January 28, 2011 in order to curb skyrocketing housing prices and to rationalize intergovernmental fiscal relations. With this survey, our research group is to poll the attitudes of residents towards the pilot LPT and then provide our analyses to policy-makers for possible improvements.

We sincerely thank you for your time and cooperation in answering the following questions.

Part I: Personal and Family Background Information

1. **What is your age?**
   A. 22–30
   B. 31–40
   C. 41–50
   D. 51–60
   E. Older than 60
   □

2. **What is your occupation?**
   A. Government
   B. Government supported entity
   C. State-owned enterprise
   D. Financial institution
   E. Private enterprise
   F. Nonprofitable organization
   G. Agriculture
   H. Self-employed

I. Unemployed
J. Retired
K. Other
☐

3. What is the number of members in your household?
A. 1
B. 2
C. 3
D. 4
E. 5 or more
☐

4. What is your average after-tax salary per year?

Please fill in the blank __________(in 10 thousand RMB Yuan).
☐

5. What is the average after-tax revenue of your family?

Please fill in the blank. __________(in 10 thousand RMB Yuan).
☐

6. What is the number of housing units that you own on state-owned land?
A. 0
B. 1
C. 2
D. 3
E. 4
F. 5 or more
☐

7. What is the number of housing units that you own on collectively owned land?
A. 0
B. 1
C. 2
D. 3
E. 4
F.5 or more
☐

8. What is the average floor space of the housing units you own (in m^2)?
A. <80
B. 80–120
C. 120–160
D. 160–200
E. >200
☐

9. **What is the average (current) market price per square meter of the housing units you own (in thousands)?**
   A. <3
   B. 3–5
   C. 5–8
   D. 8–10
   E. 10–15
   F. 15–20
   G. 20–30
   H. >30
   □

10. **Where do you live (the location of your primary residence)?**

    Please fill in the blank. ___________

Part II: Knowledge about the Local Property Tax

11. **Have you heard of the pilot local property tax (LPT)?**
    A. Yes
    B. No
    □

12. **Do you support the LPT on residential housing?**
    A. Yes
    B. No
    C. I do not care.
    □

13. **How large should the eligibility of LPT be in your mind?**
    A. New purchases and the second unit or more.
    B. Second or more units even if they were purchased earlier.
    C. New purchases only.
    D. All housing units, regardless of purchase date or number of units.
    □

14. **What should the method be to calculate LPT in your mind?**
    A. Floor space * unit price * flat amount per unit.
    B. Assessed value * flat rate.
    C. # of units * fixed amount per unit.
    □

15. **When should LPT be paid in your mind, by whom?**
    A. Onetime payment by purchaser.
    B. Onetime payment by seller.
    C. Once a year by owner.
    □

16. Do you think you are a taxpayer if LPT is levied?

A. Yes
B. No
□

17. What is the amount of LPT you can afford per year?

A. <500
B. 500–1000
C. 1000–2000
D. 2000–3000
E. 3000–4000
F. 4000–5000
G. >5000

Part III: Opinion on Pilot Local Property Tax in Shanghai and Chongqing

LPT in Shanghai

- Eligibility: Newly purchased second (or more) housing units
- Assessed Value: 70 % of market price
- Tax Rate: 0.4–0.6 %
- Tax Exemption: 60 m^2 per household member
- Calculation: ***Property Tax = (FS - 60 × N) × MP × 70% × TR***

FS— Floor space
N— Number of household member
MP— Market price/m^2
TR— Tax rate

18. What is your opinion about the LPT in Shanghai?

A. Satisfied
B. Roughly satisfied
C. Not satisfied
D. It doesn't matter
□

19. What is your opinion about the exempted area per household member in Shanghai?

A. Too large
B. Too small
C. Appropriate
□

20. What do you think about the assessment ratio and tax rate of LPT in Shanghai?

A. Better to lower the rate
B. Better to raise the rate
C. Appropriate

LPT in Chongqing

- Eligibility
  - Detached housing including earlier purchase
  - Newly purchased apartments with the market price/m^2 exceeding twice of the average in the last 2 years (luxury housing)
- Assessed Value: 100 % of market price
- Tax Rate: 0.5–1.2 %
- Tax Exemption: 100 or 180 m^2
- Calculation: ***Property Tax = (FS - 100 or 180)*** × ***MP*** × ***TR***

FS— Floor space
MP— Market price/m^2
TR— Tax rate

21. What is your opinion about the LPT in Chongqing?
A. Satisfied
B. Roughly satisfied
C. Not satisfied
D. It doesn't matter
□

22. What is your opinion about the exempted area per unit in Chongqing?
A. Too large
B. Too small
C. Appropriate
□

23. What do you think about exempting luxury housing (detached house excluded) brought before 01/28/2011 in Chongqing?
A. Appropriate. Earlier purchases should not be taxed.
B. Not appropriate. All purchases should be taxed.
□

24. What is your opinion about the criteria of luxury housing in Chongqing?
A. Too high
B. Too low
C. Appropriate
□

25. What is your opinion about LPT on detached houses (villas)?
A. Earlier purchases should not be taxed.
B. All purchases should be taxed.
C. I don't know.
□

26. Do you think the LPT will help suppress housing prices?
A. Yes
B. No
C. I don't know

Part IV: Your Suggestions on Improving the Local Property Tax

27. Who should pay LPT among owners by the number of housing units owned?

A. Top 10%
B. Top 30%
C. Top 50%
D. Top 70%
E. All
□

28. What is your opinion on categories of housing that should be subject to LPT?

A. All purchases past and new.
B. Only purchases made after LPT implementation.
C. All detached houses old and new purchases as well as ordinary housing bought after LPT implementation.

29. What is your opinion on exempted floor space?

A. 40 m^2 or less each household member
B. 40–60 m^2 each household member
C. Over 60 m^2 each household member
D. 80 m^2 or less per household
E. 100–120 m^2 per household
F. Over 120 m^2 per household
□

30. What do you think should be the effective tax rate of LPT?

A. Less than 0.1%
B. 0.1–0.3%
C. 0.3–0.5%
D. >0.5%
□

31. What is your attitude towards LPT after the concept is clarified?

A. Support
B. Oppose
C. I don't care

Appendix 8.3 Survey Instrument for Government Officials

Questionnaire on Pilot Local Property Tax in China

Please file out "Questionnaire of Pilot Local Property Tax in China (For Residents)" first if you are a government official, and then fill in this questionnaire.

Our research group sincerely thank you for your cooperation, patience, and time.

Please Read the Following First The ultimate goal of levying a local property tax on residential housing is much more than to control skyrocketing housing prices; it is also to help make local governments more responsible and accountable to their taxpayers. In the short run, Chinese governments may levy LPT only on luxury housing units or nonprimary housing units. In the long run, however, the tax base will cover most, even all, housing units for efficiency and equity reasons, with reasonable exemptions.

The ideal LPT is not only a tool to raise own-source revenue for local governments; it also serves as an effective tool to improve local governance. Specifically, an ideal LPT should have the following characteristics. First, revenues from LPT should belong to local governments at full local discretion and be devoted to key public services highly related to the daily lives of local residents. These include education, public safety, public health, recreation, and road. Second, tax rates should be determined locally in accord with total local expenditure needs. As such, the rate varies across different localities. Third, the budget and budgeting process should be transparent so that local residents can evaluate the performance of local officials and government by comparing what they pay with what they gain from public expenditure. The selection or appointment of local officials should be based on their prior performance and future plan.

Questions:

Part I: Your Opinion about the Local Property Tax

1. **Is it feasible for LPT to be an own-source revenue for local governments?**
   A. Feasible
   B. Not feasible
   C. I don't know
   □

2. **Is it feasible for localities to determine their own LPT rate by local needs?**
   A. Feasible
   B. Not feasible
   C. I don't know
   □

3. **Is it feasible for localities to supplement local public services financing with LPT revenue?**
   A. Feasible
   B. Not feasible
   C. I don't know

4. **Do you think that local residents will require more transparency of local governments if China levies LPT?**
   A. Yes
   B. No
   C.I don't know
   □

5. **Do you think that local residents will require local governments to publish performance reports if China adopts LPT?**
   A. Yes
   B. No
   C. I don't know
   □

6. **Do you think that local residents could participate in budgetary decision-making after paying LPT?**
   A. Yes
   B. No
   C. I don't know
   □

7. **Is it feasible to increase democracy in electing top local officials?**
   A. Feasible
   B. Not feasible
   C. I don't know
   □

8. **Is it feasible to increase local government efficiency with LPT and public choice?**
   A. Infeasible
   B. Worth a try
   C. Feasible
   D.I don't know

Part II: Information about You and Your Working Unit (Agency Affiliation)

1. **Which department of government are you in?**
   A. General office
   B. Finance
   C. Revenue
   D. Education
   E. Public Health
   F. Police
   G. Transportation
   H. Housing
   I. Land
   J. Other

2. **What is the administrative rank of your agency/unit?**
   A. Ministry/province
   B. Department
   C. Division
   D. Subdivision
   E. Section
   F. Others
   □

3. **What is the administrative rank of your position?**
   A. Ministry/province
   B. Department
   C. Division
   D. Subdivision
   E. Section
   F. Other

4. **Please specify the city where your working unit is located.**
   City:________________

Appendix 9.1 Sampling Method (with Hebei Province as Example)

1. Capital city: the selected district code is 130102, and county code is 130122. Where the first two digits indicate province, the middle two indicate city (the capital city is always 01), and the last two digits are a denotation of urban districts if they are from 01 to 19 and counties if they are larger than 20. To randomize our samples, we selected 02 for districts and 22 for counties in each province. There were two exceptions to this randomization rule. The first is with two jurisdictions that are small and thereby do not have jurisdictions with the 02 and 22 coded. The second exception is with two samples (with codes 02 and 22) that are geographically too close to each other. In these cases, the next numbers in the code series (03 or 23, or higher) are selected.[1]
2. Prefecture-level city: it must be at least 2 h driving distance away from the capital city and at the middle level of social economic status in the province. Sometimes, the selected prefecture-level city can better represent the typical characteristics of the province.
   In Hebei Province, the selected district code is 130302, and county code is 130322. The only difference from the areas in capital city lies on the two middle digits, since they denote different cities. For prefecture-level cities, the same sampling rules apply to district and county codes as that in capital cities.

Appendix 9.2 List of Main Official Data Sources for Variables

- China Population Census 2000 and 2010
- China Statistical Yearbook 1994–2011
- Compendium of Fiscal Statistics for Prefectures, Cities and Counties in the Country 1994–2009
- Demographic Data in Cities and Counties of China 1994–2010

[1] For the case that the two places (02 and 22) are geographically too close to each other, the option is just changing 22 to 23 until we get a satisfied available county sample. Otherwise, we change 02 to 03 and repeat the above steps.

Appendix 9.3 Full Versions of Tables 9.2, 9.6, 9.7 (A&B), and 9.8–9.13 (and more)

Table 9.2 Distribution of household disposable income in cities and townships from 1994 to 2010 (in RMB Yuan). (Source: China Statistical Yearbook, Schedule 10-7 (2012, 2011, 2010, 1999, 1998); 9-6 (2009, 2008); 10-6 (2006, 2005, 2004, 2003, 2002, 2001); 10-5 (2000); 9-8 (1997, 1996); 9-4 (1995))

Household groups (%)	Group	*2011*	*2010*	*2009*	*2008*	*2007*	*2006*	*2005*	*2004*	*2003*
Poverty within lowest (5)	Households in poverty	5398	4739	4198	3734	3358	2839	2496	2313	2099
Lowest (10)	Lowest income	6876	5948	5253	4754	4210	3569	3135	2862	2590
Low (10)	Low income	10,672	9285	8162	7363	6505	5541	4885	4429	3970
Low-mid (20)	Lower-middle income	14,498	12,702	11,244	10,196	8901	7554	6711	6024	5377
Mid (20)	Middle income	19,545	17,224	15,400	13,984	12,042	10,270	9190	8167	7279
Mid-high (20)	Upper-middle income	26,420	23,189	21,018	19,254	16,386	14,049	12,603	11,051	9763
High (10)	High income	35,579	31,044	28,386	26,250	22,234	19,069	17,203	14,971	13,123
Highest (10)	Highest income	58,842	51,432	46,826	43,614	36,785	31,967	28,773	25,377	21,837
Total average		21,810	19,109	17,175	15,781	13,786	11,759	10,493	9422	8472
Number of households		65,655	65,607	65,506	64,675	59,305	56,094	54,496	50,430	48,028
Gini coefficient (raw estimate)		0.32	0.32	0.32	0.33	0.32	0.32	0.33	0.32	0.32
Gini coefficient (adjusted)		*0.47*	*0.47*	*0.48*	*0.49*	*0.48*	*0.49*	*0.49*	*0.48*	*0.47*
		2002	*2001*	*2000*	*1999*	*1998*	*1997*	*1996*	*1995*	*1994*

Table 9.2 (continued)

Household groups (%)	Group	*2011*	*2010*	*2009*	*2008*	*2007*	*2006*	*2005*	*2004*	*2003*
Poverty within lowest (5)	Households in poverty	1957	2465	2325	2326	2199	2161	1937	1723	1352
Lowest (10)	Lowest income	2409	2803	2653	2618	2477	2430	2156	1924	1525
Low (10)	Low income	3649	3856	3634	3492	3303	3223	2809	2506	2012
Low-mid (20)	Lower-middle income	4932	4947	4624	4364	4107	3966	3397	3041	2461
Mid (20)	Middle income	6657	6366	5898	5512	5119	4895	4146	3698	3007
Mid-high (20)	Upper-middle income	8870	8164	7487	6905	6371	6045	5075	4512	3707
High (10)	High income	11,773	10,375	9434	8632	7878	7461	6190	5504	4565
Highest (10)	Highest income	18,996	15,115	13,311	12,084	10,962	10,251	8433	7538	6263
Total average		7703	6860	6280	5854	5425	5160	4377	3893	3179
Number of households		45,317	43,840	42,220	40,044	39,080	37,890	36,370	35,520	34,940
Gini coefficient (raw estimate)		0.31	0.26	0.25	0.23	0.23	0.22	0.21	0.21	0.22
Gini coefficient (adjusted)		*0.46*	*0.38*	*0.37*	*0.35*	*0.34*	*0.33*	*0.31*	*0.31*	*0.32*

The grouping of surveyed households into quintiles was to rank the households by their disposable income and cut-off into quintiles, with the first and last quintiles further broken into two. These seven groups are given the group names shown in column 2. The bottom 5% are households in poverty

Note that the Gini coefficient here is only a raw estimate which is severely underestimated since only five points are used in the calculation. The appropriate estimation (adjusted) would be about 1.5 times as described raw estimate here. The results are consistent with the official Gini coefficients (in the past decade) just released by the State Statistics Bureau in January 2013. The calculation method is available upon request

Table 9.6 Effective Tax Rate (ETR) for each province and year from 1995 to 2010

Code	Province	1995 (%)	1996 (%)	1997 (%)	1998 (%)	1999 (%)	2000 (%)	2001 (%)	2002 (%)	2003 (%)	2004 (%)	2005 (%)	2006 (%)	2007 (%)	2008 (%)	2009 (%)	2010 (%)
11	Beijing	0.50	0.52	0.39	0.51	0.53	0.65	0.70	0.78	0.89	0.95	0.82	0.78	0.58	0.58	0.55	0.44
12	Tianjin	0.78	0.86	1.02	1.08	1.21	1.18	1.24	1.29	1.39	1.22	0.94	0.92	0.85	0.98	0.88	0.82
13	Hebei	0.95	0.94	0.90	1.00	1.08	1.06	1.12	1.27	1.33	1.31	1.20	1.18	1.05	1.10	1.03	1.06
14	Shanxi	1.00	1.06	1.03	1.17	1.22	1.33	1.25	1.53	1.73	1.54	1.41	1.61	1.59	1.56	1.48	1.29
15	Neimenggu	0.71	1.07	1.23	1.55	1.58	1.59	1.66	1.81	1.98	1.93	1.86	1.78	1.64	1.60	1.46	1.39
21	Liaoning	0.61	0.75	0.76	0.71	0.73	0.75	0.77	0.92	0.94	0.96	0.90	0.95	0.96	1.01	1.02	1.05
22	Jilin	0.69	0.89	0.93	1.02	1.00	0.99	1.01	1.21	1.41	1.25	1.33	1.43	1.32	1.35	1.20	1.07
23	Heilongjiang	0.66	0.69	0.85	0.89	0.96	0.91	0.99	1.20	1.24	1.30	1.29	1.32	1.21	1.14	1.05	0.98
31	Shanghai	0.74	0.72	0.79	0.78	1.02	0.99	1.00	1.00	0.97	0.90	0.85	0.89	0.81	0.93	0.66	0.62
32	Jiangsu	0.70	0.75	0.85	0.85	0.94	0.91	0.92	1.03	1.02	0.96	0.86	0.92	0.93	1.04	0.91	0.87
33	Zhejiang	0.97	1.01	0.96	1.02	1.04	1.12	1.27	1.27	1.26	1.21	0.91	0.89	0.84	0.84	0.69	0.65
34	Anhui	1.09	1.37	1.25	1.29	1.32	1.35	1.46	1.32	1.31	1.18	1.01	1.10	1.12	1.08	1.02	0.92
35	Fujian	0.49	0.55	0.69	0.74	0.80	0.94	1.06	1.32	1.21	1.18	1.08	0.93	0.82	0.92	0.85	0.82
36	Jiangxi	1.16	1.28	1.37	1.80	1.74	1.62	1.73	1.81	1.86	1.62	1.58	1.46	1.34	1.41	1.22	1.13
37	Shandong	0.91	1.05	1.06	1.07	1.14	1.17	1.28	1.28	1.33	1.24	1.13	1.19	1.15	1.25	1.11	1.08
41	Henan	1.60	0.93	1.00	1.00	1.09	0.94	1.04	1.18	1.29	1.26	1.19	1.18	1.16	1.26	1.16	1.07
42	Hubei	0.73	0.85	0.80	0.83	0.94	0.96	0.98	1.09	1.11	1.07	0.86	0.85	0.79	0.89	0.84	0.89
43	Hunan	1.13	1.08	1.16	1.30	1.31	1.37	1.32	1.40	1.44	1.46	1.41	1.28	1.20	1.24	1.13	1.03
44	Guangdong	0.62	0.70	0.67	0.72	0.79	0.83	0.87	0.98	1.16	1.11	0.90	0.90	0.77	0.85	0.85	0.85
45	Guangxi	1.13	0.99	1.07	1.03	1.08	1.04	1.04	1.17	1.20	1.14	1.21	1.21	1.21	1.22	1.13	1.11
46	Hainan	0.59	0.73	0.55	0.74	0.85	0.72	0.85	1.02	0.96	0.84	0.75	0.64	0.66	0.57	0.52	0.43
50	Chongqing			1.02	0.93	1.09	1.22	1.26	1.29	1.37	1.32	1.24	1.27	1.03	1.10	0.99	0.88
51	Sichuan	0.72	0.82	0.84	0.95	0.99	1.11	1.17	1.24	1.26	1.20	1.04	0.94	0.82	0.81	0.81	0.78
52	Guizhou	1.22	1.33	1.37	1.16	1.34	1.27	1.50	1.65	1.64	1.70	1.63	1.51	1.43	1.34	1.22	1.09
53	Yunnan	0.79	1.22	1.20	1.05	1.04	0.99	0.95	1.02	1.04	1.13	1.06	1.02	1.08	1.08	1.03	1.08
54	Xizang		2.85			2.25	1.73	1.30	1.26	1.10	0.73	1.31	1.20	0.91	0.86	1.18	1.09
61	Shannxi	0.75	0.95	0.84	0.98	1.33	1.18	1.06	1.22	1.36	1.24	1.10	0.99	1.01	1.05	1.01	0.92

Table 9.6 (continued)

Code	Province	1995 (%)	1996 (%)	1997 (%)	1998 (%)	1999 (%)	2000 (%)	2001 (%)	2002 (%)	2003 (%)	2004 (%)	2005 (%)	2006 (%)	2007 (%)	2008 (%)	2009 (%)	2010 (%)
62	Gansu	0.72	0.71	0.84	0.94	1.15	1.12	1.21	1.49	1.62	1.28	1.25	1.39	1.19	1.40	1.17	1.03
63	Qinghai	0.70	0.84	0.84	0.81	0.94	1.18	1.36	1.42	1.35	1.40	1.26	1.32	1.23	1.23	1.27	1.14
64	Ningxia	0.83	0.85	0.76	0.92	0.94	1.02	1.04	0.96	1.11	1.09	1.15	1.24	1.38	1.39	1.17	1.18
65	Xinjiang	0.90	0.98	1.01	1.07	1.15	1.16	1.26	1.35	1.39	1.58	1.34	1.35	1.28	1.24	1.12	1.09
Average		*0.84*	*0.98*	*0.94*	*1.00*	*1.12*	*1.11*	*1.15*	*1.25*	*1.30*	*1.23*	*1.16*	*1.15*	*1.08*	*1.11*	*1.02*	*0.96*

ETR were calculated from the *China Statistical Yearbook* series and the *Population Census* in 2000 and 2010
Chongqing was established as "municipality directly under the central government" in 1997
No data are available for Xizang (Tibet) in 1995, 1997, and 1998

Table 9.7A Average total income and property tax payment (per capita) by province 1994–2010 (in RMB *Yuan*)

Code	Province	Inc.	Pay.	Inc.	Pay.	Inc.	Pay.	Inc.	Pay.	Inc.	Pay.	Inc.	Pay.
		1994		*1995*		*1996*		*1997*		*1998*		*1999*	
11	Beijing	5086	232	6238	279	7339	345	7862	380	8521	443	9239	483
12	Tianjin	3982	169	4931	212	5976	275	6621	333	7126	389	7671	430
13	Hebei	3180	146	3923	178	4446	212	4982	240	5116	272	5395	298
14	Shanxi	2566	112	3307	143	3706	155	4008	178	4118	197	4362	218
15	Neimenggu	2504	103	2874	110	3446	152	3968	190	4389	236	4799	266
21	Liaoning	3063	113	3708	137	4210	165	4547	192	4646	204	4925	227
22	Jilin	2581	106	3176	125	3806	163	4206	180	4224	190	4499	213
23	Heilongjiang	2599	97	3377	135	3769	152	4110	184	4292	202	4620	234
31	Shanghai	5890	278	7196	326	8191	384	8476	405	8825	445	10,989	613
32	Jiangsu	3779	171	4647	206	5188	243	5807	285	6064	314	6587	359
33	Zhejiang	5070	239	6225	282	6960	319	7366	351	7884	415	8476	460
34	Anhui	3049	124	3797	156	4515	194	4620	205	4799	230	5102	260
35	Fujian	3676	133	4511	159	5176	199	6201	284	6545	311	6914	347
36	Jiangxi	2776	123	3381	152	3782	177	4091	198	4274	221	4746	269
37	Shandong	3445	163	4265	202	4893	234	5217	259	5414	287	5841	319
41	Henan	2619	107	3302	137	3757	164	4112	187	4238	208	4554	240
42	Hubei	3360	149	4032	167	4367	190	4694	213	4849	225	5235	263
43	Hunan	3893	182	4705	213	5060	231	5249	248	5475	281	5856	306
44	Guangdong	6378	324	7445	358	8166	403	8616	447	8905	479	9206	505
45	Guangxi	4001	181	4809	215	5045	220	5140	238	5441	282	5648	297
46	Hainan	3977	180	4803	218	4968	230	4918	222	4895	232	5385	280
50	Chongqing							5343	217	5487	232	5916	262
51	Sichuan	3313	137	4005	161	4485	186	4788	205	5160	243	5510	272
52	Guizhou	3227	144	3935	164	4226	173	4458	199	4580	209	4953	257
53	Yunnan	3486	147	4113	165	4999	224	5616	262	6100	296	6235	315
54	Xizang	4025	169			6567	289					6956	313

Table 9.7A (continued)

Code	Province	Inc.	Pay.	Inc.	Pay.	Inc.	Pay.	Inc.	Pay.	Inc.	Pay.	Inc.	Pay.
		1994		*1995*		*1996*		*1997*		*1998*		*1999*	
61	Shannxi	2686	117	3311	140	3811	170	4022	186	4244	211	4679	246
62	Gansu	2659	108	3156	127	3355	131	3613	156	4034	193	4502	219
63	Qinghai	2813	101	3320	119	3834	145	4016	167	4258	183	4727	222
64	Ningxia	2989	122	3387	138	3616	146	3864	160	4146	188	4509	225
65	Xinjiang	3184	147	4184	196	4689	231	4879	231	5042	253	5360	286
		2000		*2001*		*2002*		*2003*		*2004*		*2005*	
11	Beijing	10,416	576	11,659	666	13,252	728	14,959	861	17,117	1014	19,533	1174
12	Tianjin	8165	462	8999	513	9839	578	10,972	643	12,280	723	13,563	782
13	Hebei	5686	312	6028	335	7015	392	7608	430	8381	483	9617	549
14	Shanxi	4745	245	5416	303	6528	384	7447	450	8429	517	9539	582
15	Neimenggu	5151	278	5561	311	6341	359	7352	420	8488	479	9565	549
21	Liaoning	5389	260	5833	291	6941	360	7833	405	8706	464	9837	520
22	Jilin	4829	229	5361	271	6523	347	7311	402	8227	450	9123	495
23	Heilongjiang	4945	253	5462	292	6334	358	6968	386	7803	437	8722	493
31	Shanghai	11,802	651	12,982	741	14,396	837	16,380	1030	18,502	1136	20,603	1276
32	Jiangsu	6841	371	7428	420	8739	519	9912	591	11,237	680	13,330	811
33	Zhejiang	9334	520	10,540	619	12,682	739	14,295	853	15,882	947	17,877	1034
34	Anhui	5332	266	5716	293	6335	325	7156	386	7994	425	9185	498
35	Fujian	7486	405	8385	476	9861	588	10,816	649	12,118	722	13,408	824
36	Jiangxi	5130	302	5546	337	6521	383	7154	430	7877	466	9042	538
37	Shandong	6522	363	7141	414	8158	483	9058	550	10,187	616	11,608	711
41	Henan	4784	256	5292	299	6516	389	7245	441	8073	496	9146	562
42	Hubei	5543	289	5889	312	7142	387	7746	420	8522	463	9395	522
43	Hunan	6261	340	6833	384	7372	427	8145	469	9190	512	10,106	573
44	Guangdong	9854	552	10,535	618	11,961	686	13,451	814	14,953	872	16,250	905
45	Guangxi	5882	321	6723	391	7757	459	8294	501	9324	547	10,022	581

Table 9.7A (continued)

Code	Province	Inc.	Pay.	Inc.	Pay.	Inc.	Pay.	Inc.	Pay.	Inc.	Pay.	Inc.	Pay.
		1994		*1995*		*1996*		*1997*		*1998*		*1999*	
46	Hainan	5416	279	5927	332	7174	383	7606	416	8122	440	8670	484
50	Chongqing	6297	299	6755	333	7663	395	8672	448	9910	525	11,079	614
51	Sichuan	5926	307	6407	341	6989	377	7488	405	8261	433	9004	481
52	Guizhou	5137	248	5467	285	6107	340	6746	375	7519	415	8385	460
53	Yunnan	6370	329	6850	368	7690	400	8203	424	9546	503	9995	530
54	Xizang	7477	363	7912	391	8627	417	9697	434	10,396	475	10,659	492
61	Shannxi	5149	276	5514	299	6747	378	7314	413	8043	448	8902	500
62	Gansu	4944	250	5414	277	6524	356	7133	394	7991	439	8738	484
63	Qinghai	5197	260	5884	307	6499	345	7155	392	7785	443	8767	491
64	Ningxia	4948	241	5582	289	6409	337	6991	383	7749	427	8745	491
65	Xinjiang	5687	304	6457	360	7453	412	7867	450	8202	473	8694	474
		2006		*2007*		*2008*		*2009*		*2010*			
11	Beijing	22,417	1386	24,576	1543	27,678	1752	30,674	1967	33,360	2118		
12	Tianjin	15,476	936	17,828	1070	21,174	1290	23,566	1431	26,942	1655		
13	Hebei	10,887	635	12,336	721	14,141	848	15,676	963	17,334	1097		
14	Shanxi	10,794	658	12,468	762	13,859	852	14,983	943	16,893	1112		
15	Neimenggu	10,812	631	12,977	742	15,195	844	16,951	931	19,014	1028		
21	Liaoning	11,230	618	13,438	749	15,836	868	17,758	981	20,015	1161		
22	Jilin	10,245	581	11,799	656	13,606	761	15,155	815	16,794	946		
23	Heilongji-ang	9722	564	10,882	618	12,264	670	13,690	743	15,096	813		
31	Shanghai	22,809	1437	26,102	1571	29,759	1805	32,403	2004	35,739	2227		
32	Jiangsu	15,249	955	17,687	1127	20,176	1282	22,495	1444	25,115	1640		
33	Zhejiang	19,954	1170	22,584	1389	24,981	1552	27,119	1656	30,135	1869		
34	Anhui	10,575	588	12,499	726	14,160	817	15,692	935	17,627	1056		
35	Fujian	15,102	943	16,983	1041	19,686	1203	21,692	1349	24,150	1517		
36	Jiangxi	10,015	611	11,984	725	13,464	798	15,047	889	16,558	997		

Table 9.7A (continued)

Code	Province	Inc.	Pay.	Inc.	Pay.	Inc.	Pay.	Inc.	Pay.	Inc.	Pay.	Inc.	Pay.
		1994		*1995*		*1996*		*1997*		*1998*		*1999*	
37	Shandong	13,223	809	15,366	941	17,549	1076	19,337	1176	21,737	1338		
41	Henan	10,339	642	12,083	738	13,908	851	15,408	949	17,142	1037		
42	Hubei	10,533	595	12,383	694	14,174	797	15,698	916	17,573	1031		
43	Hunan	11,146	634	12,998	762	14,577	827	16,078	927	17,657	1038		
44	Guangdong	17,726	1020	19,619	1098	21,679	1238	24,117	1396	26,897	1574		
45	Guangxi	10,624	647	13,183	807	15,393	923	17,033	1052	18,742	1149		
46	Hainan	10,082	552	11,792	635	13,599	751	14,909	818	16,930	964		
50	Chongqing	12,549	705	13,441	733	15,218	816	16,990	934	18,991	1064		
51	Sichuan	10,117	556	12,010	644	13,685	727	15,324	835	17,129	950		
52	Guizhou	9439	535	11,066	629	12,186	686	13,793	805	15,139	887		
53	Yunnan	10,848	587	12,296	676	14,118	753	15,680	838	17,479	973		
54	Xizang	9541	528	11,952	668	13,648	770	14,979	852	16,539	958		
61	Shannxi	9938	559	11,482	642	13,847	789	15,311	873	17,065	975		
62	Gansu	9586	548	10,860	613	11,669	643	12,918	720	14,307	804		
63	Qinghai	9803	583	11,428	676	12,867	761	14,150	830	15,481	918		
64	Ningxia	10,002	578	11,793	697	14,119	818	15,551	905	17,537	1043		
65	Xinjiang	9689	553	11,303	631	12,479	680	13,602	743	15,422	876		

For each year, the first column is per capita income and the second column is per capita property tax payment
Property tax payments are calculated from the *China Statistical Yearbook* series according to formula described in the chapter
Chongqing was established as "municipality directly under the central government" in 1997
No data are available for Xizang (Tibet) in 1995, 1997, and 1998

Table 9.7B Average LPT payment as ratio of per capita income by province 1994–2010

Code	Province	*1994 (%)*	*1995 (%)*	*1996 (%)*	*1997 (%)*	*1998 (%)*	*1999 (%)*	*2000 (%)*	*2001 (%)*	*2002 (%)*
11	Beijing	4.6	4.5	4.7	4.8	5.2	5.2	5.5	5.7	5.5
12	Tianjin	4.3	4.3	4.6	5.0	5.5	5.6	5.7	5.7	5.9
13	Hebei	4.6	4.5	4.8	4.8	5.3	5.5	5.5	5.6	5.6
14	Shanxi	4.4	4.3	4.2	4.4	4.8	5.0	5.2	5.6	5.9
15	Neimenggu	4.1	3.8	4.4	4.8	5.4	5.5	5.4	5.6	5.7
21	Liaoning	3.7	3.7	3.9	4.2	4.4	4.6	4.8	5.0	5.2
22	Jilin	4.1	3.9	4.3	4.3	4.5	4.7	4.7	5.1	5.3
23	Heilongjiang	3.7	4.0	4.0	4.5	4.7	5.1	5.1	5.3	5.6
31	Shanghai	4.7	4.5	4.7	4.8	5.0	5.6	5.5	5.7	5.8
32	Jiangsu	4.5	4.4	4.7	4.9	5.2	5.4	5.4	5.6	5.9
33	Zhejiang	4.7	4.5	4.6	4.8	5.3	5.4	5.6	5.9	5.8
34	Anhui	4.1	4.1	4.3	4.4	4.8	5.1	5.0	5.1	5.1
35	Fujian	3.6	3.5	3.8	4.6	4.8	5.0	5.4	5.7	6.0
36	Jiangxi	4.4	4.5	4.7	4.8	5.2	5.7	5.9	6.1	5.9
37	Shandong	4.7	4.7	4.8	5.0	5.3	5.5	5.6	5.8	5.9
41	Henan	4.1	4.1	4.4	4.6	4.9	5.3	5.4	5.7	6.0
42	Hubei	4.4	4.1	4.3	4.5	4.6	5.0	5.2	5.3	5.4
43	Hunan	4.7	4.5	4.6	4.7	5.1	5.2	5.4	5.6	5.8
44	Guangdong	5.1	4.8	4.9	5.2	5.4	5.5	5.6	5.9	5.7
45	Guangxi	4.5	4.5	4.4	4.6	5.2	5.3	5.5	5.8	5.9
46	Hainan	4.5	4.5	4.6	4.5	4.7	5.2	5.2	5.6	5.3
50	Chongqing				4.1	4.2	4.4	4.7	4.9	5.1
51	Sichuan	4.1	4.0	4.2	4.3	4.7	4.9	5.2	5.3	5.4
52	Guizhou	4.4	4.2	4.1	4.5	4.6	5.2	4.8	5.2	5.6
53	Yunnan	4.2	4.0	4.5	4.7	4.8	5.0	5.2	5.4	5.2
54	Xizang	4.2		4.4			4.5	4.9	4.9	4.8
61	Shannxi	4.4	4.2	4.5	4.6	5.0	5.3	5.4	5.4	5.6
62	Gansu	4.0	4.0	3.9	4.3	4.8	4.9	5.1	5.1	5.5
63	Qinghai	3.6	3.6	3.8	4.2	4.3	4.7	5.0	5.2	5.3
64	Ningxia	4.1	4.1	4.0	4.1	4.5	5.0	4.9	5.2	5.3
65	Xinjiang	4.6	4.7	4.9	4.7	5.0	5.3	5.3	5.6	5.5
Code	Province	*2003 (%)*	*2004 (%)*	*2005 (%)*	*2006 (%)*	*2007 (%)*	*2008 (%)*	*2009 (%)*	*2010 (%)*	
11	Beijing	5.8	5.9	6.0	6.2	6.3	6.3	6.4	6.3	
12	Tianjin	5.9	5.9	5.8	6.0	6.0	6.1	6.1	6.1	
13	Hebei	5.6	5.8	5.7	5.8	5.8	6.0	6.1	6.3	
14	Shanxi	6.0	6.1	6.1	6.1	6.1	6.2	6.3	6.6	
15	Neimenggu	5.7	5.6	5.7	5.8	5.7	5.6	5.5	5.4	
21	Liaoning	5.2	5.3	5.3	5.5	5.6	5.5	5.5	5.8	
22	Jilin	5.5	5.5	5.4	5.7	5.6	5.6	5.4	5.6	
23	Heilongjiang	5.5	5.6	5.6	5.8	5.7	5.5	5.4	5.4	
31	Shanghai	6.3	6.1	6.2	6.3	6.0	6.1	6.2	6.2	
32	Jiangsu	6.0	6.1	6.1	6.3	6.4	6.4	6.4	6.5	
33	Zhejiang	6.0	6.0	5.8	5.9	6.2	6.2	6.1	6.2	
34	Anhui	5.4	5.3	5.4	5.6	5.8	5.8	6.0	6.0	
35	Fujian	6.0	6.0	6.1	6.2	6.1	6.1	6:2	6.3	

Table 9.7B (continued)

36	Jiangxi	6.0	5.9	6.0	6.1	6.0	5.9	5.9	6.0	
37	Shandong	6.1	6.0	6.1	6.1	6.1	6.1	6.1	6.2	
41	Henan	6.1	6.1	6.1	6.2	6.1	6.1	6.2	6.0	
42	Hubei	5.4	5.4	5.6	5.6	5.6	5.6	5.8	5.9	
43	Hunan	5.8	5.6	5.7	5.7	5.9	5.7	5.8	5.9	
44	Guangdong	6.1	5.8	5.6	5.8	5.6	5.7	5.8	5.9	
45	Guangxi	6.0	5.9	5.8	6.1	6.1	6.0	6.2	6.1	
46	Hainan	5.5	5.4	5.6	5.5	5.4	5.5	5.5	5.7	
50	Chongqing	5.2	5.3	5.5	5.6	5.5	5.4	5.5	5.6	
51	Sichuan	5.4	5.2	5.3	5.5	5.4	5.3	5.5	5.5	
52	Guizhou	5.6	5.5	5.5	5.7	5.7	5.6	5.8	5.9	
53	Yunnan	5.2	5.3	5.3	5.4	5.5	5.3	5.3	5.6	
54	Xizang	4.5	4.6	4.6	5.5	5.6	5.6	5.7	5.8	
61	Shannxi	5.6	5.6	5.6	5.6	5.6	5.7	5.7	5.7	
62	Gansu	5.5	5.5	5.5	5.7	5.6	5.5	5.6	5.6	
63	Qinghai	5.5	5.7	5.6	5.9	5.9	5.9	5.9	5.9	
64	Ningxia	5.5	5.5	5.6	5.8	5.9	5.8	5.8	5.9	
65	Xinjiang	5.7	5.8	5.4	5.7	5.6	5.5	5.5	5.7	

Table 9.8 LPT revenue as ratio of local expenditure 1995–2009

Id	County	1995 (%)	1996 (%)	1997 (%)	1998 (%)	1999 (%)	2000 (%)	2001 (%)	2002 (%)	2003 (%)	2004 (%)	2005 (%)	2006 (%)	2007 (%)	2008 (%)	2009 (%)
110102	0	24	18	15	16	15	16	14	15	16	17	16	15	10	11	9
110105	0	34	28	22	22	21	21	20	21	24	26	25	23	20	19	19
110108	0	25	12	20	17	16	15	17	18	19	20	21	21	19	17	17
110228	1	27	26	23	25	16	16	16	13	14	14	16	16	17	16	11
120101	0	25	26	28	27	22	23	17	19	19	19	16	15	14	13	12
120102	0	43	36	48	51	48	45	38	37	35	35	32	33	16	31	28
120104	0	46		49	49	45	42	44	41	42	36	32	30	26	26	27
120223	1	33	34	38	43	48	53	44	41	39	34	31	32	14	24	23
130102	0	21	22	18	17	16	15	13	13	11	10	11	14	11	12	12
130123	1	21	17	14	14	13	13	11	10	10	11	10	10	10	9	10
130302	0	19	21	16	15	15	13	11	13	12	10	11	10	9	9	9
130322	1	21	21	21	21	23	18	14	15	14	13	12	11	9	7	8
140106	0	25	21	23	17	17	18	17	20	18	16	16	16	16	14	14
140122	1	11	11	11	11	11	10	10	12	11	9	8	8	6	6	7
140502	0	19	18	16	14	17	18	18	18	18	7	18	12	14	14	13
140522	1	18	14	15	14	14	13	11	12	12	13	10	4	9	9	8
150102	0	20	22	25	27	21	17	14	14	12	13	14	13	10	10	9
150122	1	9	12	11	10	12	10	9	9	6	4	4	4	5	5	4
150402	0	12	12	14	15	15	13	12	12	12	11	11	11	11	11	9
150422	1	18	18	18	19	18	16	14	11	9	8	9	10	9	8	8
210102	0	15	16	15	13	16	15	16	16	15	13	12	11	11	10	11
210122	1	23	31	33	35	39	40	40	56	44	38	37	33	23	20	18
210202	0	10	10	11	10	11	12	11	11	10	11	12	12	12	12	12
210224	1	6	8	7	8	7	7	7	7	7	9	7	6	7	7	8
220102	0					29	27	28	30	27	27	25	25	24	21	18
220122	1	34	34	31	29	31	35	32	34	29	27	25	19	19	16	14
220502	0					36	34	26	32	33	29	27	29	29	27	23

Table 9.8 (continued)

Id	County	1995 (%)	1996 (%)	1997 (%)	1998 (%)	1999 (%)	2000 (%)	2001 (%)	2002 (%)	2003 (%)	2004 (%)	2005 (%)	2006 (%)	2007 (%)	2008 (%)	2009 (%)
220523	1	17	21	22	21	18	18	17	18	19	17	15	13	12	10	8
230102	0	27	24	22	19	17	17	14	8	7	14	13	12	12	11	12
230125	1	35	32	30	28	29	28	25	9	9	22	20	17	15	13	13
230202	0						43	33	29	26	26	27	25	21	17	17
230221	1	25	25	29	23	31	37	31	27	29	26	23	23	18	16	14
310101	0	9	8	7	8	9	10	13	13	13	12	11	11	12	13	13
310103	0	23	20	17	15	18	18	14	13	12	11	10	10	9	9	9
310104	0	27	30	22	22	27	26	19	20	19	17	16	17	15	16	17
310110	0	38	37	33	33	42	43	41	32	30	27	25	25	24	25	25
310230	1	34	35	31	33	40	44	30	29	29	25	21	20	15	17	16
320102	0					12	10	8	8	9	9	10	11	12	13	14
320124	1	16	16	17	17	16	14	13	14	13	12	14	14	14	11	9
320302	0					35	39	38	41	39	35	46	55	55	57	49
320322	1	30	30	31	31	32	34	31	33	33	30	29	27	22	22	20
330102	0					14	15	14	13	11	11	12	12	14	9	10
330122	1	26	23	24	29	25	25	17	19	19	17	16	18	20	17	15
330302	0					26	22	23	23	23	25	23	26	27	25	22
330322	1	15	14	14	16	16	14	13	13	11	12	12	11	10	10	11
340102	0					14			10	12	10	8	11	11	9	14
340122	1	18	18	17	17	16	13	13	12	13	12	11	10	9	8	8
340202	0								7	7	7	9	4	5	5	4
340222	1	10	9	9	9	11	10	8	8	8	6	6	7	7	6	6
350102	0					20	20	22	27	28	32	27	33	24	22	25
350122	1	15	17	22	20	19	21	21	28	25	27	30	25	19	17	20
350402	0					21	19	23	24	21	20	23	24	22	22	20
350423	1	7	8	10	13	16	16	17	19	20	19	21	21	17	15	13
360102	0	20	20	16	21	21	15	16	13	13	10	10	11	11	10	11

Table 9.8 (continued)

Id	County	1995 (%)	1996 (%)	1997 (%)	1998 (%)	1999 (%)	2000 (%)	2001 (%)	2002 (%)	2003 (%)	2004 (%)	2005 (%)	2006 (%)	2007 (%)	2008 (%)	2009 (%)
360122	1	14	14	14	15	11	12	13	10	10	9	8	7	7	6	5
360702	0					11	13	13	11	12	10	11	11	9	8	7
360722	1					14	16	14	12	12	11	11	10	10	9	8
370102	0	27	26	24	21	19	19	17	17	16	15	15	14	13	13	11
370124	1	24	11	10	12	13	17	15	15	15	13	14	12	13	13	13
370602	0	18	17	17	16	17	17	17	16	16	15	15	14	13	13	13
370682	1	48	43	38	31	29	27	24	21	21	20	20	19	21	23	23
410102	0					12	10	11	10	12	11	10	10	9	9	10
410122	1	18	16	14	15	16	15	13	12	11	11	10	9	8	7	6
410302	0					12	13	11	10	9	9	8	7	8	7	7
410322	1	13	12	12	11	11	12	12	10	13	11	9	8	8	8	7
420102	0					13	12	10	12	11	10	10	9	8	8	8
420111	0					16	14	13	17	16	14	15	15	15	12	11
420502	0					44	35	46	45	46	38	42	33	33	31	31
420525	1	20	18	17	15	15	14	13	13	13	13	12	8	9	8	6
430102	0		14	12	12	10	10	9	6	6	4	3	3	3	3	3
430122	1	21	16	15	16	15	17	14	12	9	8	8	6	6	4	4
430412	0	9	7	8	6	6	6	5	5	5	5	5	4	4	3	3
430422	1	29	29	27	30	27	29	23	18	19	18	19	16	14	11	1
440103	0					14	12	10	11	13	14	10	11	10	10	11
440104	0					11	9	8	8	11	11	13	13	13	13	15
440106	0					6	8	8	9	10	9	8	8	10	10	11
440183	1	24	24	26	25	26	2	23	20	19	18	14	15	13	13	13
440507	0					14	16	16	20	34	31	24	24	24	23	25
440523	1	10	11	13	14	16	16	18	12	14	19	17	16	14	13	16
450102	0						7	7	7	5	5	7	7	8	9	8

Table 9.8 (continued)

Id	County	1995 (%)	1996 (%)	1997 (%)	1998 (%)	1999 (%)	2000 (%)	2001 (%)	2002 (%)	2003 (%)	2004 (%)	2005 (%)	2006 (%)	2007 (%)	2008 (%)	2009 (%)
450122	1	12	10	12	11	9	9	10	12	11	12	12	11	10	10	10
450302	0						11	9	8	7	7	7	8	9	9	8
450322	1	17	16	16	17	15	14	12	12	10	10	9	8	9	7	7
460105	0		18	22	22	14	11	11	12	16	15	14	14	14	14	12
469001	1	9	8	7	5	8	7	6	6	6	5	5	4	4	4	2
469005	1	17	17	14	13	16	14	14	12	13	10	9	9	8	6	5
469033	1	26	24	21	19	19	15	16	15	13	12	11	10	2	8	6
500102	0				8	8	8	7	7	7	8	10	10	10	9	7
500222	1			30	25	29	29	21	20	20	16	20	19	15	12	10
510104	0	6	7	6	7	12	5	4	3	4	3	3	3	2	2	2
510122	1	6	5	7	7	6	7	7	7	6	6	6	5	4	4	4
510302	0	11	11	16	21	21	24	22	16	14	12	18	16	14	12	12
510322	1	18	17	24	29	29	31	23	20	18	16	13	13	12	11	10
520102	0	13	12	12	10	10	8	6	5	5	5	5	5	5	4	4
520122	1		11	9	9	9	7	6	5	5	5	4	4	4	3	3
520203	0	20	19	17	15	17	14	10	9	9	8	7	8	8	5	6
520221	1	20	19	17	16	16	13	11	10	10	9	8	8	8	6	6
530102	0	2	2	2	3	2	2	2	3	3	4	4	4	4	4	3
530122	1	5	5	5	5	5	5	5	6	6	6	5	4	4	3	3
530502	0							8	8	8	7	7	7	7	6	5
530522	1							6	6	6	6	5	5	4	4	4
540102	0		2			1	5	4	4	4	4	3	3	3	3	3
540122	1		6			5	5	4	3	2	2	2	2	2	2	2
542122	1		9			7	7	5	5	4	4	3	4	3	3	3
542124	1		7			5	6	5	3	3	3	2	2	2	2	2
610102	0	13	11	11	9	9	9	8	10	10	9	10	9	9	9	8
610122	1	27	25	22	25	28	25	21	23	22	21	23	20	15	12	11

Table 9.8 (continued)

Id	County	1995 (%)	1996 (%)	1997 (%)	1998 (%)	1999 (%)	2000 (%)	2001 (%)	2002 (%)	2003 (%)	2004 (%)	2005 (%)	2006 (%)	2007 (%)	2008 (%)	2009 (%)
542124	1		7			5	6	5	3	3	3	2	2	2	2	2
610102	0	13	11	11	9	9	9	8	10	10	9	10	9	9	9	8
610122	1	27	25	22	25	28	25	21	23	22	21	23	20	15	12	11
610302	0	14	15	18	17	18	16	16	19	20	20	18	15	13	12	12
610322	1	25	29	30	26	28	25	21	21	22	21	20	16	13	12	10
620102	0	9	8	8	9	9	10	9	9	5	5	9	9	7	7	6
620122	1	10	7	8	9	8	9	8	8	7	6	7	5	5	4	4
620502	0	15	13	15	16	15	14	13	13	12	11	12	10	9	6	5
620522	1	23	18	19	22	21	19	16	17	16	16	16	13	11	7	6
630102	0	19	18	19	18	20	21	17	20	22	20	19	18	16	12	10
630121	1	14	12	12	13	12	12	11	11	11	10	9	9	8	7	6
632802	1	8	7	7	8	8	7	6	6	5	4	3		2	2	2
632822	1	6	7	7	8	9	8	6	5	5	7	5		4	3	3
640104	0					22	15	17	16	15	15	16	17	16	16	14
640122	1	13	12	11	11	12	11	9	9	9	10	9	9	7	6	5
640402	0	22	19	16	14	15	12	10	9	12	14	12	13	13	10	9
640422	1	22	17	15	14	14	13	10	11	13	14	13	13	11	11	9
650102	0					15	17	15	17	16	15	14	13	12	10	10
650121	1	8	9	8	8	7	7	7	5	5	4	4	5	5	4	5
652101	1	19	17	14	12	11	11	15	11	11	11	10	9	9	7	6
652122	1	10	10	8	9	9	6	6	8	8	8	7	5	5	4	5
Average	19	17	18	18	18	17	15	15	15	14	14	13	12	11	11	

Table 9.9 Predicted LPT revenue as ratio of local expenditure 2010–2020

Id	County	2010 (%)	2011 (%)	2012 (%)	2013 (%)	2014 (%)	2015 (%)	2016 (%)	2017 (%)	2018 (%)	2019 (%)	2020 (%)
110102	0	5.7	5.9	6.1	6.3	6.4	6.6	6.7	6.8	6.9	7.0	7.1
110105	0	34.9	33.4	32.2	31.2	30.3	29.6	28.9	28.4	27.9	27.4	27.0
110108	0	16.4	16.5	16.6	16.7	16.8	16.8	16.9	16.9	17.0	17.0	17.1
110228	1	14.2	14.3	14.3	14.3	14.3	14.3	14.3	14.3	14.3	14.3	14.3
120101	0	12.0	12.1	12.1	12.1	12.2	12.2	12.2	12.3	12.3	12.3	12.3
120102	0	22.1	22.3	22.6	22.8	23.0	23.2	23.4	23.5	23.7	23.8	23.9
120104	0	33.9	33.6	33.2	33.0	32.7	32.5	32.3	32.1	32.0	31.8	31.7
120223	1	29.0	28.6	28.3	28.0	27.8	27.6	27.4	27.2	27.0	26.9	26.8
130102	0	11.6	11.6	11.5	11.5	11.4	11.4	11.4	11.4	11.3	11.3	11.3
130123	1	9.6	9.5	9.5	9.4	9.4	9.4	9.3	9.3	9.3	9.2	9.2
130302	0	8.3	8.3	8.3	8.3	8.4	8.4	8.4	8.4	8.4	8.5	8.5
130322	1	10.3	10.2	10.0	9.9	9.8	9.7	9.6	9.5	9.4	9.4	9.3
140106	0	15.5	15.5	15.5	15.5	15.5	15.5	15.5	15.5	15.5	15.5	15.6
140122	1	7.2	7.2	7.2	7.2	7.2	7.2	7.2	7.2	7.2	7.2	7.2
140502	0	14.0	14.1	14.1	14.2	14.2	14.2	14.2	14.3	14.3	14.3	14.3
140522	1	5.9	6.0	6.1	6.1	6.2	6.3	6.3	6.4	6.4	6.5	6.5
150102	0	10.8	10.7	10.7	10.7	10.7	10.6	10.6	10.6	10.6	10.6	10.6
150122	1	5.0	5.0	4.9	4.9	4.9	4.8	4.8	4.8	4.8	4.7	4.7
150402	0	11.0	11.0	11.0	11.0	11.0	11.1	11.1	11.1	11.1	11.1	11.1
150422	1	6.8	6.9	6.9	7.0	7.1	7.1	7.2	7.2	7.3	7.3	7.4
210102	0	9.8	9.9	10.0	10.0	10.1	10.1	10.2	10.2	10.3	10.3	10.4
210122	1	26.1	26.0	25.9	25.8	25.7	25.6	25.6	25.5	25.4	25.4	25.3
210202	0	20.4	19.8	19.3	18.8	18.4	18.1	17.8	17.6	17.3	17.1	16.9
210224	1	7.4	7.4	7.4	7.4	7.4	7.5	7.5	7.5	7.5	7.5	7.5
220102	0	13.6	13.8	14.0	14.2	14.4	14.6	14.7	14.9	15.0	15.1	15.2
220122	1	14.1	14.2	14.3	14.4	14.5	14.6	14.7	14.8	14.8	14.9	15.0
220502	0	25.8	25.6	25.4	25.3	25.2	25.1	25.0	24.9	24.9	24.8	24.7

Table 9.9 (continued)

Id	County	2010 (%)	2011 (%)	2012 (%)	2013 (%)	2014 (%)	2015 (%)	2016 (%)	2017 (%)	2018 (%)	2019 (%)	2020 (%)
220523	1	11.5	11.5	11.4	11.4	11.3	11.3	11.2	11.2	11.2	11.2	11.1
230102	0	9.1	9.2	9.3	9.4	9.5	9.5	9.6	9.6	9.7	9.7	9.8
230125	1	15.7	15.6	15.5	15.4	15.3	15.2	15.1	15.1	15.0	15.0	14.9
230202	0	17.9	17.5	17.2	16.9	16.6	16.4	16.3	16.1	15.9	15.8	15.7
230221	1	18.9	18.8	18.8	18.7	18.6	18.6	18.6	18.5	18.5	18.4	18.4
310101	0	8.7	9.0	9.3	9.6	9.9	10.1	10.3	10.5	10.7	10.8	11.0
310103	0	10.6	10.5	10.4	10.3	10.2	10.1	10.1	10.0	9.9	9.9	9.8
310104	0	18.3	18.2	18.1	18.0	17.9	17.8	17.8	17.7	17.6	17.6	17.5
310110	0	30.8	30.4	30.1	29.8	29.5	29.3	29.1	28.9	28.7	28.6	28.4
310230	1	10.4	10.9	11.3	11.6	12.0	12.2	12.5	12.7	12.9	13.1	13.3
320102	0	12.8	12.9	13.0	13.1	13.1	13.2	13.2	13.3	13.3	13.3	13.4
320124	1	18.3	17.7	17.3	16.9	16.5	16.2	16.0	15.8	15.6	15.4	15.2
320302	0	52.7	53.0	53.3	53.5	53.7	53.8	54.0	54.1	54.3	54.4	54.5
320322	1	28.5	28.2	28.0	27.8	27.6	27.4	27.2	27.1	27.0	26.9	26.8
330102	0	10.3	10.3	10.2	10.2	10.2	10.2	10.1	10.1	10.1	10.1	10.1
330122	1	19.9	19.8	19.7	19.5	19.4	19.4	19.3	19.2	19.1	19.1	19.0
330302	0	22.9	23.0	23.1	23.1	23.2	23.2	23.2	23.3	23.3	23.3	23.3
330322	1	11.1	11.1	11.1	11.1	11.1	11.1	11.1	11.1	11.1	11.1	11.1
340102	0	6.3	6.6	6.8	7.1	7.3	7.5	7.6	7.8	8.0	8.1	8.2
340122	1	7.9	7.9	8.0	8.0	8.0	8.1	8.1	8.1	8.1	8.2	8.2
340202	0	42.7	26.8	20.6	17.3	15.2	13.8	12.8	12.1	11.4	11.0	10.6
340222	1	9.3	9.0	8.8	8.6	8.5	8.3	8.2	8.1	8.0	7.9	7.9
350102	0	52.4	48.2	45.2	42.9	41.1	39.6	38.4	37.3	36.5	35.7	35.0
350122	1	33.0	32.1	31.4	30.8	30.3	29.8	29.4	29.0	28.7	28.4	28.2
350402	0	21.2	21.2	21.1	21.1	21.1	21.1	21.1	21.1	21.1	21.1	21.1
350423	1	17.7	17.9	18.0	18.1	18.2	18.3	18.4	18.5	18.6	18.7	18.7
360102	0	11.2	11.2	11.2	11.2	11.2	11.2	11.2	11.2	11.2	11.2	11.2

Table 9.9 (continued)

Id	County	2010 (%)	2011 (%)	2012 (%)	2013 (%)	2014 (%)	2015 (%)	2016 (%)	2017 (%)	2018 (%)	2019 (%)	2020 (%)
360122	1	11.2	10.7	10.3	9.9	9.6	9.4	9.2	9.0	8.8	8.6	8.5
360702	0	6.3	6.4	6.4	6.5	6.5	6.6	6.6	6.7	6.7	6.8	6.8
360722	1	8.0	8.0	7.9	7.9	7.9	7.9	7.8	7.8	7.8	7.8	7.8
370102	0	11.7	11.7	11.8	11.9	11.9	11.9	12.0	12.0	12.0	12.1	12.1
370124	1	13.5	13.6	13.6	13.6	13.6	13.7	13.7	13.7	13.7	13.7	13.8
370602	0	11.2	11.4	11.5	11.6	11.8	11.9	12.0	12.1	12.1	12.2	12.3
370682	1	28.9	28.3	27.8	27.3	26.9	26.6	26.2	26.0	25.7	25.5	25.3
410102	0	7.7	7.8	7.9	7.9	8.0	8.1	8.1	8.2	8.2	8.2	8.3
410122	1	5.7	5.8	5.8	5.9	6.0	6.0	6.1	6.1	6.2	6.2	6.2
410302	0	7.4	7.3	7.2	7.2	7.2	7.1	7.1	7.1	7.1	7.0	7.0
410322	1	8.4	8.4	8.4	8.4	8.4	8.4	8.4	8.4	8.4	8.4	8.4
420102	0	7.7	7.7	7.6	7.6	7.6	7.5	7.5	7.5	7.5	7.5	7.4
420111	0	11.3	11.3	11.4	11.4	11.4	11.4	11.5	11.5	11.5	11.5	11.5
420502	0	31.9	31.6	31.3	31.1	31.0	30.8	30.7	30.6	30.4	30.3	30.3
420525	1	7.9	7.8	7.8	7.7	7.7	7.6	7.6	7.6	7.5	7.5	7.5
430102	0	2.8	2.7	2.7	2.7	2.7	2.7	2.7	2.7	2.7	2.7	2.7
430122	1	6.7	6.5	6.4	6.2	6.1	6.0	5.9	5.8	5.7	5.7	5.6
430412	0	3.7	3.6	3.6	3.6	3.6	3.6	3.6	3.5	3.5	3.5	3.5
430422	1	15.4	15.2	15.0	14.8	14.6	14.5	14.3	14.2	14.1	14.0	13.9
440103	0	10.3	10.2	10.2	10.2	10.2	10.2	10.2	10.2	10.2	10.1	10.1
440104	0	15.8	15.7	15.7	15.6	15.6	15.6	15.5	15.5	15.5	15.5	15.4
440106	0	9.5	9.6	9.7	9.8	9.9	10.0	10.0	10.1	10.1	10.2	10.2
440183	1	14.8	14.7	14.6	14.5	14.4	14.4	14.3	14.3	14.2	14.2	14.1
440507	0	30.1	29.8	29.6	29.4	29.2	29.1	28.9	28.8	28.7	28.6	28.5
440523	1	15.9	16.1	16.2	16.3	16.3	16.4	16.5	16.6	16.6	16.7	16.7
450102	0	8.4	8.5	8.5	8.6	8.7	8.7	8.7	8.8	8.8	8.8	8.9
450122	1	11.0	11.0	11.1	11.1	11.2	11.2	11.2	11.2	11.3	11.3	11.3

Table 9.9 (continued)

Id	County	2010 (%)	2011 (%)	2012 (%)	2013 (%)	2014 (%)	2015 (%)	2016 (%)	2017 (%)	2018 (%)	2019 (%)	2020 (%)
450302	0	8.2	8.2	8.3	8.3	8.3	8.3	8.3	8.3	8.3	8.3	8.3
450322	1	8.2	8.2	8.1	8.1	8.1	8.1	8.0	8.0	8.0	8.0	8.0
460105	0	14.8	14.9	15.0	15.1	15.1	15.2	15.3	15.3	15.4	15.4	15.5
469001	1	3.6	3.6	3.5	3.5	3.5	3.5	3.4	3.4	3.4	3.4	3.4
469005	1	8.3	8.1	8.0	7.8	7.7	7.6	7.5	7.4	7.4	7.3	7.2
469033	1	5.4	5.4	5.4	5.4	5.4	5.4	5.4	5.4	5.4	5.4	5.4
500102	0	9.2	9.2	9.2	9.2	9.2	9.2	9.2	9.2	9.2	9.2	9.2
500222	1	11.2	11.2	11.1	11.1	11.0	11.0	11.0	10.9	10.9	10.9	10.9
510104	0	2.8	2.7	2.7	2.7	2.6	2.6	2.6	2.6	2.5	2.5	2.5
510122	1	4.7	4.7	4.7	4.6	4.6	4.6	4.5	4.5	4.5	4.5	4.5
510302	0	14.5	14.6	14.6	14.6	14.7	14.7	14.7	14.8	14.8	14.8	14.8
510322	1	12.2	12.1	12.1	12.0	12.0	11.9	11.9	11.8	11.8	11.7	11.7
520102	0	3.1	3.2	3.2	3.2	3.3	3.3	3.3	3.4	3.4	3.4	3.4
520122	1	3.5	3.4	3.4	3.3	3.3	3.3	3.3	3.2	3.2	3.2	3.2
520203	0	7.4	7.3	7.2	7.1	7.1	7.0	7.0	6.9	6.9	6.8	6.8
520221	1	5.1	5.1	5.2	5.2	5.3	5.3	5.3	5.4	5.4	5.4	5.5
530102	0	2.8	2.9	3.0	3.0	3.1	3.2	3.2	3.3	3.3	3.4	3.4
530122	1	3.7	3.7	3.6	3.6	3.6	3.6	3.6	3.6	3.6	3.6	3.6
530502	0	4.5	4.6	4.6	4.6	4.6	4.6	4.6	4.6	4.6	4.6	4.6
530522	1	4.2	4.1	4.0	3.9	3.8	3.8	3.8	3.7	3.7	3.6	3.6
540102	0	3.5	3.5	3.6	3.6	3.6	3.6	3.7	3.7	3.7	3.7	3.7
540122	1	1.9	1.9	1.9	1.9	1.9	1.9	1.9	1.9	1.8	1.8	1.8
542122	1	3.3	3.3	3.3	3.3	3.3	3.3	3.2	3.2	3.2	3.2	3.2
542124	1	2.2	2.2	2.2	2.2	2.2	2.1	2.1	2.1	2.1	2.1	2.1
610102	0	8.6	8.6	8.7	8.7	8.7	8.7	8.7	8.7	8.7	8.7	8.7
610122	1	14.4	14.3	14.2	14.2	14.1	14.1	14.0	14.0	13.9	13.9	13.9
610302	0	14.4	14.4	14.4	14.4	14.5	14.5	14.5	14.5	14.5	14.5	14.5

Table 9.9 (continued)

Id	County	2010 (%)	2011 (%)	2012 (%)	2013 (%)	2014 (%)	2015 (%)	2016 (%)	2017 (%)	2018 (%)	2019 (%)	2020 (%)
610322	1	13.3	13.2	13.1	13.1	13.0	13.0	12.9	12.9	12.8	12.8	12.8
620102	0	6.4	6.5	6.5	6.6	6.6	6.7	6.7	6.8	6.8	6.8	6.9
620122	1	5.0	5.0	5.0	4.9	4.9	4.9	4.9	4.9	4.9	4.9	4.9
620502	0	5.0	5.1	5.2	5.2	5.3	5.4	5.4	5.5	5.5	5.6	5.6
620522	1	6.4	6.5	6.6	6.7	6.7	6.8	6.9	6.9	7.0	7.0	7.1
630102	0	14.2	14.2	14.2	14.1	14.1	14.1	14.1	14.1	14.1	14.1	14.1
630121	1	19.1	17.5	16.3	15.3	14.6	14.0	13.5	13.0	12.6	12.3	12.0
632802	1	2.5	2.4	2.4	2.4	2.4	2.4	2.4	2.4	2.4	2.4	2.4
632822	1	3.6	3.6	3.6	3.6	3.6	3.6	3.6	3.5	3.5	3.5	3.5
640104	0	10.9	11.2	11.4	11.6	11.8	11.9	12.1	12.2	12.3	12.4	12.5
640122	1	7.0	7.0	7.0	7.0	7.0	7.0	7.0	7.0	7.0	7.0	7.0
640402	0	13.6	13.4	13.2	13.0	12.9	12.8	12.7	12.6	12.5	12.4	12.4
640422	1	16.0	15.6	15.2	14.9	14.7	14.4	14.2	14.1	13.9	13.8	13.6
650102	0	7.2	7.3	7.3	7.4	7.5	7.5	7.6	7.6	7.7	7.7	7.8
650121	1	4.0	3.9	3.9	3.8	3.7	3.6	3.6	3.5	3.4	3.4	3.3
652101	1	8.0	8.0	7.9	7.9	7.8	7.8	7.7	7.7	7.7	7.7	7.6
652122	1	5.1	5.1	5.0	5.0	5.0	4.9	4.9	4.9	4.9	4.8	4.8

Table 9.10 25 % LPT revenue as ratio of education expenditure 1998–2007

Id	County	1998 (%)	1999 (%)	2000 (%)	2001 (%)	2002 (%)	2003 (%)	2004 (%)	2005 (%)	2006 (%)	2007 (%)
110102	0	21	20	22	23	23	27	30	33	37	20
110105	0	25	24	26	27	28	32	37	39	32	22
110108	0	31	30	29	30	29	32	34	35	36	28
110228	1	28	26	23	26	25	27	28	30	32	24
120101	0	21	20	20	16	18	19	18	16	15	12
120102	0	31	31	29	25	27	27	27	25	27	12
120104	0	32	32	33	32	30	31	30	30	31	27
120223	1	30	32	33	29	28	29	25	25	26	12
130102	0	17	15	14	13	11	11	9	8	8	6
130123	1	12	11	10	8	8	8	8	8	8	8
130302	0	10	9	8	7	8	9	8	8	9	9
130322	1	16	13	11	11	11	10	10	10	12	8
140106	0	32	32	33	31	35	34	24	22	20	17
140122	1	14	12	11	12	12	12	10	11	11	9
140502	0	16	17	16	18	17	16	7	20	19	16
140522	1	13	13	10	9	10	10	13	9	9	8
150102	0	25	18	13	12	12	10	11	11	11	8
150122	1	13	13	12	10	9	8	7	6	7	5
150402	0	16	18	14	12	12	13	13	14	12	12
150422	1	23	23	21	15	13	13	12	14	13	8
210102	0	14	13	14	13	14	16	13	11	11	13
210122	1	19	21	22	22	25	25	24	25	25	22
210202	0	18	19	22	22	23	23	17	19	18	16
210224	1	14	14	11	12	11	12	13	9	12	9
220102	0		25	24	23	30	28	35	28	27	17
220122	1	25	24	22	22	24	23	21	21	20	18
220502	0		42	39	40	50	61	58	61	48	38

Table 9.10 (continued)

Id	County	1998 (%)	1999 (%)	2000 (%)	2001 (%)	2002 (%)	2003 (%)	2004 (%)	2005 (%)	2006 (%)	2007 (%)
220523	1	23	22	23	24	21	24	22	24	25	15
230102	0	15	12	12	10	5	5	10	11	12	11
230125	1	19	21	19	18	6	6	16	19	17	15
230202	0			20	16	16	15	17	18	18	11
230221	1	27	28	35	23	20	24	23	17	19	16
310101	0	13	16	19	19	17	17	16	17	18	18
310103	0	15	18	21	16	16	16	15	15	15	15
310104	0	24	30	34	26	31	35	35	32	32	30
310110	0	31	39	44	43	38	40	39	38	38	41
310230	1	33	40	41	34	31	32	37	37	31	31
320102	0		11	10	9	11	12	12	14	15	15
320124	1	18	16	14	13	15	15	17	16	18	14
320302	0		28	37	34	38	44	43	58	74	47
320322	1	23	25	27	25	27	32	32	32	35	21
330102	0		35	19	16	14	13	13	13	13	13
330122	1	24	23	23	16	21	23	19	17	19	20
330302	0		28	27	24	28	29	30	33	36	29
330322	1	22	21	22	17	17	14	16	13	15	16
340102	0		19			11	14	12	15	12	11
340122	1	17	12	10	8	9	9	7	7	8	7
340202	0					9	10	5	7	3	4
340222	1	16	15	11	9	9	9	6	7	10	11
350102	0		19	21	17	23	25	28	25	27	24
350122	1	16	16	17	16	25	20	24	24	21	19
350402	0		25	26	24	25	28	24	29	30	22
350423	1	12	15	16	15	17	17	19	22	21	18
360102	0	22	27	22	24	25	26	21	26	26	20

Table 9.10 (continued)

Id	County	1998 (%)	1999 (%)	2000 (%)	2001 (%)	2002 (%)	2003 (%)	2004 (%)	2005 (%)	2006 (%)	2007 (%)
360122	1	17	15	15	14	11	12	11	10	10	8
360702	0		22	19	21	21	22	23	24	23	15
360722	1		19	18	14	14	13	13	13	13	12
370102	0	18	20	18	17	18	20	21	21	24	16
370124	1	18	21	21	19	21	23	21	21	21	16
370602	0	13	16	17	17	18	19	19	15	15	13
370682	1	21	25	23	19	19	19	18	19	20	20
410102	0		17	10	10	10	12	13	16	16	15
410122	1	17	16	16	13	13	14	12	12	11	9
410302	0		11	11	12	11	13	12	11	15	11
410322	1	10	10	10	9	8	9	8	10	10	8
420102	0		16	14	8	9	9	9	9	9	8
420111	0		18	17	14	17	19	20	23	22	18
420502	0		59	47	62	44	44	43	43	23	24
420525	1	23	24	24	20	19	18	12	14	12	11
430102	0	20	21	21	20	12	9	6	6	6	4
430122	1	19	18	20	14	13	12	9	13	13	9
430412	0	9	10	9	10	8	9	8	10	10	7
430422	1	36	34	32	25	14	15	16	20	21	16
440103	0		29	22	14	15	18	20	16	18	15
440104	0		25	19	12	13	15	15	18	21	17
440106	0		17	16	15	15	16	16	14	15	14
440183	1	35	29	31	23	22	23	24	20	19	13
440507	0		15	18	16	17	25	24	23	24	21
440523	1	23	24	21	21	18	22	25	25	27	26
450102	0			32	26	13	10	9	13	12	13
450122	1	13	11	10	11	12	13	12	12	10	10

Table 9.10 (continued)

Id	County	1998 (%)	1999 (%)	2000 (%)	2001 (%)	2002 (%)	2003 (%)	2004 (%)	2005 (%)	2006 (%)	2007 (%)
450302	0			10	9	7	8	8	8	8	9
450322	1	13	11	11	9	9	8	7	7	7	7
460105	0	16	14	11	13	12	12	11	12	12	12
469001	1	11	13	10	8	9	7	8	7	7	7
469005	1	12	19	19	17	13	13	11	9	9	9
469033	1	21	17	11	16	15	16	12	10	10	2
500102	0	21	20	20	17	16	17	18	22	21	13
500222	1	22	21	23	18	17	17	18	21	19	16
510104	0	11	19	10	8	8	7	7	8	7	4
510122	1	8	9	10	8	7	8	8	9	7	5
510302	0	35	39	40	31	25	27	27	32	30	22
510322	1	28	29	32	21	19	20	20	20	16	13
520102	0	14	13	11	10	10	10	9	9	6	5
520122	1	9	8	8	6	7	6	6	6	6	5
520203	0	13	15	13	10	10	10	8	6	8	7
520221	1	15	16	13	11	11	11	9	8	8	7
530102	0	6	6	5	5	5	6	7	6	7	6
530122	1	7	7	6	7	6	6	6	6	5	5
530502	0				7	7	7	6	7	7	7
530522	1				6	6	5	5	5	5	5
540102	0		1	5	4	4	4	4	4	4	3
540122	1		4	4	3	2	2	1	1	2	1
542122	1		9	9	9	6	6	5	3	4	3
542124	1		6	7	5	3	3	3	2	2	1
610102	0	11	13	15	13	14	16	16	16	9	8
610122	1	16	17	16	14	15	15	16	17	14	13
610302	0	19	21	18	15	17	19	18	15	14	8

Table 9.10 (continued)

Id	County	1998 (%)	1999 (%)	2000 (%)	2001 (%)	2002 (%)	2003 (%)	2004 (%)	2005 (%)	2006 (%)	2007 (%)
610322	1	23	23	18	14	14	15	16	14	11	9
620102	0	10	11	10	9	11	6	6	10	11	7
620122	1	8	6	6	6	6	5	5	5	5	4
620502	0	14	14	13	12	13	11	11	11	10	8
620522	1	17	16	14	13	13	12	12	12	10	8
630102	0	21	27	28	20	23	25	24	22	20	20
630121	1	12	12	12	10	9	9	9	9	8	8
632802	1	6	6	7	5	5	5	5	5	6	4
632822	1	11	13	13	7	6	6	9	9	8	5
640104	0		28	16	25	24	13	13	13	14	11
640122	1	11	13	10	10	9	10	10	10	9	7
640402	0	11	12	10	9	9	11	11	10	12	10
640422	1	12	12	11	10	11	12	12	11	11	8
650102	0		14	13	14	16	16	12	16	16	10
650121	1	11	9	9	8	5	6	6	7	6	4
652101	1	13	12	11	9	9	10	10	9	8	7
652122	1	13	10	9	8	9	9	9	9	8	6
Average		18	19	18	16	16	16	16	16	16	13

Table 9.11 25 % LPT revenue as ratio of health expenditure 2003–2007

Id	County	2003 (%)	2004 (%)	2005 (%)	2006 (%)	2007 (%)
110102	0	37	42	42	33	31
110105	0	70	118	112	97	65
110108	0	96	126	142	110	80
110228	1	105	122	92	106	71
120101	0	76	57	68	62	53
120102	0	123	129	107	131	54
120104	0	132	135	114	119	102
120223	1	151	125	127	114	48
130102	0	69	75	67	102	49
130123	1	107	165	127	52	38
130302	0	81	137	141	155	42
130322	1	96	61	51	49	30
140106	0	49	43	46	53	48
140122	1	54	43	50	43	36
140502	0	75	23	76	70	56
140522	1	51	63	53	39	36
150102	0	52	69	57	62	55
150122	1	30	32	24	22	32
150402	0	45	45	58	54	59
150422	1	89	147	118	106	52
210102	0	101	96	58	78	47
210122	1	329	193	141	121	113
210202	0	71	62	64	85	70
210224	1	33	54	48	31	38
220102	0	114	123	102	104	54
220122	1	245	217	214	115	91
220502	0	134	144	149	145	114
220523	1	169	190	198	88	57
230102	0	40	92	79	57	44
230125	1	91	245	251	141	86
230202	0	186	179	186	193	155
230221	1	193	175	176	164	72
310101	0	104	108	111	119	86
310103	0	98	95	89	97	50
310104	0	129	120	174	185	97
310110	0	357	368	376	342	138
310230	1	124	109	108	86	70
320102	0	44	52	58	64	59
320124	1	70	77	82	91	62
320302	0	207	224	279	369	482
320322	1	183	134	158	114	99
330102	0	39	45	48	52	60
330122	1	82	63	57	63	56
330302	0	91	91	99	115	70
330322	1	63	68	49	44	51
340102	0	62	68	74	87	75
340122	1	60	68	63	45	44
340202	0	76	46	54	26	18

Table 9.11 (continued)

Id	County	2003 (%)	2004 (%)	2005 (%)	2006 (%)	2007 (%)
340222	1	44	31	26	25	38
350102	0	113	103	136	161	125
350122	1	154	171	182	107	102
350402	0	91	87	90	115	101
350423	1	93	93	96	118	61
360102	0	67	41	65	64	42
360122	1	45	43	39	22	22
360702	0	90	68	64	62	30
360722	1	150	105	87	85	34
370102	0	86	79	68	58	67
370124	1	67	62	65	67	51
370602	0	100	87	83	90	70
370682	1	217	252	223	197	89
410102	0	44	47	36	55	53
410122	1	134	118	92	47	33
410302	0	51	55	43	51	34
410322	1	180	130	132	119	46
420102	0	110	125	99	85	37
420111	0	64	72	68	67	66
420502	0	167	157	200	193	177
420525	1	57	46	48	47	39
430102	0	45	36	32	31	22
430122	1	47	38	47	29	24
430412	0	52	51	40	15	19
430422	1	246	202	224	130	65
440103	0	45	46	44	50	43
440104	0	43	34	54	51	55
440106	0	58	47	38	43	41
440183	1	145	125	87	104	77
440507	0	227	292	168	180	123
440523	1	63	86	105	85	74
450102	0	34	41	52	51	55
450122	1	60	69	52	37	34
450302	0	37	39	76	62	57
450322	1	51	54	54	57	36
460105	0	58	49	48	44	39
469001	1	45	37	37	32	20
469005	1	106	145	108	63	34
469033	1	108	102	52	38	6
500102	0	50	51	61	73	42
500222	1	120	107	103	83	59
510104	0	28	26	28	36	20
510122	1	20	17	19	17	15
510302	0	56	45	81	78	42
510322	1	155	217	73	52	39
520102	0	17	19	17	20	21
520122	1	16	19	18	17	13
520203	0	46	44	38	27	23

Table 9.11 (continued)

Id	County	2003 (%)	2004 (%)	2005 (%)	2006 (%)	2007 (%)
520221	1	46	49	45	29	21
530102	0	13	19	15	15	14
530122	1	41	53	49	27	20
530502	0	35	32	33	20	19
530522	1	25	27	25	16	14
540102	0	22	23	27	20	18
540122	1	8	7	5	6	5
542122	1	12	11	7	8	7
542124	1	7	7	6	6	5
610102	0	26	43	33	35	31
610122	1	84	80	88	80	40
610302	0	94	98	71	66	48
610322	1	117	128	134	90	57
620102	0	17	17	30	32	16
620122	1	25	27	27	24	19
620502	0	70	75	81	74	30
620522	1	101	116	127	106	31
630102	0	148	66	102	83	67
630121	1	42	35	33	22	18
632802	1	73	33	39	70	25
632822	1	15	22	21	21	13
640104	0	129	116	124	139	129
640122	1	60	73	71	89	50
640402	0	89	90	78	44	37
640422	1	84	78	80	65	37
650102	0	167	154	130	132	131
650121	1	28	27	22	23	19
652101	1	43	55	29	39	27
652122	1	28	26	22	29	18
Average		87	87	84	76	55

Table 9.12 25 % LPT revenue as ratio of public safety expenditure 1995–2007

Id	1995 (%)	1996 (%)	1997 (%)	1998 (%)	1999 (%)	2000 (%)	2001 (%)	2002 (%)	2003 (%)	2004 (%)	2005 (%)	2006 (%)	2007 (%)
110102	82	64	71	86	58	56	52	58	59	59	57	63	54
110105	104	104	98	95	75	53	77	80	77	73	68	55	40
110108	115	49	95	118	100	83	71	74	79	85	76	84	63
110228	109	115	134	150	101	102	90	79	83	70	72	84	74
120101	79	86	89	93	65	64	48	57	58	55	45	43	35
120102	140	121	142	152	113	106	88	92	98	91	84	77	34
120104	132		121	132	135	104	129	107	105	98	80	72	51
120223	157	140	138	159	158	146	104	105	96	90	93	100	50
130102	40	36	35	33	30	28	24	22	27	22	24	67	50
130123	72	68	54	45	49	45	36	39	35	36	37	40	38
130302	35	39	33	34	28	27	24	26	27	27	29	30	25
130322	72	89	93	102	59	58	48	52	49	42	39	38	31
140106	45	33	41	28	33	36	34	39	44	40	58	118	79
140122	40	32	37	41	44	36	42	54	54	43	30	29	24
140502	46	41	38	37	48	49	41	48	45	37	102	78	95
140522	82	58	69	55	56	51	47	58	52	57	34	32	39
150102	137	121	134	110	100	85	101	111	102	104	85	100	101
150122	52	49	53	60	64	61	39	56	42	36	35	38	30
150402	28	25	32	35	37	38	35	41	46	38	36	39	40
150422	91	99	126	141	122	102	85	72	81	72	66	68	65
210102	33	30	35	31	29	25	25	27	27	25	24	20	27
210122	90	96	79	124	134	127	128	140	132	135	116	128	93
210202	146	71	112	97	92	120	97	94	98	93	79	81	38
210224	31	28	39	37	36	34	33	38	48	36	28	29	27
220102					290	228	199	197	180	85	112	127	101
220122	148	164	132	116	126	137	147	137	161	144	151	111	95
220502					70	61	63	84	85	76	66	63	60

Table 9.12 (continued)

Id	1995 (%)	1996 (%)	1997 (%)	1998 (%)	1999 (%)	2000 (%)	2001 (%)	2002 (%)	2003 (%)	2004 (%)	2005 (%)	2006 (%)	2007 (%)
220523	120	103	71	71	81	78	74	82	80	80	73	69	51
230102	56	43	44	35	34	37	30	17	16	36	33	38	31
230125	130	131	99	81	94	90	83	35	30	103	104	98	69
230202						213	207	176	102	83	169	165	138
230221	123	125	110	138	120	135	123	123	113	123	117	111	97
310101	22	26	22	23	26	29	39	31	30	29	30	31	32
310103	45	37	38	38	43	43	36	32	34	30	30	32	22
310104	96	89	90	77	85	96	60	62	60	51	51	51	57
310110	92	83	86	89	107	117	98	82	89	67	70	75	64
310230	133	117	136	143	167	189	154	177	168	139	128	117	106
320102					102	81	55	47	50	45	40	45	40
320124	57	42	58	62	92	60	58	44	40	35	37	46	47
320302					134	137	137	140	69	98	113	113	144
320322	158	156	155	140	170	159	157	167	179	134	137	141	128
330102					51	52	33	36	34	33	29	35	36
330122	123	88	93	104	101	69	56	71	63	56	48	54	53
330302					48	54	60	63	63	73	78	86	37
330322	51	43	45	59	52	49	40	48	47	40	33	35	38
340102					84			66	80	46	62	85	48
340122	75	74	77	59	53	59	45	49	55	34	38	43	51
340202								41	43	24	16	21	24
340222	84	99	93	95	48	44	40	39	38	29	33	35	39
350102					104	128	134	180	166	117	92	108	122
350122	81	70	59	73	55	55	57	83	80	87	81	97	64
350402					95	104	99	104	124	120	114	141	114
350423	30	25	34	40	47	51	52	64	66	64	74	70	55
360102	71	64	66	75	84	76	61	59	60	41	24	16	17

Table 9.12 (continued)

Id	1995 (%)	1996 (%)	1997 (%)	1998 (%)	1999 (%)	2000 (%)	2001 (%)	2002 (%)	2003 (%)	2004 (%)	2005 (%)	2006 (%)	2007 (%)
360122	89	42	88	65	42	46	33	35	40	35	30	26	24
360702					148	156	138	98	102	86	67	74	74
360722					47	49	51	49	52	39	50	53	42
370102	70	58	52	48	41	44	33	30	29	31	36	29	25
370124	146	117	108	99	100	92	52	67	71	58	66	68	67
370602	53	46	54	45	44	48	50	52	58	60	145	139	53
370682	186	140	165	140	131	118	126	124	123	123	79	86	92
410102					72	62	61	59	56	47	46	53	30
410122	55	49	52	35	36	34	43	49	43	46	38	34	31
410302					29	45	54	40	38	34	39	35	31
410322	76	57	35	42	46	37	50	44	40	39	34	33	38
420102					36	33	29	21	23	17	17	17	14
420111					27	23	21	24	27	27	33	35	31
420502					139	134	182	186	230	218	187	140	121
420525	90	76	79	71	70	61	50	79	58	44	38	39	37
430102		34	34	59	47	51	30	40	29	31	24	23	17
430122	106	68	67	91	92	95	91	60	38	38	42	32	27
430412	22	21	24	18	14	14	12	14	13	13	13	10	11
430422	166	216	78	156	90	93	65	66	60	56	56	59	61
440103					21	18	17	17	20	21	17	17	18
440104					15	14	12	11	14	14	18	17	19
440106					14	15	15	13	13	12	11	13	13
440183	60	57	50	55	47	56	55	60	47	41	28	32	27
440507					37	37	45	105	258	191	113	118	126
440523	60	57	64	66	38	70	40	42	48	55	57	53	50
450102						9	8	13	11	13	22	20	19
450122	61	53	63	54	48	44	50	46	46	54	44	50	51

Table 9.12 (continued)

Id	1995 (%)	1996 (%)	1997 (%)	1998 (%)	1999 (%)	2000 (%)	2001 (%)	2002 (%)	2003 (%)	2004 (%)	2005 (%)	2006 (%)	2007 (%)
450302						50	37	43	26	23	24	32	20
450322	56	42	45	47	65	53	41	48	35	42	43	48	25
460105		75	79	71	67	52	60	52	108	112	92	89	69
469001	37	36	36	35	33	29	29	36	29	24	20	18	18
469005	71	69	68	66	83	74	72	50	53	45	36	37	36
469033	148	198	190	153	112	82	79	68	62	71	55	55	9
500102				47	40	42	44	38	40	42	49	55	39
500222			96	77	124	121	82	94	83	78	88	98	69
510104	9	12	11	14	27	13	13	11	7	7	7	7	6
510122	32	16	26	21	23	21	28	26	20	21	20	15	13
510302	12	13	22	28	28	38	40	31	26	23	35	39	32
510322	77	62	91	156	137	175	137	148	86	93	78	83	66
520102	28	22	24	23	23	18	17	13	13	10	8	8	9
520122		52	40	34	45	36	30	32	27	22	20	23	21
520203	79	63	57	52	59	54	49	46	47	44	43	46	42
520221	87	66	69	63	58	48	40	52	48	44	40	39	42
530102	6	7	7	7	6	5	5	5	5	6	7	7	7
530122	18	17	19	22	24	22	20	19	21	22	17	17	14
530502							42	33	28	29	29	25	23
530522							33	29	27	26	22	20	18
540102		15			7	30	20	18	17	13	11	17	11
540122		31			24	24	17	13	13	12	10	9	7
542122		39			33	31	30	23	18	17	14	13	12
542124		34			26	22	20	16	14	12	11	10	8
610102	19	14	13	11	20	13	13	15	13	17	15	14	14
610122	100	98	94	81	91	78	65	69	69	49	67	67	59
610302	104	83	91	79	131	114	122	137	180	159	110	147	102

Table 9.12 (continued)

Id	1995 (%)	1996 (%)	1997 (%)	1998 (%)	1999 (%)	2000 (%)	2001 (%)	2002 (%)	2003 (%)	2004 (%)	2005 (%)	2006 (%)	2007 (%)
610322	118	129	174	146	175	169	126	134	139	150	151	125	85
620102	30	25	28	28	27	28	25	26	15	14	23	23	18
620122	48	42	44	45	43	46	37	42	43	48	41	34	37
620502	81	55	76	72	70	74	70	78	97	93	80	59	52
620522	116	86	103	111	123	111	92	116	94	71	65	101	74
630102	28	27	38	36	36	38	32	111	126	120	96	93	74
630121	73	82	75	82	75	80	69	81	58	64	64	57	54
632802	21	21	23	25	39	27	25	23	29	18	21	20	12
632822	21	29	31	34	35	33	25	23	24	34	32	26	17
640104					103	84	76	52	64	54	61	66	69
640122	63	51	49	55	57	49	46	48	42	42	40	42	29
640402	150	130	127	124	129	98	90	84	143	250	245	285	194
640422	147	153	146	155	163	109	102	98	116	113	110	113	89
650102					77	73	77	63	71	72	74	61	48
650121	29	38	28	30	31	34	20	15	17	15	16	21	16
652101	57	60	39	42	49	43	50	44	48	44	37	33	26
652122	84	71	62	50	52	43	37	38	45	35	31	28	26
Average	78	67	71	72	70	67	61	62	63	59	57	58	48

Table 9.13 25 % LPT revenue as ratio of public construction expenditure 1995–2006

Id	1995 (%)	1996 (%)	1997 (%)	1998 (%)	1999 (%)	2000 (%)	2001 (%)	2002 (%)	2003 (%)	2004 (%)	2005 (%)	2006 (%)
110102	121	58	34	38	36	27	21	26	29	42	35	42
110105	423	100	86	76	76	124	72	161	264	208	96	87
110108	67	23	47	33	23	28	30	37	44	49	47	60
110228			212	209	151	60	42	39	49	32	35	41
120101	64	80	179	103	40	32	63	26	29	31	22	29
120102			989									
120104			866	783	343						·869	329
120223		439							595			
130102		744	648	584				162	54	27	42	541
130123	354	132	137	284	32	58	235	51	32	70	309	54
130302						568			155	58	121	193
130322		330						351	220	228	111	156
140106						171				550	176	163
140122	79	189	456	68	284	211	189			166	459	523
140502												
140522												
150102	54	45	72	49	61	60	36	29	26	60	61	77
150122	269	258	91	106	53	15	16	16	8	14	3	4
150402	421	296	526	103	416	95	65	68	37	93	65	55
150422			557	254	35	19	24	15	10	17	19	25
210102								306				
210122												
210202	57	77	151	137	96	244	82	124	51	37	27	32
210224	11	69	32	18	22	15	10	28	18	63	12	11
220102					145	304	553	362	103	96	153	449
220122									165	136	171	74
220502					214				402	533	71	92
220523									70	120	61	35

Table 9.13 (continued)

Id	1995 (%)	1996 (%)	1997 (%)	1998 (%)	1999 (%)	2000 (%)	2001 (%)	2002 (%)	2003 (%)	2004 (%)	2005 (%)	2006 (%)
230102											141	777
230125	340	291										212
230202												
230221							465					395
310101	12	12	12	7	10	10	22	23	21	14	11	12
310103	171	164	119	116	107	102	49	30	28	21	16	17
310104	126	87	29	36	51	56	42	27	15	13	12	14
310110	146	178	192	213	330	442	433	365	56	42	36	29
310230	60	116	196	502	474	654	144	162	433	246	149	77
320102					30	31	25	23	23	22	29	39
320124				834	128	94	72	319	449	431	143	294
320302												
320322								860	343		391	
330102					464	443	753					
330122		457	621			428	518	47	33	42	67	48
330302					896		116	158	168	379	83	436
330322	162	93	186	189	275	270	87	40	67	37	47	62
340102					41			19	28	29	6	15
340122		74	69	47	31	43	596	338	129	66	30	29
340202								27	43	43	96	31
340222	28	28	47	163	185	574	215	139	86	46	61	29
350102					377	795				216	49	109
350122	39	203	712									
350402									29	33	49	99
350423			121									
360102	112	168	200		61	64	82	27	32	37	30	40
360122	507	639	297	345	9	12	25	17	21	26	36	25
360702					677	468	476	249	50	23	32	36

Table 9.13 (continued)

Id	1995 (%)	1996 (%)	1997 (%)	1998 (%)	1999 (%)	2000 (%)	2001 (%)	2002 (%)	2003 (%)	2004 (%)	2005 (%)	2006 (%)
360722					78	119	71	38	43	86	154	47
370102												
370124								935				
370602												
370682												
410102					66	28	55	92		427	42	42
410122	365	267	335	238	167	309	142	44	28	38	28	29
410302							519		51	71	93	49
410322	912		854	70	59	109	26	37	72	75	24	16
420102												
420111												
420502												
420525												
430102		32	46	87	58	29	41	35	23	14	6	5
430122	253	80	97	869	244	828	303	107	47	17	26	36
430412												
430422												
440103					76	32	38	33	36	814	55	147
440104					24	15	26	25	45	123	141	141
440106					6	11	26	40	48	22	15	14
440183		740	804	716	965	876		439	224	207	112	80
440507										946		
440523	88	191	251	140	330	29	249	17	187		90	
450102						18	24	16	10	12	19	15
450122	369	72	245		895					223		
450302						92	65	21	19	16	14	17
450322							217	109	55	119	49	24
460105					190	45	27	52	348			
469001										267	99	107

Table 9.13 (continued)

Id	1995 (%)	1996 (%)	1997 (%)	1998 (%)	1999 (%)	2000 (%)	2001 (%)	2002 (%)	2003 (%)	2004 (%)	2005 (%)	2006 (%)
469005												
469033									65	100	105	67
500102				17	18	16	8	6	9	19	29	30
500222			570	319	592	535	93	10	174	101	70	93
510104	31	25	27	29	52	25	39	28	31	35	46	10
510122	184	289	197	73	13	12	18	74	63	57	56	59
510302	239	265	157	355		464				11		173
510322	896	788	743	512		791	106	147	72	67	53	56
520102	233			270							42	91
520122												
520203					674			895	184	153	114	137
520221												
530102	3	3	4	5	2	3	4	20	9	11	11	8
530122	242	541					64	153	169	75	103	28
530502							241	31	124	48	124	43
530522							39	14	28	54	41	24
540102					3	13	9	12	15	9	10	7
540122											17	18
542122												
542124												
610102												
610122												
610302												
610322												
620102	60	855	28	45	110	144	97	58	43	32	44	19
620122	107	33	59	124	74	20	17	25	24	17	30	31
620502	763	687		349	268	357	55	93	73	113	186	76
620522		492	188	253	528	425	34	71	76	100	52	53

Table 9.13 (continued)

Id	1995 (%)	1996 (%)	1997 (%)	1998 (%)	1999 (%)	2000 (%)	2001 (%)	2002 (%)	2003 (%)	2004 (%)	2005 (%)	2006 (%)
630102		403	281	127	235		176	267	680	340	144	124
630121		311				698	654		903	553	158	122
632802					101	100		88		6	5	21
632822									227	122	97	16
640104					75	26	150	102	144	105	219	184
640122						49	13	23	19	41	44	70
640402						25	16	13	27	35	22	29
640422						25	10	17	29	42	29	26
650102					23	187	73	186	227	48	50	41
650121	226	46	31	59	70	55	80	32	33	28	10	22
652101	866	152	162	91	84	62		57	79	79	121	97
652122	15	33	20	64	112	14	38	50	24	33	11	6
Average	237	243	265	215	193	193	136	124	114	121	84	94

The percentage larger than 1000 % were deleted as outliers
The averages were based on calculation without outliers
Full table is available on request

Table 9.14 Simulated LPT revenue 1995–2010 (in 10 thousand *Yuan*)

Id	County	1995	1996	1997	1998	1999	2000	2001	2002	2003	2004	2005	2006	2007	2008	2009	2010
110102	0	14,531	17,282	19,267	22,210	23,836	27,033	32,489	36,975	45,668	54,980	66,615	81,376	91,439	101,045	113,403	110,859
110105	0	25,382	30,845	34,439	41,046	44,956	52,680	64,156	73,890	92,076	118,971	151,518	186,696	211,657	235,827	265,734	261,542
110108	0	26,302	16,845	35,402	43,014	47,369	55,106	68,680	81,424	103,122	132,577	169,933	212,621	242,645	271,957	309,452	306,074
110228	1	7725	9188	10,115	12,089	12,974	14,556	17,684	19,700	24,339	30,393	37,435	45,689	50,739	55,621	61,694	59,023
120101	0	5697	6972	8426	8877	9896	11,106	10,543	13,053	15,117	17,356	18,150	19,294	22,615	26,774	29,738	33,829
120102	0	7358	9197	10,883	12,710	14,074	15,795	16,317	18,895	21,549	25,056	28,733	35,297	20,811	48,738	53,652	60,538
120104	0	8545		13,165	14,727	16,493	18,756	21,839	22,888	25,570	29,181	33,005	40,658	48,422	57,088	63,456	72,979
120223	1	5815	7269	8601	10,087	10,995	12,340	12,802	14,653	16,651	19,107	21,728	26,546	15,960	37,330	41,620	47,599
130102	0	1074	1428	1607	1775	1892	2078	2047	2385	2626	2941	3407	4044	4729	5742	6804	8271
130123	1	1768	1941	2169	2530	2601	2803	2251	2562	2788	3129	3587	4273	5027	6167	7375	9069
130302	0	1295	1648	1808	2042	2176	2271	2456	3036	3428	3950	4626	5563	6655	8237	9845	12,597
130322	1	1705	1977	2169	2397	2554	2609	2763	3227	3510	3925	4492	5318	6205	7562	8937	10,809
140106	0	2032	2217	2502	1785	1953	2200	2727	3628	4342	5037	5936	7067	8586	9987	11,522	13,533
140122	1	466	493	547	595	636	700	849	1095	1278	1444	1671	1965	2375	2756	3194	3776
140502	0	733	774	860	978	1136	1250	1636	2069	2511	2987	3579	4374	5443	6417	7541	9033
140522	1	1299	1372	1564	1700	1817	2000	2424	2977	3477	4861	4555	5342	6391	7312	8424	9910
150102	0	1033	1371	1787	2258	1807	1915	2189	2515	2944	3368	3978	4833	6223	7704	9272	10,993
150122	1	517	723	871	1047	1145	1174	1300	1501	1762	2046	2385	2858	3650	4448	5340	6262
150402	0	775	1066	1283	1597	1747	1853	2052	2374	2749	3163	3717	4504	6346	7778	9221	10,753
150422	1	1004	1332	1604	1928	2169	2162	2462	2783	3268	3691	4303	5182	6547	7918	9386	10,861
210102	0	4048	4852	5429	5590	6061	6787	7552	9186	10,512	12,044	13,522	15,995	19,889	23,599	27,771	35,699
210122	1	3213	3791	4241	4436	4907	5602	6233	7643	8624	9983	11,276	13,556	17,032	20,163	23,840	29,467
210202	0	2377	2805	3138	3283	3560	4094	4315	5285	5884	6689	7450	8874	11,119	13,352	15,781	19,399
210224	1	578	682	763	799	866	970	1079	1307	1473	1675	1581	1875	2333	2767	3258	3981
220102	0					4061	4491	5261	6779	7422	8313	9397	11,321	13,170	15,781	17,556	21,515
220122	1	5108	6590	7075	7235	7766	8449	9573	12,167	13,948	15,333	16,933	19,058	22,044	26,479	29,525	35,911
220502	0					2137	2283	2673	3441	3958	4350	4805	5724	6522	7743	8525	10,252

Table 9.14 (continued)

Id	County	1995	1996	1997	1998	1999	2000	2001	2002	2003	2004	2005	2006	2007	2008	2009	2010
220523	1	1719	2237	2380	2499	2565	2664	3105	3813	4411	4841	5321	6399	7304	8679	9531	11,454
230102	0	3382	3677	4337	4609	4832	5879	6082	3949	4170	9031	10,377	12,245	13,811	15,301	17,388	19,596
230125	1	2941	3197	3771	3875	4530	4912	5621	2527	2718	8350	9427	10,935	12,234	13,527	15,280	17,364
230202	0						2496	2765	3331	3542	3969	4498	5270	5865	6424	7197	8186
230221	1	2843	3091	3645	3941	4455	4590	5529	6747	7179	8119	9323	10,866	12,131	13,364	15,039	16,901
310101	0	6933	7924	7838	8329	11,096	13,482	34,968	39,024	46,545	52,301	58,934	67,706	76,034	88,156	98,195	91,592
310103	0	9657	11,152	11,456	11,993	17,106	20,224	18,829	20,608	24,705	27,729	31,180	35,291	39,113	45,008	50,091	46,324
310104	0	20,057	24,065	25,323	28,317	39,760	48,874	40,886	54,602	66,660	76,109	87,384	99,831	111,968	130,637	147,716	138,602
310110	0	26,248	31,401	32,558	36,646	49,931	60,671	66,708	66,434	81,377	92,717	106,502	121,205	135,232	156,978	177,036	166,101
310230	1	16,095	19,076	21,102	22,987	30,513	34,830	32,816	39,513	47,803	54,136	69,046	78,719	87,521	100,638	112,485	104,919
320102	0					3148	3404	3961	5222	6210	7628	9772	12,349	15,768	18,949	23,330	27,742
320124	1	2015	2332	2721	2967	3313	3404	3864	4908	5621	6633	8294	10,251	12,832	15,228	18,731	22,269
320302	0					1905	2213	2512	3252	3845	4588	7185	10,468	13,315	15,826	19,540	25,676
320322	1	5553	6426	7566	8323	9526	10,043	11,400	14,451	16,697	18,905	23,608	29,355	37,204	43,877	54,447	65,918
330102	0					3711	4041	4939	5925	7094	8192	9103	10,663	13,419	15,281	17,383	19,597
330122	1	2640	3000	3252	3999	4386	5051	6174	7430	8932	10,251	11,319	13,235	16,620	18,833	21,417	24,145
330302	0					5736	6567	9724	12,034	14,778	17,262	19,281	22,662	28,850	33,025	37,787	42,601
330322	1	812	923	1084	1300	1462	1642	2007	2344	2811	3203	3532	4150	5252	5962	6811	7679
340102	0					758			1320	1696	2052	2751	3524	4773	5749	7603	10,688
340122	1	2353	2890	2971	3244	3591	3733	3912	4216	4937	5457	6970	8823	11,757	13,910	16,716	20,413
340202	0								422	520	603	1156	1423	1913	2271	2775	8908
340222	1	1008	1215	1238	1339	1483	1561	1636	1809	2143	2354	3024	3764	4976	5862	7122	5298
350102	0					2717	3180	3988	5675	6989	8620	10,810	13,561	15,486	18,196	21,906	25,208
350122	1	1805	2253	3275	3594	3946	4619	5529	7123	8106	9385	11,359	13,798	16,249	19,472	23,418	27,372
350402	0					841	984	1178	1517	1775	2082	2544	3092	3653	4344	5238	6060
350423	1	414	509	728	799	970	1136	1360	1697	1944	2262	2740	3320	3864	4528	5441	6332
360102	0	913	1094	1159	1286	1744	1720	2121	2485	2869	2806	3544	4303	5593	6483	7595	8930

Table 9.14 (continued)

Id	County	1995	1996	1997	1998	1999	2000	2001	2002	2003	2004	2005	2006	2007	2008	2009	2010
360122	1	1278	1458	1602	1769	2061	2400	2632	2912	3310	3619	4463	5452	6892	7949	9216	11,061
360702	0					1490	1684	1925	2198	2717	3088	3760	4534	5795	7082	8321	9772
360722	1					2029	2293	2554	2901	3312	3681	4443	5415	7019	7925	9304	11,042
370102	0	2268	2667	2919	3209	3639	4185	4898	5760	6816	7765	9017	10,427	12,273	14,111	15,850	18,620
370124	1	1915	1986	2129	2358	2568	2843	3206	3740	4241	4757	5584	6522	7866	9352	107,19	12,800
370602	0	2570	2894	3223	3733	4281	4896	5788	6743	7801	8945	10,528	12,340	14,771	17,325	19,675	23,436
370682	1	4535	5107	5474	5829	6350	7028	7925	9200	10,364	11,468	13,396	15,475	18,605	22,062	25,217	30,017
410102	0					1556	1691	2311	2640	3121	3638	4445	5384	6886	8424	10,133	12,294
410122	1	1358	1580	1730	1859	2107	2265	2620	3331	3785	4329	5236	6333	8018	9832	10,133	13,913
410302	0					292	440	539	655	733	822	974	1171	1474	1801	2166	2628
410322	1	912	1062	1162	1249	1394	1522	1734	2162	2423	2761	3312	3953	4970	6016	7163	8539
420102	0					4047	4404	4688	5731	6178	6807	8202	9683	11,670	13,652	16,153	18,937
420111	0					3851	4124	4465	6151	7122	8333	10,903	13,328	15,070	16,981	19,731	22,604
420502	0					2415	2167	3125	3481	3864	4250	5200	6107	7378	8563	10,043	11,618
420525	1	1031	1131	1221	1195	1371	1468	1563	1845	1908	2088	2490	2882	3440	3974	4680	5420
430102	0		1059	1145	1302	1381	1498	1706	1960	2185	2481	3070	3544	4593	5248	6099	7025
430122	1	2668	2702	2709	3025	3207	3479	3786	4135	4455	4844	5891	6656	8225	6960	7674	8869
430412	0	173	183	191	210	223	242	267	295	319	349	423	481	615	684	819	951
430422	1	3465	3687	3854	4285	4543	4977	5546	5796	6299	6860	8422	9731	12,284	13,812	16,351	18,930
440103	0					7849	8468	9602	11,075	13,646	14,657	20,139	24,032	27,541	32,516	39,347	43,769
440104	0					6642	7140	7940	9058	11,062	11,790	32,882	39,237	45,269	53,567	64,990	72,181
440106	0					7397	8800	10,340	12,702	15,831	17,841	17,710	21,994	26,965	33,000	41,511	47,554
440183	1	7585	8581	9933	10,861	11,774	13,449	15,141	17,707	21,867	23,812	22,699	27,620	31,968	38,064	46,428	51,826
440507	0					2566	2989	3324	4048	8849	9767	10,090	12,344	14,494	17,498	21,563	24,464
440523	1	727	812	915	987	1057	1162	1293	1545	1908	2049	2069	2463	2827	3346	4068	4548
450102	0						439	522	852	870	941	2009	2309	3033	3634	4395	5440
450122	1	1800	1808	1893	2161	2220	2341	2654	3239	3495	3840	4496	5232	6945	8354	10,131	12,394
450302	0						402	468	539	593	651	757	870	1145	1355	1624	1991

Table 9.14 (continued)

Id	County	1995	1996	1997	1998	1999	2000	2001	2002	2003	2004	2005	2006	2007	2008	2009	2010
450322	1	1257	1243	1301	1486	1561	1646	1958	2261	2456	2752	3204	3707	4906	5880	7095	8896
460105	0		638	599	602	707	625	721	853	1837	1956	2215	2627	3191	3932	4564	6116
469001	1	484	491	461	463	598	573	661	740	805	854	965	1111	1341	1641	1887	2483
469005	1	2518	2552	2442	2454	2881	2762	3245	3698	3986	4214	4669	5482	6643	8228	9542	12,679
469033	1	2179	2258	2119	2176	2554	2345	2765	3170	3461	3744	4235	4918	1447	7440	8700	11,664
500102	0				4998	5538	6305	6915	8281	9371	11,126	14,880	17,609	19,402	22,373	27,000	32,168
500222	1			4378	4356	4783	5397	5972	7054	7979	9440	12,581	14,827	16,260	18,677	22,317	26,288
510104	0	667	928	973	1258	2618	1500	1669	1863	2011	2182	2671	3257	3942	4591	5625	7072
510122	1	1415	1503	2567	2957	2967	3395	3724	4119	4559	5036	6233	7566	9314	10,824	13,208	15,367
510302	0	325	371	540	723	803	947	1027	935	1001	1059	2305	2894	3544	4080	4852	5878
510322	1	1935	2208	3269	3806	4223	4777	5179	5728	6249	6760	6828	8435	10,425	12,166	14,816	17,870
520102	0	930	945	1031	1081	1280	1238	1428	1725	1972	2237	2697	3258	4051	4314	5664	7202
520122	1		494	539	564	669	632	714	859	950	1051	1247	1484	1829	2019	2521	3299
520203	0	1142	1181	1289	1363	1616	1581	1815	2148	2384	2661	3186	3826	4721	5234	6627	8832
520221	1	1374	1417	1570	1645	1951	1844	2142	2505	2794	3152	3773	4544	5576	6233	7958	10,576
530102	0	694	935	1074	1204	1303	1386	1583	1738	1891	2847	3263	3685	4437	5238	6084	7460
530122	1	445	585	655	745	770	814	891	948	1001	1175	1309	1534	1912	2187	2583	3222
530502	0							2771	2941	3102	3679	4098	4793	5978	6943	8249	10,437
530522	1							1979	2112	2236	2654	2964	3495	4366	5060	5999	7576
540102	0		102			93	373	382	406	434	498	545	624	872	1227	1496	1332
540122	1		102			93	107	107	112	120	128	134	152	208	268	320	352
542122	1		152			140	160	187	192	194	207	223	263	360	457	558	683
542124	1		102			93	107	107	117	117	124	132	151	195	249	309	349
610102	0	1183	1457	1566	1709	1936	2138	2275	2891	3170	3445	3962	4535	5462	6953	8155	9878
610122	1	1604	1892	2055	2243	2636	2866	3049	3821	4162	4552	5032	5796	6984	8845	10,426	12,623
610302	0	684	837	946	1032	1318	1410	1597	2024	2489	2752	3171	3704	4541	5823	7040	8680
610322	1	1288	1612	1729	1887	2183	2457	2614	3067	3341	3615	4068	4636	5547	7103	8382	10,144
620102	0	1384	1402	1617	2048	2336	2644	3079	3990	2616	2910	6088	7167	8480	9390	11,054	13,373

Table 9.14 (continued)

Id	County	1995	1996	1997	1998	1999	2000	2001	2002	2003	2004	2005	2006	2007	2008	2009	2010
620122	1	326	321	370	470	522	584	638	822	924	1030	1170	1375	1627	1796	2123	2582
620502	0	1160	1182	1386	1688	1905	2129	2366	2999	3357	3794	4418	5222	6157	6768	7999	9710
620522	1	1078	1082	1271	1550	1752	1923	2215	2809	3131	3526	4129	4839	5683	6237	7312	8800
630102	0	484	564	619	724	892	1070	1124	1283	1523	1767	1992	2461	3003	3521	4116	4977
630121	1	1018	1246	1336	1483	1743	2094	2302	2555	2890	3339	3817	4644	5657	6594	7662	9067
632802	1	127	148	163	207	243	279	321	358	412	475	548	702	875	1034	1227	1468
632822	1	127	178	196	241	284	326	321	319	364	536	600	748	897	1044	1210	1434
640104	0					1204	1311	1616	1912	2932	3592	4496	5902	7821	9938	12,294	16,030
640122	1	540	551	579	704	834	874	1039	1233	1341	1565	1898	2383	3107	3906	4767	6076
640402	0	1557	1621	1738	1996	2409	2476	2944	3425	3692	4291	5058	6361	8342	8930	10,899	13,868
640422	1	1366	1426	1500	1761	2085	2184	2598	2993	3474	4048	4832	6106	7953	10,020	12,325	15,722
650102	0					2429	2645	3303	3909	4631	4937	5045	6016	7328	8408	9884	12,250
650121	1	859	1019	971	1032	997	1008	1126	684	782	844	861	1047	1279	1419	1673	2095
652101	1	1213	1416	1349	1433	1557	1511	1877	2146	2421	2597	2625	3157	3827	4231	4932	6168
652122	1	1112	1246	1187	1261	1370	1259	1577	1802	1985	2132	2155	2577	3102	3430	4014	5027

Table 9.15 LPT revenue as ratio of own-source revenue 1995–2009

Id	County	1995 (%)	1996 (%)	1997 (%)	1998 (%)	1999 (%)	2000 (%)	2001 (%)	2002 (%)	2003 (%)	2004 (%)	2005 (%)	2006 (%)	2007 (%)	2008 (%)	2009 (%)
110102	0	25	20	18	18	18	12	12	12	13	14	14	13	9	7	8
110105	0	34	28	25	24	22	14	14	14	16	17	18	18	122	14	14
110108	0	32	15	26	25	22	20	20	19	22	23	24	24	91	20	19
110228	1	149	141	140	116	68	70	49	25	30	32	50	64	58	54	48
120101	0	25	27	29	27	26	29	22	30	25	24	18	16	205	13	12
120102	0	73	74	77	77	75	72	64	75	49	40	37	38	18	34	32
120104	0	68		86	85	84	85	85	88	44	37	32	29	364	26	26
120223	1	44	47	51	53	68	75	65	70	95	68	60	60	28	48	43
130102	0	16	17	16	15	14	14	11	14	12	4	4	5	4	5	5
130123	1	29	22	18	17	17	16	17	19	21	21	21	21	20	19	19
130302	0	14	16	15	14	14	14	13	20	21	21	20	18	14	14	14
130322	1	27	26	26	24	28	22	24	31	31	37	37	34	25	24	24
140106	0	13	12	13	12	12	14	15	20	20	19	19	19	19	17	17
140122	1	24	22	20	20	21	24	25	35	27	21	23	19	16	17	21
140502	0	27	23	22	21	22	22	24	33	35	17	30	19	26	23	23
140522	1	22	19	19	17	17	17	17	23	22	24	18	5	15	15	15
150102	0	25	25	26	28	23	22	23	26	8	7	8	8	8	7	6
150122	1	26	27	24	25	24	22	20	20	14	8	5	6	7	7	6
150402	0	21	21	20	22	22	21	22	23	23	20	11	13	13	13	13
150422	1	41	36	37	45	46	56	66	61	57	52	54	60	47	42	43
210102	0	19	21	19	15	16	16	16	15	16	14	13	12	11	10	12
210122	1	74	63	57	75	82	87	96	122	100	90	106	80	56	43	37
210202	0	11	11	11	12	12	13	12	14	11	13	12	11	11	11	11
210224	1	8	10	11	11	11	10	9	12	13	33	17	14	15	16	16
220102	0					49	43	53	76	56	46	50	53	44	41	33
220122	1	129	80	67	54	58	80	75	81	63	127	142	107	86	69	61
220502	0					62	64	40	68	77	61	56	51	45	41	38

Table 9.15 (continued)

Id	County	1995 (%)	1996 (%)	1997 (%)	1998 (%)	1999 (%)	2000 (%)	2001 (%)	2002 (%)	2003 (%)	2004 (%)	2005 (%)	2006 (%)	2007 (%)	2008 (%)	2009 (%)
220523	1	90	46	43	37	34	33	44	57	67	60	57	44	40	41	41
230102	0	32	27	26	22	18	18	15	11	10	19	18	17	17	15	16
230125	1	72	53	44	43	48	54	61	23	24	90	69	68	56	51	55
230202	0						48	40	49	45	42	48	49	38	33	35
230221	1	54	48	52	56	59	81	140	73	89	206	191	186	174	158	136
310101	0	8	7	7	8	9	11	16	17	17	15	15	16	154	17	18
310103	0	24	22	19	20	26	28	22	23	22	20	13	13	12	10	11
310104	0	31	31	27	26	34	39	26	28	26	23	20	21	143	18	19
310110	0	46	45	39	41	52	57	51	42	38	35	30	41	204	38	40
310230	1	63	64	48	51	65	72	56	61	55	46	38	53	47	46	48
320102	0					14	12	9	10	15	15	16	9	9	10	10
320124	1	25	25	26	26	26	21	21	25	20	19	23	23	20	15	13
320302	0					42	48	46	52	44	38	31	36	31	32	31
320322	1	50	48	52	49	53	54	51	58	58	58	59	49	45	41	36
330102	0					20	18	15	16	12	7	7	7	6	4	4
330122	1	45	45	44	45	40	33	21	28	25	24	22	23	25	23	23
330302	0					16	15	14	16	17	22	19	20	20	21	22
330322	1	41	35	33	35	37	29	25	34	33	36	32	27	30	28	30
340102	0					22			13	15	20	20	21	22	20	22
340122	1	23	25	21	21	21	20	23	24	24	23	23	20	18	17	18
340202	0								6	6	8	5	2	3	3	3
340222	1	13	11	10	10	13	13	12	13	13	10	10	11	12	10	10
350102	0					18	18	19	27	29	30	25	26	14	13	16
350122	1	19	20	25	23	22	23	26	34	33	37	41	43	33	31	31
350402	0					22	23	21	22	19	20	21	23	22	21	22
350423	1	9	10	14	20	29	33	36	48	48	49	61	64	60	57	58
360102	0	16	17	15	15	18	15	24	43	41	22	16	17	19	19	20

Table 9.15 (continued)

Id	County	1995 (%)	1996 (%)	1997 (%)	1998 (%)	1999 (%)	2000 (%)	2001 (%)	2002 (%)	2003 (%)	2004 (%)	2005 (%)	2006 (%)	2007 (%)	2008 (%)	2009 (%)
360122	1	25	22	20	23	24	22	23	21	22	17	17	15	15	14	14
360702	0					14	21	22	24	24	19	20	19	17	13	15
360722	1					19	22	24	26	24	23	25	28	30	27	27
370102	0	32	30	27	23	21	20	19	21	21	11	10	10	10	9	8
370124	1	39	15	14	18	17	23	21	25	25	29	27	25	26	26	26
370602	0	27	25	22	22	23	22	21	26	23	21	19	17	16	16	16
370682	1	55	50	45	35	32	30	26	28	27	29	25	24	27	32	36
410102	0					12	10	11	13	13	11	10	9	9	9	9
410122	1	29	24	23	24	29	28	32	30	28	24	22	20	16	13	11
410302	0					27	22	11	12	14	13	12	10	11	10	10
410322	1	20	16	15	14	15	15	21	24	26	22	18	15	15	15	15
420102	0					16	15	12	17	16	13	12	11	11	10	10
420111	0					23	21	18	33	30	24	24	23	21	18	17
420502	0					51	43	56	83	73	57	66	63	59	55	56
420525	1	36	35	30	23	24	24	23	37	34	32	32	29	26	22	18
430102	0		14	11	12	11	10	10	10	7	5	4	4	4	4	4
430122	1	30	19	19	21	23	25	20	20	15	12	12	11	11	8	9
430412	0	13	12	12	11	11	12	11	11	11	10	10	8	7	5	5
430422	1	43	37	36	37	36	36	36	35	37	46	53	52	57	46	41
440103	0					18	19	18	24	27	26	18	14	13	13	14
440104	0					12	13	13	18	22	22	20	18	53	18	20
440106	0					7	10	10	13	14	13	10	11	91	11	13
440183	1	32	42	42	38	37	35	31	27	26	23	17	17	15	14	15
440507	0					12	14	15	27	55	56	38	39	38	38	41
440523	1	25	29	32	40	56	55	58	69	80	80	75	82	85	84	84
450102	0						5	4	5	4	3	8	12	12	14	14
450122	1	17	15	17	14	13	14	17	20	20	23	30	32	37	38	34

Table 9.15 (continued)

Id	County	1995 (%)	1996 (%)	1997 (%)	1998 (%)	1999 (%)	2000 (%)	2001 (%)	2002 (%)	2003 (%)	2004 (%)	2005 (%)	2006 (%)	2007 (%)	2008 (%)	2009 (%)
450302	0						9	7	7	7	6	9	83	9	9	8
450322	1	32	26	23	24	22	21	23	29	24	22	19	18	15	13	14
460105	0		80	83	76	93	75	78	65	116	87	10	92	107	53	48
469001	1	16	15	18	16	22	20	20	25	24	28	36	35	28	22	16
469005	1	27	25	22	21	27	22	22	26	27	29	29	28	27	26	23
469033	1	61	53	43	40	39	29	39	42	41	78	115	109	21	71	58
500102	0				14	13	14	13	15	15	18	24	25	21	18	16
500222	1			39	36	44	46	48	50	47	46	54	52	42	34	25
510104	0	6	7	6	7	12	8	5	5	4	4	4	3	3	2	2
510122	1	7	5	8	8	7	9	10	10	10	8	8	6	4	5	5
510302	0	14	14	21	26	27	43	43	31	29	24	40	106	100	143	170
510322	1	26	24	33	35	40	52	53	59	60	67	71	101	66	59	63
520102	0	15	13	12	10	10	7	6	7	6	5	5	5	5	5	5
520122	1		20	18	17	19	16	15	14	13	12	10	10	10	9	10
520203	0	48	37	36	32	39	33	32	33	29	23	26	31	35	32	28
520221	1	77	52	49	44	43	36	37	36	33	28	23	23	22	18	18
530102	0	3	3	3	3	3	3	3	4	3	4	5	4	4	4	4
530122	1	7	7	7	9	8	9	10	12	11	12	10	8	8	7	5
530502	0							19	21	20	21	19	18	18	18	16
530522	1							18	20	20	21	19	17	14	13	12
540102	0		7			3	13	11	11	11	11	11	10	9	9	9
540122	1		94			54	58	42	37	36	31	29	25	17	18	12
542122	1		60			77	61	64	67	60	54	49	44	42	42	41
542124	1		48			29	29	26	27	27	26	13	13	12	25	27
610102	0	12	10	10	9	9	9	8	12	6	6	6	7	6	6	6
610122	1	65	64	61	53	61	57	56	61	55	54	97	108	112	111	98
610302	0	12	12	13	12	15	16	19	25	27	26	32	33	30	31	30

Table 9.15 (continued)

Id	County	1995 (%)	1996 (%)	1997 (%)	1998 (%)	1999 (%)	2000 (%)	2001 (%)	2002 (%)	2003 (%)	2004 (%)	2005 (%)	2006 (%)	2007 (%)	2008 (%)	2009 (%)
610322	1	61	53	51	43	42	43	45	51	50	48	66	57	50	50	44
620102	0	6	6	6	7	7	8	7	9	10	9	14	14	13	12	13
620122	1	37	31	33	33	30	28	27	36	35	32	44	37	32	27	23
620502	0	21	17	20	20	21	22	24	28	40	38	39	33	34	30	29
620522	1	60	45	52	57	48	53	73	79	87	99	127	132	128	118	12
630102	0	64	49	46	21	16	21	20	25	27	27	25	26	25	24	21
630121	1	29	31	34	32	32	28	27	27	26	25	24	25	26	26	33
632802	1	19	19	21	21	22	20	20	20	19	20	19	17	14	12	12
632822	1	20	23	22	26	27	26	23	21	26	43	32	33	32	29	25
640104	0					21	18	18	19	25	23	23	26	28	29	32
640122	1	32	19	17	17	20	21	23	24	25	23	26	26	23	17	13
640402	0	122	85	96	79	81	82	83	81	117	18	228	241	205	160	165
640422	1	360	167	153	166	187	206	202	202	211	214	268	303	343	359	373
650102	0					13	14	13	16	15	14	13	10	10	8	10
650121	1	12	12	9	9	8	8	38	29	25	17	16	17	16	15	11
652101	1	21	20	17	16	18	17	19	20	22	22	15	15	16	15	16
652122	1	13	10	8	9	9	6	7	8	9	9	6	6	6	5	6
Average		38	32	31	30	30	30	30	32	32	33	34	35	41	30	30

References

An, Tifu, and Haiyong Wang. 2005. Research on development of real property market and tax reform in China. *Review of Economic Research* 43:19–28. **安体富 王海勇**:"我国房地产市场发展和房地产税收制度改革研究",《经济研究参考》, 2005年第43期, 第19–28页。

An, Tifu, and Jing Ge. 2012. Analysis on issues of reforming real property tax in China: Revelation from tax pilot in Chongqing and Shanghai. *Review of Economic Research* 45:12–21. **安体富 葛静**:"关于房产税改革的若干问题探讨 - 基于重庆、上海房产税试点的启示"《经济研究参考》, 2012年第45期, 第12–21页。

Anderson, John. 2011. The path to property taxation. In *China's local public finance in transition*, eds. Joyce Yanyun Man and Yu-Hung Hong, 145–164. Cambridge: Lincoln Institute of Land Policy.

Cai, C. 1990. *History of public finance in Sui and Tang dynasties and the period of five dynasties*. Beijing: China Financial and Economic Publishing House. 蔡次薛:隋唐五代财政史, 中国财政经济出版社,1990年2月。

Carlson, R. H. 2004. *A brief history of property tax*. Retrieved from IAAO Conference on Assessment Administration. https://secure.sauder.ubc.ca/re_creditprogram/course_resources/courses/content/443/carlson.pdf.

Chen, M. 2010. *Real property tax in Tang Dynasty (Dissertation of Master Degree)*. Shanghai: Shanghai University. 陈敏:唐代房屋税研究, 上海大学历史学硕士学位论文, 2010年4月。

David K., and H. R. Hildebrand. 1977. *Analysis of ordinal data*. California: SAGE.

Dillman, D. A. 2000. *Mail and internet surveys: The tailored design method*. New York: Wiley.

Gao, Peiyong, and Dehua Wang. 2012. *Report on fiscal policy in China 2012/2013: Housing security in the context of urbanization*. China Financial and Economic Publishing House. 高培勇,汪德华:《中国财政政策报告2012/2013:新型城市化背景下的住房保障》, 中国财政经济出版社, 2012 年版。

Greene, W. H. 2012. *Econometric analysis*. 7th ed. Boston: Prentice Hall.

Gu, Cheng. 2011. Rethinking the reform of the real property tax. *Research on Financial and Economic Issues* 4:91–97. 谷成:"房产税改革再思考",《财经问题研究》, 2011年第4期, 第91–97 页。

He, B. 2000. *Population and related issues after early Ming dynasty 1368~1953*. Beijing: SDX. 何炳棣:明初以降人口及其相关问题 1368—1953, 三联书店, 2000年11月。

Hong, Yu-Hung, and Diana Brubaker. 2011. Integrating the proposed property tax with the public leasehold system. In *China's local public finance in transition*, ed. Joyce Yanyun Man and Yu-Hung Hong, 165–190. Cambridge: Lincoln Institute of Land Policy.

Hou, Yilin. 2008. The logic of government reforms. In *Public finance and government reform*, ed. C Zhu , H. Yilin and J. Ma (in Chinese). Shanghai: Shanghai People's Press.

Hou, Yilin. 2009. A theoretical analysis of China's financial administration reforms on the division of taxing power and outlay responsibilities 1978–2008. *Journal of Public Administration* 2 (2): 36–72.

Hu, J. 1998. *A history of economic thought in China*. Shanghai: Shanghai University of Finance and Economics Press. 胡寄窗:中国经济思想史(上、中、下), 上海财经大学出版社, 1998年12月。

Ivanyna, M., and A. Shah. 2012. *How close is your government to its people? Worldwide indicators on localization and decentralization*. Retrieved from World Bank. http://elibrary.worldbank.org/docserver/download/6138.pdf?expires=1363189005&id=id&accname=guest&checksum=E4F819EFDDA647DF1E1E1F70DD46AA95.

Jean M., and S. P. Converse. 1986. *Survey questions: Handcrafting the standardized questionnaire*: California: SAGE.

Jia, Kang. 2011. Reform real property tax: American model and China's selection. *People's Tribune* 48–50. 贾康:"房产税改革:美国模式和中国选择",《人民论坛》, 2011年3月, 第48-50页。

Kalton, G. 1983. *Introduction to survey sampling*. California: SAGE.

Lang, Xianping. 2010. Don't learn the experience from America in levying real property tax. *IT Times Weekly* 17:14. 郎咸平:"别学美国征房产税",《中国经济信息》, 2010年第17期, 第14页。

Li, Y. 1997. *A history of state-owned land in China*. Yunnan: Yunan Press.李埏:中国古代土地国有制史, 云南出版社, 1997年1月。

Liang, F. 2008. *A statistics on household, land and taxation in Chinese history*. Beijing: Zhonghua. 梁方仲:中国历代户口、田地、田赋统计, 中华书局, 2008年11月。

Liu, Rong. 2011. Experience and revelation of the real property tax from other countries. *Reform* 3:145–148. 刘蓉:"房产税税制的国际比较与启示",《改革》, 2011年第3期, 第145-148页。

Liu, Shangxi. Real property tax is not omnipotent and it can't be endowed with so many functions. 刘尚希:"房产税不是 '万能税',不可赋予太多功能" http://finance.people.com.cn/GB/18064949.htmlã

Ma, Guoqiang, and Jing Li. 2011. Goals and stages of the real property tax reform. *Reform* 2:130–132. 马国强 李晶:"房产税改革的目标与阶段性"《改革》, 2011年第2期,第130–132页。

Mooney, C. Z. 1997. *Monte Carlo Simulation*. California: SAGE

Ni, Hongri. Some proposals on real estate tax reform in China. International Taxation in China February 2011: 5–8. 倪红日:"对我国房地产税制改革的几点建议",《涉外税务》, 2011年2月,第5-8页。

Qi, X. 1987. *A history of economy in Song dynasty*. Shanghai: Shanghai People. 漆侠:宋代经济史(上、下),上海人民出版社, 1987年2月。

Shah, Anwar, and Sana Shah. 2009. The new vision of local governance and the evolving roles of local governments. *Journal of Public Administration* 3:004.

Sun, Y. 2003. *A history of Chinese taxation*. Beijing: Chinese Tax Press.孙翊刚, 陈光焱:中国赋税史, 中国税务出版社, 2003年12月。

Wooldridge, J. M. (2009). *Introductory econometrics: A modern approach*. 4th ed. Mason: South Western, Cengage Learning.

Xia, Shangmo. 2011. Can real property tax narrow income gap and suppress real property price? *Taxation Research* 4:19–25. 夏商末:"房产税:能够调节收入分配不公和抑制房价上涨吗",《税务研究》, 2011年第4期, 第19-25页。

Xiang, H. 2006. *A history of public finance in China*. Beijing: China Financial and Economic. 项怀诚、贾康:中国财政通史(共12卷),中国财政经济出版社, 2006年7月。

Xing, T. 2002. *A history of household class in China*. Yunnan: University Press of Yunnan. 刑铁:户等制度史纲,云南大学出版社, 2002年5月。

Yang, J. 1985. Household class and land in Tang dynasty. *Historical Research* (3):100–110. 杨际平:唐代户等与田产,历史研究,1985年第3期, 100–110页。

Yang, Bin. 2007. An argument on the reform of real estate tax and pattern of intergovernmental fiscal relation in China. *Taxation Research* 3:43–48. 杨斌:"关于房地产税费改革方向和地方财政收入模式的论辩",《税务研究》, 2007年第3期,第43–48页。

Zhang, Qi'an, and Shangxi Liu: There should be three stages in expanding real property tax. 张启安:"刘尚希:房产税推广应走三步"http://finance.china.com.cn/news/gnjj/20121216/1190992.shtmlã.

Zhang, S. 1998. *Ancient taxation in China*. Beijing: The Commercial Press. 张守军:中国古代的赋税与劳役,商务印书馆, 1998年12月。

Zhang, Z. 1986. *A brief history of taxation in Tang dynasty and the period of five dynasties*. Beijing: The Commercial Press. 张泽咸:唐五代赋役草, 商务印书馆, 1986年10月。

Zheng, X. 1994. *Chinese taxation history*. Xiamen: University Press of Xiamen. 郑学檬:中国赋役制度史, 厦门大学出版社, 1994 年 8 月。

MIX
Papier aus verantwortungsvollen Quellen
Paper from responsible sources
FSC® C105338
FSC
www.fsc.org

If you have any concerns about our products,
you can contact us on
ProductSafety@springernature.com

In case Publisher is established outside the EU,
the EU authorized representative is:
Springer Nature Customer Service Center GmbH
Europaplatz 3, 69115 Heidelberg, Germany

Printed by Libri Plureos GmbH
in Hamburg, Germany